UNBUTTONING AMERICA

UNBUTTONING AMERICA:

A Biography of "Peyton Place"

ARDIS CAMERON

CORNELL UNIVERSITY PRESS
ITHACA AND LONDON

First published 2015 by Cornell University Press
First paperback printing 2024

Library of Congress Cataloging-in-Publication Data

Cameron, Ardis, author.
   Unbuttoning America : a biography of "Peyton Place" / Ardis Cameron.
      pages cm
   Includes bibliographical references and index.
   ISBN 978-0-8014-5364-9 (cloth)
  1. Metalious, Grace. Peyton Place. 2. Popular literature—United States—History and criticism. 3. Literature and society—United States—History—20th century. 4. Books and reading—United States—History—20th century. 5. Sex in literature. I. Title.
   PS3525.E77P4335   2015
   813'.54—dc23   2014044855

ISBN 978-1-5017-7597-0 (pbk)
ISBN 978-0-8014-5609-1 (epub)
ISBN 978-0-8014-5610-7 (pdf)

Cover design by Kimberly Glyder

To Nancy, always

A novel is an act of hope. It allows us to imagine that things may be other than they are.

Hilary Mantel

CONTENTS

ACKNOWLEDGMENTS

Books are collective acts that depend upon the kindness, generosity, expertise, and goodwill of many people. Debts like this are never adequately repaid; they just grow. When books become longtime projects, like this one, they envelop the lives of more and more people, deepening a writer's debts. To my friends, students, colleagues, and family, who lived with *Peyton Place* and me for the past ten years, I am deeply grateful for your understanding, patience, curiosity, advice, and sense of humor. Your comradeship sustained me and made this book possible.

I am especially grateful to the Metalious family, who generously provided me with their mother's correspondence and shared as well their memories, some painful, most poignant and loving—all of them invaluable to this book. Without the help of Marsha Metalious in particular, this project would never have gotten off the ground. Not only did she answer my endless questions, but she offered encouragement and friendship as well. Thanks also to Grace Metalious's daughter Cindy, and to Grace's former husband George Metalious for enduring multiple interviews and never losing patience. To Grace Metalious's grandson Joseph Duprey, I offer my thanks. (I will never forget that dinner in Paris.)

I am also grateful to the late Laurose (Laurie) Wilkins and her family, Wendy Wilkins, Joanne Wilkins Pugh, and John Wilkins, who spent endless hours with me in the kitchen Grace loved so much, and who were kind enough to offer me their stories as well as many fine meals. Thanks too to those who generously gave their time to discuss the early years of *Peyton Place* and the publishing landscape in the 1950s: Leona Nevler, John Chandler, Alan "Bud" Brandt, Howard Goodkind, James Silberman, Charlotte Sheedy, and Sterling Lord. If residents of Gilmanton, New Hampshire, were reluctant to put *Peyton Place* on their town library shelves, they were more than willing to talk to me about its controversial author. My thanks especially to Richard and Betty Arms, Helene Roberts, Darryl Thompson, Joe and Meg Hempel, David Sellin, Linda Clarke, John Collins, and Eric Seline. For showing me the Manchester, New Hampshire, of Grace's youth, a special thanks to Robert B. Perreault, whose dedication to preserving the Franco-American heritage inspires all who meet him.

Librarians and archivists have always been the invisible heroes of history—their knowledge, expertise, and passion are the wind behind history's sail. My thanks to the many who assisted me at the Rare Book and Manuscript Library, Columbia University; the Hachette Livre archives, Paris; the Motion Picture and Television Reading Room at the Paley Center for Media in New York; the American Antiquarian Society; the Gale Memorial Library in Laconia, New Hampshire; the New Hampshire State Library; the Camden (Maine) Public Library; and the Gilmanton (New Hampshire) Historical Society. A special thank you to Jane Klain, Jackie Penny, and Barbra Dyer. For all the years of help at the Glickman Family Library at the University of Southern Maine, thanks go especially to Loraine Lowell, Michelle Dustin, Carolyn Hughes, Pat Prieto, and Bill Sargent. Zipp Kellogg and Casandra Fitzherbert were there from the beginning, introducing me to new sources, technologies, and a dazzling array of materials only they could have pulled out of cyberspace. You are all amazing.

I owe the readers of *Peyton Place* an enormous debt of gratitude as well. In email, interviews, letters, and at public presentations, they generously shared their stories and, at times, the marginalia from their dog-eared copies. Some asked to remain anonymous, others were audience members whose names were never given, but most were my students, neighbors, friends, friends of friends, and readers who wanted to tell their stories of

Peyton Place. They brought new questions, critique, excitement, and inspiration. Although I cannot remember all of their names, I owe a special thanks to June Carter, Rosemary Caldwell, Elizabeth DeWolfe, Sarah Goss, Ann Zill, Bill Snyder, Aud Miller, Marilyn Zacks, Fred Goal, Nancy Marcotte, Shauna Baxter, Kate Cone, Ann Colford, Cynthia Richardson, Rea Turret, Sarah Cowperthwaite, Penny Davis-Dublin, David Jester, Lynn Chabot, Tracy Morreau, Pat Fox, Adrienne and Deborah Briskey, Pat Shearman, Nancy Barton, Bjorn Swenson, Marcia Howell, Shirley Stenberg, Marie Sacks, Peter Sullivan, Cynthia Richardson, Nancy Masterton, Barbara Knowles, Lynn Bushnell, Elizabeth Fairlamb, Sally Pember, Nancy Kavanagh, Chris Clawson, Jane Guerin Young, Nancy Guerin, Pat Clawson, and Jimmy Von Ruhr. To David Richards I am doubly indebted. The many articles and documents sent my way were welcome presents, but the gift of Pee Wee Reese was a treasure I'll never forget. A special thanks to Susan Stamberg for taking the other side of the mike.

Additionally, I want to thank Claire Potter, Susan Yohn, Elaine Abelson, Franca Iacovetta, Kathi Kern, Barbra Sicherman, and Carol Groneman, whose own work offered wonderful examples to follow and whose provocative discussions at the "Little Berks" gave the hard work of scholarship a collective and much-needed lift. I also owe a debt of gratitude to Emily Toth, whose early appreciation for *Peyton Place* and recognition of its significance in American culture helped preserve an invaluable oral archive. To colleagues at USM who offered encouragement from the start, my thanks to Kent Ryden, Donna Cassidy, Matthew Edney, and Joe Conforti.

It was while I was completing the final stages of this book that the war against public universities stormed into Maine. If not for the extraordinary and tireless efforts of Jerry LaSala, Mark Lapping, Luisa Deprez, Eve Raimon, Wendy Chapkis, Rayne Carroll, Susan Feiner, Nancy Gish, Lydia Savage, and especially Jeannine Uzzi to try to save the humanities at USM, and the American and New England Studies program in particular, I could never have finished this project. Nor could I have managed without the extraordinary team of graduate assistants and administrative assistants who, over the years, provided invaluable research skills and professionalism. I am especially indebted to Madeleine Winterfalcon, Lauren Webster, Michele Morgan, Rachael Miller, Melanie Mackenzie, Cassie Kane, Kerrianne Falco, and Arline Palmer, whose research skills, organizational wizardry, and wicked humor put me in debt I can never repay.

Joan Scott, Judy Smith, Christina Simmons, and Nancy Hewitt read many versions of this book in manuscript, and it reflects their careful reading and thoughtful discussions. Since the book's inception, Joan Scott has engaged in so many discussions over it I cannot imagine it without her supportive and enthusiastic voice in my head. I also thank the generous and skilled editors at Cornell University Press, Amanda Heller and Sara Ferguson; Max Richman; and especially Michael J. McGandy, who gave my work discipline, insight, and a second life.

It is important to acknowledge as well the role of sabbatical leaves. Without them, a book like this could never be written, and teachers would grow musty and stale. I am indebted to the previous administrations at USM for understanding the critical and essential relationship between scholarship and teaching. My thanks especially to Mark Lapping, Joseph Wood, Devinder Malhotra, John Wright, and Luisa Deprez, and to my colleagues who awarded me both two sabbatical leaves and a USM Trustee Professorship. A National Endowment for the Humanities Senior Research Fellowship and a John Simon Guggenheim Memorial Fellowship provided me with the essential time and funding to begin this project and sustain it over the long years of research and writing. This book would never have been possible without such generous funding.

Finally, I thank those friends who nourished me with both their intellectual warmth and fabulous food. It is not an easy thing to live with an obsessed academic. Thanks to Doris for everything and to my dad, whose memory this book honors. Thank you, Ezra and Carmen Scott-Henning, for going camping with me and making me laugh so, so much, and to Don Scott and Steve Caton for your many charms. To Dylan, Katie, Ben, Lily, Tim, Maeghan, Will, and Nico, and all their parents, thanks for pulling me into your fantastic adventures and reminding me that there is life beyond words. And to Nancy Hewitt, Cheryl Lewis, Norine Kotts, Freddie Wachsberger, Sylvia Newman, Lucy Steele, Dottie Abbott, Jean Redpath, Anne MacKay, Joan Scott, Nancy and Bart Green, Philip Osgood, Lydia Cassatt, and Nancy MacKay—a most heartfelt thank you for your kindness, love, and for always being there. And for Nancy, to whom this book is dedicated, my deepest gratitude for all the things she knows so well.

Unbuttoning America

Introduction

SMALL TALK

I had the story, bit by bit, from various people, and, as generally happens in
such cases, each time it was a different story.

EDITH WHARTON, *ETHAN FROME*

This is what I had. It was the summer of 1964 and my best friend had
just learned that her mother was having an affair with a neighbor of ours.
More fascinated than upset, my friend recounted to our small group of
intimates the clues that had finally forced her errant mom to come clean:
the book of matches from the Essex House, "the pill" (thinly boxed and
tucked into the corner drawer), the "secret" late-night phone calls, the sudden errands down the road. My friend spilled all. She talked of divorce,
abortion, and "free love." Then, as we sat dazed by the revelations and
somewhat uncertain of our feelings, she looked at us with an air of worldly
knowledge and whispered, "Welcome to Peyton Place."

As it did for many Americans who came of age in the heady years of
the early sixties, the story of *Peyton Place* came to me like this in the kinds
of small talk exchanged between friends, whispered in locker rooms,
and spoken between you and me. I knew that it had been a controversial
"dirty" novel and a popular film, and I was vaguely aware of a television
show—that blurry blue light in the parental bedroom—but like many of

my friends, I had no memory of *Peyton Place* outside these emblematic conversations about marital strife and sexual scandal. Seemingly remote from the worldly noises of civil rights, the War on Poverty, Vietnam, or even the "sexual revolution," *Peyton Place* silently infiltrated the invisible everyday.[1] Like the many rumored affairs of my friend's mother, it was "just talk."

But talk is never as small or as cheap as we imagine. Putting names to unspeakable acts, uttering in private what cannot be said in public, pushing the illicit and unconventional forward with the whispered vocabulary of racy books, "dirty talk" is a weighty and signifying practice that sets into motion constitutive linguistic events. For many of us, the erotic possibilities of a more exciting "elsewhere" slipped into talk of *Peyton Place* and produced what was missing "in here." Among my friends who longed to escape the boredom of suburban New Jersey, talk of *Peyton Place* produced an endless improvisation that played itself out against "real life." When my friend's mother became the talk of the town, parents used *Peyton Place* to map the terrain of the moral "Other" and "the bad woman." She in turn dismissed our town as just another Peyton Place. Her daughter tellingly used it to signal a grand interruption in the drift of ordinary events and assumed identities.

"Welcome to Peyton Place" was simultaneously enticement and warning, a conceptual site of desire and undoing where conventional wisdom slipped into dangerous critique and fantasy.[2] People talked about *Peyton Place*, some acted it out, while a few, including the writer Barbara Wolfson, "did" *Peyton Place*.[3] Journalists used it to conjure up for suburban readers the small-town mendacity and hypocrisy they believed they had left behind. For neighbors who wanted to register social disapproval or rant against a rise in marital infidelity, premarital sex, out-of-wedlock pregnancy, and other "irregularities," *Peyton Place* became a cautionary tale. The telling itself was often an exercise in autobiography as neighbors compared themselves and others to characters in the book. Personal histories came into view: "I felt just like that," a neighbor whispered. Snippets of talk were dropped like crumbs in a thickening forest of doubt and wonder: "What do you think?" "Imagine that?" "Really?" And when my friend's father stormed out with the Essex House matches in his hand, he shouted, "I live in goddamn Peyton Place!"

Small talk could mean big trouble.

Published in 1956, *Peyton Place* quickly became America's top-selling novel. In an age when the average first novel sold two thousand copies, it sold sixty thousand within the first ten days. Amazingly, within three months it headed the *New York Times* best-seller list, where it stayed number one for another fifty-nine weeks. Soon, even these figures were dwarfed as *Peyton Place* rapidly edged out middlebrow "quality" best-sellers, including *God's Little Acre* and *Gone With the Wind*, to become, at 12 million copies sold, the century's best-selling novel to date. In the end, an astonishing one in twenty-nine Americans bought the book, and almost everyone had something to say about it.[4] A "literary phenomenon" that touched a national nerve, it was written by an unknown housewife, a daughter of New England's mills, the wife of a small-town schoolteacher, and the mother of three young children. It was Grace Metalious's first novel, the first piece of writing she ever sold.

Sales moved in rushing waves. Soldiers, teenagers, married women, unmarried women, husbands, salesclerks, and teachers dog-eared their favorite pages and then passed the book around. "I found a hardcover copy [of *Peyton Place*]," a reader recalled, "at a flea market in Geneva, Switzerland, stamped, remarkably enough, with a booksellers [*sic*] address in New Delhi."[5] *Peyton Place* raced around; its story of incest, murder, abortion, class inequality, poverty, female sexuality, and social hypocrisy sounded a clarion call difficult, perhaps, to imagine in today's tell-all culture of digital reproduction and personal invasion. Hidden under beds and read by flashlight, *Peyton Place* came out during private moments and in confidential chats with friends. "I heard my mother and her best friend whispering in the kitchen. As soon as I entered, they whipped a book into a bag, but they were too slow. I had caught my mother reading *Peyton Place*, a book banned by our own town library." Everyone and their sister, it seemed, was talking about *Peyton Place*. "Even if they hadn't read it," readers noted over and over again, "they sure had something to say." In a decade known for its silence and quiescence, *Peyton Place* set tongues wagging and emotions soaring.

And, bit by bit, *Peyton Place* unfurled across the nation. Between 1956 and 1964 it morphed into a feature film, a book sequel, a film sequel, a popular New York City nightclub, a "family" motel, a Pocketbook soap opera, and the nation's first "television novel," an episodic drama that one in three Americans watched three times a week for two years, then weekly for three more (drawing 60 million viewers, more than twice *American Idol*'s 25 million at the height of its much touted popularity).

The storyline of *Peyton Place* is deceptively simple, but like *Uncle Tom's Cabin*, it unleashed a "torrent of energy" and emotion understandably difficult for modern readers to grasp.[6] Based on the "true" story of patricide in the small New Hampshire village of Gilmanton Iron Works, *Peyton Place* follows the lives of three women who struggle to come to terms with their identity as women and as sexual persons amidst the constraints of class prejudice and gender conventions. Allison MacKenzie, very much like her youthful author, Grace Metalious, is a restless, insecure girl, "plump in all the wrong places," who is "all thumbs," and has "a head full of silly dreams."[7] Growing up in a fatherless household with the silence that surrounds his absence, Allison longs to escape, dreaming, like her creator, of becoming a famous author. Her working mother, Constance, whom Allison believes to be widowed, leads a lonely and sexually frustrated life, haunted by the fear that her long-ago adulterous love affair with a married man will be revealed and ruin both herself and her daughter, the offspring of that passionate relationship.

It is Allison's friend Selena Cross, however, who witnesses the unfairness of female sexuality in its starkest terms. Sexually abused by her stepfather, Lucas, for years, Selena becomes pregnant by him yet knows that no one will believe her story. "Dark"-complexioned with "slightly slanted" eyes, Selena has a "gypsyish beauty" which represents the dangerous edges of unregulated female sexuality in the American imagination. Despite her hard work and good reputation in town, she understands that people will blame her. She is a dweller of a tar shack. Her mother, who cleans house for the MacKenzie family, was abused by Lucas as well and has only a slim grasp on reality. In the end, Selena manages to get the much-loved town doctor, Doc Swain, to perform an abortion. Although he risks going to prison, he convinces himself, and the novel's readers, too, that his choice is the correct one: Selena's is the life he must save. His anger and moral outrage are directed at Lucas, whom he forces to leave town, and at the myopic law, which he breaks.

Selena rebuilds her life until, one snowy night just before Christmas, Lucas returns, his knock on the front door as icy and bleak as the December landscape. Filled with booze, revenge, and ugliness, he approaches Selena. "'Be nice to me honey,' same as before." As he attacks, Selena picks up the fire tongs and smashes in the side of his head. "Blood bathed her face" (297). Terrified and alone, Selena and her younger brother bury his body in the sheep pen, where the ground is still moist and warm.

Denounced at the time by conservatives for its corrupting influence and sexual frankness, the novel was dismissed as well by progressives for its trivial, soapy content. A few years later, celebrity feminists accused it of encouraging female passivity and contributing to "the mounting sex-hunger of American women."[8] But for millions of readers, *Peyton Place* broke through the "obsolete embargoes" they lived under.[9] "I'm sure you're writing about my town," they wrote the young author. "I live in Peyton Place." "I was born there," some confessed, "but I left a few years ago." If critics found the townspeople shocking and scandalous, readers knew them as friends, neighbors, and kin. "Your characters are all true to life!" a New Hampshire reader wrote. "One of them is my uncle!"[10]

From Detroit, Michigan; Troy, New York; Davenport, Florida; San Diego, California; Belfast, Maine; Kirkwood, Mississippi; Hobart, Indiana, and hundreds of other towns and cities across America, readers weighed in on *Peyton Place*. Not "earthy" they insisted, but "down-to-earth," authentic, and real. Dirty? Maybe. Not because the book made sex speak in a time of sexual repression, though (sex was everywhere in the fifties), but because it tunneled beneath official discourse, uprooting the contradictions and ambiguities through which sex and gender spoke. In a decade marked by the coalescing of a dominant conception of normality, *Peyton Place* muddied the moral certainties and stale platitudes of a nation. "I was living in the Midwest during the 1950's," recalled the writer Emily Toth, "and I can tell you it was boring. Elvis Presley and *Peyton Place* were the only two things in that decade that gave you hope there was something going on out there."[11]

My friends and I opened our dictionaries and put our ears to the ground. Allison MacKenzie, Norman Page, Betty Anderson, and Selena Cross offered a vocabulary for things some of us could not yet imagine but for others had already happened. Girl trouble came in great bursts of personal humiliation and isolated despair: expulsions from the Girl Scouts, suspensions from school, teen pregnancies, a mother overhearing her daughter in the confessional telling the priest that she was having sex with her boyfriend. Gender trouble was not a problem that had no name; it had too many.

Only later did we think of these years as plotted and purposeful, our vast outrage and vague discomfort confined to reading illicit books, watching edgy foreign films, analyzing the lyrics of Bob Dylan and Leonard Cohen, and protesting the hypocrisy that governed the restrictions of our girlhood in small and at times self-destructive rebellions: smoking, drinking, hitchhiking, resisting dress codes, cutting our hair short, and demanding the same rights as our brothers in the boys' school down the road. Only later would we look back and see "a thousand lives, a hundred thousand lives marching in union," as Melissa Fay Greene perceptively reminds us.[12] But in the beginning, we felt quite alone, our music and our books the covert compass we used to reset our paths, reorient our futures.

That cultural guardians and literary critics had little use for *Peyton Place* meant nothing to readers who put the novel to artful use, inserting themselves into its adventurous scenes, plots, and characters, drawing upon its action, dialogue, and vocabulary to tell themselves into the imaginative scenarios and fantasies the novel conjured up and set in motion. For some, the women of *Peyton Place* echoed their own dreams and desires, while for others, the story of Selena, Norman, and Allison offered a way to understand, to make meaningful—even, in a sense, to make up—experiences they had once thought beyond words.[13] They confronted as well the "iron bars" of systematic class and ethnic discrimination and the "unhappier variations" of traditional family life.[14] And to those millions on the discursive and material margins of postwar "normality," *Peyton Place* offered a language of critique and possibility; it was a story they could literally get into, a way to live "as if."[15] *Peyton Place* made a world of difference.

Perhaps it is because we can touch the recent past so intimately through our parents and grandparents that it becomes paradoxically the most foreign of all historical territories; it is a profound cultural shock to discover how very different our world is today, once, of course, we move beyond the bourbon old-fashioneds, saddle shoes, and Schiffli-embroidered dresses. To read *Peyton Place* today is to ponder the sexual quicksand on which women (and men) walked. For the unhappily pregnant, abortion was illegal, a perilous "immoral terrain" of extreme personal danger and secrecy, yet so much in demand that the American Medical Association estimated about a million abortions were performed every year in the decade before 1960. Contraception was difficult to find, and in a few states it was illegal for a doctor even to discuss family planning with an unmarried woman. As Gunnar Myrdal noted in *An American Dilemma*, "birth control is taboo as a subject for polite conversation."[16] Medical schools cautioned future physicians, therapists, and psychiatrists "not to inquire about a patient's past history of abuse, and when they learned of it, to doubt its veracity."[17] When it came to rape, wife beating, or incest, official policy was committed to a simple rule of thumb: first avoid the subject, then deny it happened, and finally, question both the story and the innocence of the woman or child.

Though a work of fiction, *Peyton Place* is nevertheless a central part of this story. Once outcasts in academia, best-selling novels now attract serious scholarly attention, their popularity no longer suspect but rather a site of pointed analysis and inquiry. Rich veins of research have suddenly opened up, revealing the emotional and psychic services that popular genres performed. Scholars have unpacked as well the cultural labor of lesbian pulps, dime novels, female sleuths, children's series, publishing factory "hacks," and the disparate writing publics they called forth and organized.[18] Historians have been especially adept at bringing print culture into their service, making legible worlds once lost. Historians have shown how in the twelfth century, "textual communities" helped promote not only a sense of collectivity but also a collective challenge to repressive traditions. Without "print languages," Benedict Anderson famously points out, individual affiliations to abstract entities like "the nation" would be difficult to imagine.[19] Nor was reading a practice confined to the salons and parlors of the genteel and influential. Far from an elite habit, vernacular reading played a critical role in shaping popular knowledge, challenging orthodoxy, and fueling working-class radicalism, providing "people with new ways to relate their doings to authority, new and old."[20]

For social historians on the trail of the ordinary and everyday, best-sellers provide an especially productive point of entry into the prosaic, calling attention not just to the practices and pleasures of reading but to the unquiet habits and productive fantasies of fans and detractors alike. "Literary texts," the critic Terry Eagleton has taught us, "do not exist on bookshelves; they are processes of signification materialized only in the practice of reading."[21]

As evidence, then, best-sellers have found their scholarly niche, although for historians they present certain difficulties. Perhaps the hardest task for historians when confronting a work of fiction is avoiding the literary pigeonholes others have created in their name. Even as scholars increasingly acknowledge *Peyton Place* as worthy of their attention, they wind up describing its merits and exploring its meanings by positioning it within academic categories readers knew little about and cared not a fig. Was *Peyton Place* part of the "revolt from the village" tradition or not? Was it a "proto-feminist" text? Despite its historical sales numbers, can we truly call it a "blockbuster"? Was it really about sex, or is it best explored as part of "whiteness studies?" Was *Peyton Place* actually about race?

When I find myself thinking like this, I turn to a story the physicist Richard Feynman told about his youth, when, while they were walking in the Catskill Mountains, a friend asked him to identify a particular bird:

> I said, "I haven't the slightest idea what kind of bird that is."
>
> He says, "It's a brown-throated thrush. Your father doesn't teach you anything."
>
> But it was the opposite. He had already taught me. "See that bird?" he says. "It's a Spencer's warbler." (I knew he didn't know the real name.) "Well, in Italian, it's a Chutto Lapittida. In Portuguese, it's a Bom da Peida. In Chinese, it's a Chung long-tah, and in Japanese, it's a Katano Tekeda. You can know the name of that bird in all the languages of the world, but when you're finished, you'll know absolutely nothing whatever about the bird. You'll only know about humans in different places and what they call the bird. So let's look at the bird and see what it's doing—that's what counts.[22]

Like birds, novels lose something of their power and wonder when we forget that more than anything else, they are unique participants in the social/cultural worlds as well as in the literary habitats we often know them by. No matter how hard we try to pin novels down to some interpretive "truth," they wriggle away from us.[23] Fiction is always up to something. Critics, politicians, reviewers, teachers, preachers, and scholars have called *Peyton Place* all sorts of names, but what counts, it seems to me, is how *Peyton Place* worked—what it did not only to the readers who couldn't put it down but also to the social, cultural, and literary truths their reading pecked apart.

For those who could find their stories nowhere else—strong women, ambitious girls, unhappy and unfaithful wives, abused children, odd boys, wayward girls, poor folk, working heroes, western tough guys, and ethnic outsiders—novels extended Clio's reach, challenging the terms on which consensus history in the fifties rested and the pipe smoke that clung to it. Unlike the mass-marketed romances produced by Mills, Boon, and

Harlequin, the sprawling, page-turning novels like *Gone With the Wind,* *Whistle Stop, Forever Amber, Kings Row, The Amboy Dukes, Mandingo*, and *Peyton Place* trafficked in the immediacy of representation documenting the emotive terrain and forgotten voices pressed up along the outskirts of power and the margins of respectability, conventionality, and normality.[24] If best-sellers like these carried the whiff of the marketplace, it was not romance that set them aflame but rather the thrill of discovery. Long before "women's history" or "history from below" found its reading public, novels like *Peyton Place* tilled their rich terrain, offering ordinary readers a meaningful *historia*, an accessible "inquest" into life that was faithful to that term but built with the fictive elements history left behind.

Where else in the years before second-wave feminism could "bad" women, sexually autonomous girls, and the victims of child sexual abuse find their stories revealed, their behaviors defended, their histories taken seriously if not in "dirty" stories like *Peyton Place?*

"I have read true books before," a fan wrote the author of *Peyton Place*, "but none stand up to yours which is fiction." He was not alone. For millions of readers the conflation of art and life was the distinguishing characteristic of a good story. Pleasure came in the novel's call to participate, the urge to identify, the ring of recognition amidst the straight talk of "how life is." In the absence of an official accounting or historical study, the undocumented undertow of human life—from sexual desire to the ambivalence of love, from dreams of home to the destructive potential of domestic life—found its best narration in tales "too shocking for words." Novels went where history often feared to go.

From this perspective novels become more than words on a printed page. Big books start big talk. Stories tell themselves into social worlds that "catch people up," force open spaces of encounter where the fixity of "this" and "that" eases its grip, becomes mutable, inconstant, transformative. Scandalous books, like good gossip, ribald rumors, and "true" stories, are always at work, constantly expanding possibilities for revision, reinvention, and transgression.[25]

For talk, no matter how small, has a habit of getting away from us; it enjoys a certain mobility and productivity that literate societies tend to ignore.[26] Literacy *records*, and so it names and frames the past. But literacy can never fully free itself from the spoken word: writing always affects an utterance; writers are mouths pinned down. This is because language is always at work, always on the make. If the truth be told, the spoken and the written word have never truly severed the friable bonds between them. As books try desperately to fix their tales by setting them into print, readers ungratefully assert their right to speak out. They see things authors know nothing about. They retell plot, character, scene, and conclusion in voices quivering with emotion or flat and affectless. Like hornets, they insert themselves into the text and maddeningly swarm around unexpected emotion, unintentional irony, plot twists not written down. They make up things that are not necessarily there, and the story takes on a life of its own. "To read well," the American philosopher Ralph Waldo Emerson instructed his audience in *The American Scholar*, "one must be an inventor." *Peyton Place* was so successful because it spawned so many fabulous inventions and gave to each a life of its own.

We can only imagine the deep emotive threads that traverse print and utterance. The descriptive difficulties of such a landscape need to be pictured too as readers merge into talkers and in conversation stories don't just take hold but take off. If print culture has historically conspired against talk, it is the spoken word, uttered "off the record" and "between you and me," that finds an honored place in the nooks and crannies of everyday life. Oral discourse, Alessandro Portelli reminds us, "runs through our fingers" and so is always on the move, difficult to pin down, more difficult to trace.[27] Even the dedicated lexicographer works in vain against the riot of rhetoricity. "Tongues, like governments," Samuel Johnson lamented, "have a natural tendency to degeneration." Corrupted by utterances spoken high and low, Johnson's painfully compiled *Dictionary* could not "embalm his language."[28] Corrupt, abused, buffeted by time and the perils of tongues untied, words can never find more than temporary shelter in books. Unpredictably they spill over into so much talk, forever outpacing the encryption of print. And talk, no matter how corrupt, is also and always a performative act, for it "requires the speaker to do something."[29] Talk makes things go.

Talkers, sociologists make clear, are essentially social actors, and ordinary talk, like other practices of everyday life, is never the passive chitchat the writing minority would have us believe. Small talk, like reading, walking, dwelling, and cooking, has "on the contrary the characteristics of a silent production."[30] It makes things happen in the very spaces where cultural activity seems most emptied of social investment and power: "talk," we like to say, "is cheap." Yet if we think of talkers as producers of culture even as they consume it, we can begin to glimpse the political dimensions of talk in all its emotive, animated, and constitutive forms as girl talk, sex talk, dirty talk, locker room talk, kitchen talk, pillow talk, and the kinds of "back talk" that small talk can quickly add up to. In the "quotidian poetics of ordinary language," the world comes to ground and we learn to make and remake a sense of things.[31] People talk, word travels, information flows, identities gel or come apart, subjectivities harden and slip, truth runs wild while stories run riot, and meaning slips and slides in the give-and-take of words in motion. The meaning of any utterance is always "a scene of conflict."[32] There is no final word when people are talking.

But the terrain of talk was long ago ceded by historians to others: anthropologists, sociologists, folklorists, ethnographers, and linguists. That the oral historian needed all of them in order to succeed lent to the positivistic professional seeking objectivity the whiff of suspicion even as it opened the historical door to subjectivity, emotion, and the vast depths of "the human heart."[33] I like to think that Grace Metalious would have understood this difficulty, her own writing being a somewhat frantic effort to pin down what her ears picked up at the rod and gun club, the grocery store in the town center, even at the school receptions where Grace, the wife of the school principal, often had to bite her tongue as she struggled to censor her speech. Absolutely nothing connects Grace Metalious more to her writing than her raconteurship, one of the few bridges to her Franco-American heritage she did not burn. She understood the power of the human voice and the longing of the storyteller to hold it captive, to press it into print like a delicate flower between the pages of a weighty, silent tome. *Peyton Place* was as much a soundscape as a literary landscape, a text in motion, a signifier on the move. In the end, all the talk would kill her, but in the beginning, in the formative years, talk was what kept Grace Metalious going.

When Metalious moved to Gilmanton, she heard the story of "the sheep pen murder" over and over again. She heard townspeople describe the dramatic torchlight procession that brought the sheriff down the lonely New Hampshire road in the summer of 1947 to the darkened farmstead of the Roberts family. She heard about how, the winter before, Barbara Roberts had killed her father and buried him in the sheep pen. She listened as patrons at the rod and gun club debated the girl's confession, listened to whether or not she had been sexually abused by her father for years. Novelists are artful gossips, observers, and snoops. And surely among all the things that bind together the village sleuth and the social historian is the shared desire to track down the hidden and hard to trace, to follow "the thick trail of talk" that lies behind the archive door and between the lines of every page. [34]

This is a story, a history, of one such trail, of how a murder in a small New England village circulated over time and across genres, ultimately pulling into its orbit a nation and the fictions it lived by. Yet the story of *Peyton Place* has not been an easy one to track. You will not find the novel in revisionist histories of the 1950s, nor will you find Grace Metalious in the canonical biographical dictionary *Notable American Women*. This disassociation from the literary has been long and continuous. Absent as well from *The Oxford Companion to American Literature*, neither book nor author makes an appearance in the more recent compendium *A New Literary History of America* by Greil Marcus and Werner Sollors. No scholarship links Metalious to the literary-cultural worlds of the postwar era. Her writing is afforded at best a meager niche in the specialized corners of "ethnic" or "women's" writing. [35]

It is not that Metalious might have eased herself into the category of fine art writing as defined by the high modernism of the fifties' "New Critics" if only her gender and ethnicity had not intervened. Building on the work of Richard Brodhead, we need instead to keep in mind that Metalious insinuated herself into the realm of authorship at a particular moment in time; a moment when definitions of the literary were under assault from "masscult" critics on the one hand and, on the other, from revolutions in publishing that reshaped the terrain of writing and the reading publics they called into being.

This is not a story, then, about a great female writer "lost" to history. Nor is it a recovery tale in search of canon revision. Rather it is an attempt to take *Peyton Place* seriously, both as an act of writerly self-realization and as a social agent, a doer of cultural, even political work. [36] *Peyton Place* was not simply an antecedent to second-wave feminism, although it was that. It was also part of a larger postwar struggle over belonging and recognition, what feminist scholar Carla Kaplan has called the "contestatory politics of voice." [37] Fictionalizing contemporary realities, *Peyton Place* composed as well a history of postwar marginalization that put gender and sexuality in direct relationship to class and ethnic disenfranchisement.

There are, historian Nancy Hewitt astutely writes, "no permanent waves" of feminist struggle, no great surges of liberation superseding one another amidst a sea of inaction and silence.[38] Like all social movements, "second-wave" feminism was a mélange of notions, ideas, emotions, needs, aspirations, ambitions, hopes, and desires that were always "in the air," commingling, overlapping, and intersecting with a diverse range of progressive moves and acts. We don't often think of scandalous books and excitable speech as among these tools of change, yet what invites more intensive collective commentary or sets into motion more forcefully the ordinary affects of life, that sentient realm of expectation and desire that "catch[es] people up in something that feels like something"?[39]

In hindsight we might argue that *Peyton Place* enfranchised suspect categories—female sexuality, gender difference, whiteness, and unconventional sex—but at the time it simply "spoke" to people, gave to readers an ideal respondent and longed-for "Listener" whose story not only echoed their own but also held up a critical mirror to the world they were given: "It does not have to be this way, it could be otherwise."[40] It spoke to readers not as a manifesto but as a yearning to be heard, to be granted a proper hearing, to have a voice in an increasingly polyvocal nation, and to find a footing in the cacophony of contentious talk, and it did so for millions of women and men, one hesitant reader at a time.

No one was less likely to call herself a feminist than Grace Metalious. Politics and collective organization held no appeal for her. Her desire was to be famous—to be a "Somebody"—and many fans saw in that fantasy a world of material security and individual aspiration that feminist activists disparaged. She had difficult relationships with other women, always preferring the company of men and needing constant validation from them. As we shall see, she was haunted, even destroyed, by the very differences *Peyton Place* celebrated. Still, to exclude her would be to define feminism very narrowly as a movement always conscious of itself, certain of its aims, aware of life's roadblocks, singular in its efforts, and available only to those who labored under its flag. Some scholars have made the link between *Peyton Place* and feminism seem clear and explicit; but for millions of readers, feminism, if it came into view at all, entered not as an uncovered truth or part of a coherent plan of action but rather as a "vague but compelling sense that something is happening."[41]

Peyton Place was not a call to social action, but it did confirm that a collective nerve had been touched. Fans felt a deep and mutual connection to both the novel's characters and the author who candidly confessed and marketed her sense of difference, of never fitting in. In the very popularity of the novel, fans felt part of something larger, their anxieties over gender and sexual identity part of a shared, if unspeakable, psychic pain. If feminism was the whisper beneath *Peyton Place*, it emerged therefore as something of a "third meaning," gathering force, in Roland Barthes's terms, as something outside the obvious, generating power not as a fixed idea or given strategy but rather as something that "maps connections, routes, and disjunctures."[42] *Peyton Place* set things in motion: doubt, fantasy, hope, complaint, shock, desire, critique, feeling, restlessness, knowledge. It was as much as anything else an exercise in rupture, a deep gash in the iron fabric of conventional ways of thinking and being.

Certainly this is part of *Peyton Place*'s legacy as a best-seller and part of Grace Metalious's historical meaning as a writer. In the years before the "problem that had no name" acquired political force, became an "ideology," or generated organized resistance, feminism was often simply a flash of singular recognition, an ache made immanent in the unfairness of things, an utterance out of character, a longing unspoken, a restlessness undefined, an inchoate stirring in the effort to say *something*. Feminism came in many big ways, of course; its history is long, ongoing, and powerful, for it causes big trouble for those who dream of foundational truths, gender and sexual fixity, to be sure, but also for the kinds of social and cultural pigeonholing that fundamentalist regimes require. But in the years before "feminism" or "sexual liberation" took on more organized agendas, they found traction in small acts and rebellions, not the least of which was the reading of "racy" books and magazines. Because of the incautious tongues of unquiet readers, the social and cultural orbs of postwar America tilted.

My *dramatis personae* in this book are readers and the many uses they made of *Peyton Place*, both during its time of publication and long afterwards, as they recalled "that book." Most were working-class wives and mothers who in their letters to Grace Metalious struggled to explain the urge to write and come to terms with the novel that had compelled them to do so. Some were men equally moved by the story, while others saw in the success of the unknown author a literary opportunity of their own. They crossed geographic and class boundaries, writing from every region of the country, some with poor spelling, leaking pens, or typewriters with chipped keys, others with schoolteacher-perfect penmanship and grammar. And they kept on writing. Between 1956 and 1965, thousands of letters poured in. Moved by them all, the young author responded, carefully noting with a neat hand the date of her reply at the upper right-hand corner.

Two images emerge from these letters and from the oral histories of readers. The first is that of a solitary figure reading *Peyton Place*, often at night, under bedcovers, a flashlight illuminating the guilty pleasures of a daring act. The second is that of parents, neighbors, churchgoers, teachers, and teenagers knotted together in heated conversation and debate. As biography, then, the story of *Peyton Place* begins here, in the sonorous materiality of history, where transgressive stories find room to maneuver and where unspoken things find collective voice. And because fiction is understood as a representation of the "real," it thus invites comment, comparison, and discussion. If stories remained the purloined treasures of readers sworn to silence, what difference would or could they make? Like many a soap opera, *Peyton Place* was always in production, creating a new text and commentary with every telling.[43] Fan mail, sex talk, or just plain talk between you and me all became integral components of *Peyton Place*'s social life, turning the purposefully muted and officially obscured realm of sexuality and difference into a site of guarded but heated commentary.

In so many ways, then, history is a story of tongues untied. Acts of reading, in other words, are social acts, at times noisy events simultaneously private and public. *Uncle Tom's Cabin* did not launch the American Civil War, nor could readers have found political traction without the kinds of grass-roots activism and reform politics that were taking shape across the nation. But Stowe's novel opened up opportunities to imagine a collectivity that was the South and an oppositional community that was the North. For those who lived beyond the printed words of radicals and the abolitionist platform, talk was often all they had and perhaps all they needed. One of the few novels written by a woman to make it into the history books, Stowe's classic was nevertheless hardly alone in its rerouting of literature from recreation and leisure to "social agent and doer of cultural work."[44] Nor was its enfranchisement of the unarticulated and unspoken unique. Some books push the reader to contemplation. Some induce reflection. *Peyton Place* ignited talk.

Was *Peyton Place* true? To those who lived outside the imaginary landscape of "normal" Americans, whose racial, sexual, class, or gendered Otherness signaled what "real" American girls and boys were not and could never become, whose lives were maimed or broken by the violations of a parent's lust or who learned with each unwanted pregnancy the bitter unfairness of female desire, for those who ached to escape the life pinned on them like the tail on the donkey, it mattered not at all. What mattered, and mattered a great deal, was that such stories got a telling, made of themselves a public record. Fiction becomes history.

No one knows what really happened that cold December night in the village of Gilmanton Iron Works. No one ever found out who murdered Sylvester Roberts, nor is there any proof that he sexually molested his daughter. All the police had were his rotting bones and a young girl's chilling confession. All Grace Metalious had was a story of New England, an outsider's ear, and a longing to tell.

The year was 1956.

1

THE NOVEL TRUTH

When I read [*Peyton Place*] at ten years old,
I knew the world around me was a lie.

JOHN WATERS

In the autumn of 1956, Mrs. John L. Harris[1] sat down to read *Peyton Place*, but her reading was fraught with difficulties. Her son, a student at Dartmouth College, "was disgusted," she wrote its author, "and my husband wasn't much better pleased." Distracted and annoyed by the men in her family, the Seattle housewife nevertheless found the story "completely fascinating," while the writing "caused me to fairly race through the pages." *Peyton Place*'s critics had simply missed the point, she fumed. "The so-called 'filth' which many people censure in your book is to me only a small part of a truly good story." Mrs. Harris urged Grace Metalious to carry on. "Please keep writing," she implored. "Your talent is too good to hide." Then she sat down to read *Peyton Place* a second time.

Mrs. Harris was hardly alone. "Finding nothing about to read on a dull evening," Frank Allen picked up a copy of *Peyton Place* that someone had left behind at his New Hampshire summer camp. He had avoided reading the novel for almost three years after his favorite literary critic, Parker Marrow, panned it. "After a few pages," Allen exclaimed in a letter to

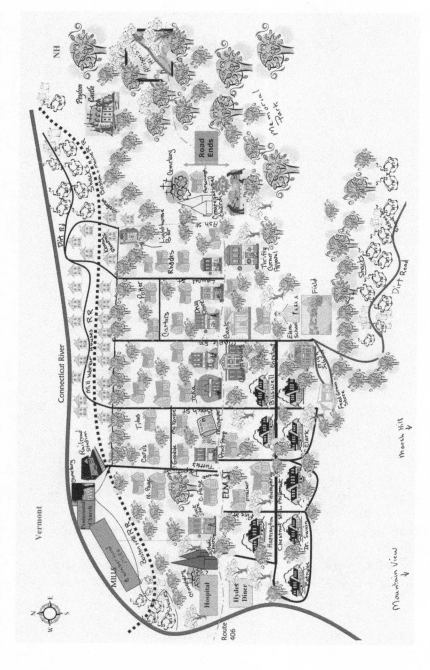

Figure 1. For some readers, Peyton Place was real enough to map. Map of *Peyton Place* by reader Deborah Briskey. Gift to the author.

Metalious, "I whistled in astonishment and thought THAT SO & SO PARKER! HE OUGHT TO BE SHOT. . . . I have taken up cudgels in your defense ever since." Even the harried cookery book writer Julia Child found in *Peyton Place* the perfect "reading-for-pure-self-indulgence." Finding a copy in paperback a year after its publication, she recommended it to her friend Avis DeVoto. "Quite enjoyed it," she confessed. Then, her vacation over, Child "soberly and happily" returned to Goethe."[2]

Despite its reputation as a form of leisure, the reading of novels has never been a trouble-free activity, especially for women, whose readerly desires and habits have long been the subject of passionate concern and controversy. Almost from the first stirrings of the genre, the novel irritated people of quality. "Novels," the Philadelphia physician Benjamin Rush warned his readers, should be avoided at all costs, for rather than "soften[ing] the female heart into acts of humanity," novels "blunt the heart to that which is real." What made the new genre "novel," in other words, was its focus on the imaginary and invented realms of human life, putting the novelist in tension with eighteenth-century calls to reason, evidence, and truth. Things only got worse. By the nineteenth century, fiction was jamming empiricist aspirations to objectivity and fact like dirt in a trigger. "History, travels, poetry, and moral essays" became, as Rush recommended, the preferred antidote to "that passion for reading novels which so generally prevails among the fair sex."[3]

Republican mothers were no less vexed over the types of fiction that women readers preferred. Popular novelists like Hannah Webster Forster wrote extensively against the dangers inherent in certain books. She lamented "the kind of reading now adopted by the generality of young ladies," which to her mind was "foreign to our manners." Susanna Rowson worried as well that the reading of novels could "vitiate the taste and corrupt the heart," joining Foster in decrying the ability of novels to promote among female readers "impure desires," "vanity," and "dissipation."[4]

At the heart of these debates was the assumption, driven by Enlightenment concerns over the relationship between reason and passion, that fiction, especially romantic, gothic, and sensational novels, overly engaged the imagination of readers, making it difficult, if not impossible, for the untutored and "primitive" to distinguish between fact and fiction, fantasy and reality. Unlike the normative educated male reader, whose reasoning capacity, it was argued, provided a more critical rendering of such materials, female, working-class, and subjugated readers were said to lack the capacity to curb readerly flights of fancy. For them, novels reduced the rational self to the imitative behavior of the "captive audience," whereby readers, too caught up in the thrills of fiction, forfeited their capacity to engage the narrative in a reasonable and productive manner. "For all of these lesser subjectivities," scholars have made clear, "the exercise of the imagination was problematic."[5] The credulous reader could literally *get lost* in a book, so closely did she identify with character, plot, and scene. Even the sober mill girls of New England, it seems, fell under the sway of sensational reading, as newspaper cartoons like the one shown here invited readers to draw connections between cheap wages and cheap fiction at the

Figure 2. Caricature of Lowell factory girls reading "cheap literature." The woman on the left is reading a French sex manual, while the pair in bed share a racy novel by Joseph Holt Ingraham. "Factory Girls," cover, *Boston City Crier and Country Advertiser*, April 1846. Courtesy American Antiquarian Society.

very time when Lowell manufacturers were seeking to prove the moral as well as the monetary benefits of female wage labor. Nothing good, it seemed, could come from the irrational mental wanderings of fiction, for "novels not only pollute the imaginations of young women," one American critic warned, but also give "false ideas of life."[6]

In the summer of 1905, Henry Dwight Sedgwick had had enough. Readers, he lamented, were nothing more than an indiscriminate "mob" rushing here and there in pursuit of the latest best-seller. "The proletariat, the lower bourgeois, and the upper bourgeois," it mattered not at all, he wrote, for each class had abandoned its better instincts and training in quest of the "mob novel." The numbers, Sedgwick reported, were shocking: "The Crisis, 405,000 copies sold, the Eternal City, 325,000, the Leopard's Spots, with its career still before it, 94,000." Like many of his literary brethren, Sedgwick worried over the state of American Letters and the nation that produced them. He explicitly linked the turbulent mass strikes that rocked his generation with the consumption of cheap novels and sensational stories, warning readers against the "Mob Spirit" that now engulfed Literature. In the grip of cheap fiction, he charged, the reader grew "more tumultuous, more passionate, more a creature of instinct and less a creature of reason." The "reading mob the bigger it grows, becomes more emotional, more excited, it reads and talks with greater avidity, is increasingly vehement in its likes and dislikes, and opinions, forces the book on its neighbors, gives, and lends more and more with the swift and sure emotions of instinct." Fiction had become a "contagion" spreading itself across the classes and undermining the educational efforts of schools and intellectuals.[7]

Sedgwick was born in 1861, seven years after the founding of the Boston Public Library, and his career as a lawyer, essayist, and historian paralleled the great boom in literacy and the mass marketing of books. Cheap paper put romance stories and dime novels into the hands of increasingly large numbers of working-class and immigrant readers, while free lending libraries not only expanded the reach of books but also gave local librarians the power to decide what kinds of books the public might check out. Publishers listened while library donors cringed. When Samuel Tilden learned that 90 percent of the books borrowed from the Boston Public Library were fiction, he came close to canceling his $2.4 million bequest to New Yorkers who hoped to establish their own free library. Literature,

Sedgwick concluded, needed new leadership: "men of natural gifts and educated taste, experienced in the humanities," who could "tame the turbulent mob spirit" as it coursed through the veins of American social and literary life. Literary men, that is, who shared his passion for Democracy and presumably the *Atlantic Monthly*. Bad novels made bad citizens.[8]

For those who sought to inflame the laboring mobs, cheap novels were blamed for making shoddy activists. Born in Russia, Rose Pastor came to the United States as a young girl of twelve and quickly found work in the cigar factories of Cleveland. Like Sedgwick, she was a "serious" reader, who turned her love of words into the literary arts, writing poetry and eventually advice columns for the *Jewish Daily News* in New York City. Moving to New York in 1903, she became active in the Socialist Party, writing on behalf of the working classes as an advocate of radical social change. Already popular among working girls on the Lower East Side, she became their heroine when she married the millionaire James Graham Phelps Stokes. Like Sedgwick, however, Pastor worried over the enormous popularity of cheap fiction and its effects on women and girls. Joining a growing chorus of progressive reformers and union leaders critical of working girls' participation in consumer culture, especially their "frivolous" pursuit of fashion and romance novels, Pastor feared that dime novels would turn wage-earning women away from political struggle and working-class organization. As Nan Enstad notes, labor activists viewed stories that "offered a fantasy of magnificent wealth bestowed on the working-girl heroine through a secret inheritance and marriage to a millionaire" with condescension and suspicion.[9] Serious times demanded serious books. "With our free circulating libraries," Pastor scolded laboring women in 1903, "what excuse is there other than ignorance for any girl who reads the crazy phantasies from the imbecile brains of Laura Jean Libbey, The Duchess, and others of their ilk! . . . I appeal to you—if you read those books—stop! stop!"[10]

It was not to be. Pastor's own marriage seemed the stuff of fantasy, her continuing radicalism living proof to readers of Laura Jean Libbey that fiction carried with it certain truths their own lives had yet to reveal, certain possibilities that might yet be played out. Readily available from pushcarts and newsstands throughout immigrant and working-class neighborhoods, dime novels joined pickles, bread, and eggs among the necessaries of daily life. But was Sedgwick right? Did cheap novels make for cheeky citizens?

Not surprisingly, proponents of women's rights were there from the beginning, defending a woman's right to read whatever her heart desired, more or less. But the relationship between fiction, fantasy, and femininity raised for feminists as well a number of troubling questions. Could the reading of gothic, romantic, and sensational novels, Mary Wollstonecraft and Jane Austen famously wondered, turn the female reader into the degraded "object of desire," leading to a "conventional, dependent, and degenerate femininity"?[11] Echoing Rose Pastor's fears, Betty Friedan saw in the "sex glutted novels" of the post–World War II era a serious erosion of "independent activity" among American women which forced them to find "their sole fulfillment through their sexual role in the home." Consciously catering to the "female hunger for sexual phantasy," Friedan opined, *Peyton Place* was another sad symptom of the feminine mystique.[12]

In the minds of both progressives and conservatives, in other words, fantasy and imagination could have only negative effects. In the minds of the former, they stirred up erotic and romantic emotions that supplanted reason, promoted female passivity, and undercut a woman's autonomy and emancipation, while to the latter group of thinkers they inspired "ambitious excess," provoking not only "disgust for all serious employments" but also a general dissatisfaction with one's station in life.[13] Only in recent years have attitudes toward the female reader begun to shift. Indeed, entire forests have surrendered themselves to the scholarly exploration of female acts of reading and the everyday uses of books. Second- and third-wave feminists have been especially astute in rethinking the effects of fantasy, repositioning the female reader as a complex social actor who is neither the passive receptor of textual messages nor extraneous to movements of social change.

Light fiction, it turns out, is serious business. For women and girls, who stood in the imaginative center of modern consumer society—men produced, women shopped—dime novels and newspaper stories called new attention to their spending habits. Hardly reflective of reality, the gendered narratives of consumption nevertheless gave women and their interests an unexpected edge by placing both at the center of modern consumer culture and rising concerns over its unpredictable emotional and psychic effects. Sharp dichotomies took hold: Was modern consumerist society and the "mass culture" it unleashed a new opiate or a potential site of rebellion and transformation? Labor historians have most often sided with Pastor, assuming, as her Enlightenment predecessors argued, that political engagement and collective action presupposed a coherent and fully formed political identity as "worker," "woman," "American."

Ladies of labor and girls of adventure, however, tell a different tale. In her powerful study of labor politics in the early twentieth century, Enstad shows that dime novels, like clothes and movies, offered girls and women who labored in constrained circumstances a way to negotiate contradictory positions. Building on the work of Wendy Brown, Judith Butler, and Joan Scott, Enstad underscores the mutability of subjectivity, arguing that women's political consciousness and actions emerged less from "clear and coherent identities" than from the contradictions laboring women experienced as terms like "worker" and "working class" increasingly took on meaning in opposition to womanhood and all things feminine, including the consumption of dime novels. "Precisely because working ladies found themselves excluded from the honorable categories of 'worker,' 'American' and 'women,'" writes Enstad, "the resources of popular culture were of particular importance in their efforts to claim identities out of contradictions, and gain a sense of dignity and worth." Unable to make sense of the categories available to describe their experiences as both wage laborers and American ladies, immigrant girls fashioned a "particular form of radicalism and their own gender and class language."[14] With fiction and fantasy, girls of toil spun new dreams and conjured different selves, reworking old identities as they went and fashioning new, aspirational, and at times political subjectivities. From this perspective, subjectivity unfolds as a process linked to "self" and "identity," but it accentuates more than either the never-ending momentum of becoming. Novels did not cause working women to go on strike in 1909, but in their ability to articulate scenarios of readerly desire, they allowed laboring women to imagine themselves in new ways. In the fantasies of fiction and fashion, female readers found common ground and a collective desire that captured—perhaps produced—their imagination as "women" in common cause. At the beginning of every good story is a reader's silent longing.

To tell the truth, readers were always a mixed lot. There was never a "universal reader," and the concept of "the female reader" was pure fiction, the rejected Other who gave to the serious reader its privileged identity. Reading itself is a deeply mediated activity. Habits of reading reflect differences in class and ethnicity as well as in gender and individual psychology. The segmentation of publishing, as Lawrence Levine pointed out, was well advanced by the turn of the twentieth century, and the notion of "the female reader," like the "mob reader," misrepresented both readership and the literary marketplace. Still, in the long and furious battle over Good Books and the dangers of reading invention and "phantasy," the "woman reader" emerged as an undifferentiated subject of concern and complaint. Historically bound together by the fetters of criticism, women across classes and regions, ethnicity, race, and sexualities now found themselves yoked together as problematic consumers of questionable taste. To pick up a "best-seller" was to confirm and mark that identity linking disparate women together as frivolous readers and femininity with the trashy and lightweight.[15] Real men read history.

Let them. The girls of toil and the ladies of leisure cared not a fig. For where, if not in novel form, could the female reader find herself an actor in a world where women's actions mattered? How else except with a novelist's pen was the history of women written? Where else did the concerns of the female reader find a telling? Of what use, George Eliot asked her readers, was Casaubon's expanding index file of "facts, facts, facts" to the busy women of *Middlemarch*, whose purposeful lives passed in front of the historian's gaze without note or notice? Of what use was History for those edited out of its pages? Novels spoke to women because History had nothing to say to them. "Women were not only not interested in history," the historian Jill Lepore writes, "they didn't trust it."[16] It simply didn't speak their language. Represented as the antidote to the stormy passions and turbulent falsehoods of fiction, History lashed itself to the oak-like mast of hard fact. It cleared its decks of subjectivity, fantasy, and desire and jettisoned undocumented lives. Women were the first to lose interest. "It tells me nothing that does not either vex or weary me," Jane Austen's heroine Catherine Morland confides in *Northanger Abbey*. "The quarrels of popes and kings, with wars or pestilences, in every page; the men all so good for nothing, and hardly any women at all—it is very tiresome: and yet I often think it odd that it should be so dull, for a great deal of it must be invention." Fiction was interesting because it gave a telling to things History would not.[17] The coquette, prostitute, spinster, society matron, factory operative, slave girl, parson's daughter, woman in the attic, girl detective, and woman behind bars all found a place in the popular archive of fiction. The difficulties readers encountered were but flies in honey. Women read the critics, heard the debates, suffered the slings and arrows of husbands and sons, and then, like Mrs. Harris, settled into the hidden lives and secret truths that every truly good story promised.

Like the category "woman," then, the "female reader" constituted an act of social engineering, shaping and defining over time the hierarchical contours of gender difference and the essential nature that separated the feminine realm from that of the masculine. But as Enstad and others have shown, the reading of melodrama, gothic, romance, and sentimental fiction could just as easily alter a reader's relationship to both. "Don't tell me that woman wasn't happy!" the deserted husband of Lulamae tells the young narrator in Truman Capote's *Breakfast at Tiffany's*. "Reading dreams. That's what started her walking down the road. Every day she'd walk a little further: a mile, and come home. Two miles, and come home. One day she just kept on." Lulamae did not simply follow her dreams, nor is it the case that stories made them up for her. Rather stories are always produced in the exchanges between text and reader so that both are subject to change, each the shifting product of fantasy. Is there ever one meaning locked into any given story? Is there truly ever one reader? In the textual fantasies Lulamae wiggled herself into, the "clear and invariable" wife her husband knew wobbled and disappeared.[18] If Lulamae couldn't make it down that road, Holly would go lightly, finding in her new name itineraries Lulamae could only dream about. The "fictive securities of reality," as Michel de Certeau put it, slip away in the reading of books, taking with them "the assurances that give the self its location on the social checkerboard."[19]

Sex upped the ante. "Reading, dear reader, is a sexual and sexually divided practice," the literary scholar Cora Kaplan writes as she sets out to probe her compulsive reading habits when, as a teenager in the 1950s, fiction became an especially powerful force in her life and "narrative pleasure lost its innocence." She confesses, "*Peyton Place, Jane Eyre, Bleak House, Nana*: in my teens, they were all the same to me, part of my sexual and emotional initiation, confirming, constructing my femininity, making plain the psychic form of sexual difference." Longish, robust novels like these collectively invited readers to identify with multiple characters, and unlike the formulaic "romance novels" of more recent years, they seldom confirmed conventional gender or sexual norms. "Rather," Kaplan argues, "they evoke powerful overlapping scenarios in which the relation of reader to character is often deliciously blurred." Novels, Kaplan theorizes, helped female readers like herself "to identify across sexual difference and to engage with narrative fantasy from a variety of subject positions and at various levels."[20]

Few readers can match Kaplan's self-awareness or capture her astute rendering of the social and psychic implications of youthful reading. But as we shall see, she was not alone in reading herself into a sexualized womanhood and, in the case of *Peyton Place*, into manhood as well. Readers tell of devouring *Peyton Place* with "heart pounding and hands straying," and in its pages coming to terms with what those inexact yet powerfully rooted concepts meant and would come to mean as they repositioned themselves within the unconventional scenarios the novel evoked.

In the language of many critics, however, *Peyton Place* was simply a "sexy" book. While serious literary critics like Carlos Baker linked *Peyton Place* to "the revolt from the village school" and compared the young author to literary lights like Sherwood Anderson, Edmund Wilson, John O'Hara, and Sinclair Lewis, the novel found cultural traction as a salacious, spicy, even "sexsational" novel, a reputation the publishing industry kindled. Even before it hit the bookshelves, the novel was marketed as so shocking that it had caused the dismissal of the author's husband from his teaching job. Pictures on the front pages of New England newspapers showed a smiling Grace Metalious surrounded by her family and her unemployed husband, George. What kind of wife could do such a thing? What kind of mother could write such a book?

Journalists, too, increasingly connected *Peyton Place* to a category of erotically infused novels loosely defined as "sex novels," best-sellers from *Anthony Adverse* and *Whistle Stop* before the war to *Forever Amber, Kings Row, The Amboy Dukes*, and *Mandingo* in the years that followed. Uneven in skillfulness and literary acclaim, they were united by their willingness to explore the intimate frontiers of everyday life. Where *Whistle Stop* adopted a gritty social realism that only hinted at sibling incest, *Forever Amber* used a sexually explicit language of pragmatic realism to relate, according to the attorney general of Massachusetts, "70 references to sexual intercourse, 39 illegitimate pregnancies, seven abortions, and 10 scenes in which women undressed in front of men who were not their husbands."[21]

Wildly popular, sex novels mirrored the narrative conventions of earlier romance, melodrama, and sentimental literature, but in these sprawling page-turners readers found complex, often dark stories with a plethora of characters who reflected the public's growing fascination with human sexuality and abnormal psychology. This was especially true in the years after World War II, when the Kinsey Reports and sex-change surgery ignited new interest in sexuality in general and in unconventional sexuality in particular. Sex novels and sexually frank magazines like *Playboy* invited readers to enter the intimate lives of the sexually diverse and socially deviant in ways unavailable in most mainstream newspapers and magazines, which, in many rural areas and conservative regions, underreported and toned down scientific studies like those of Alfred Kinsey.

Indeed, part of the "rawness" of the sex novel was its ability to represent human behaviors and emotions "in the flesh," as it were: as knowledge unprocessed and unadulterated by social probity and conventional politeness. "Dirt" took readers down below, where the unfiltered truth was hidden.[22] Desire and difference hovered over every page—sexual desire to be sure, but also the kinds of yearning and dislocation not easily translated into political understandings. And unlike the pulps, which they tend to be confused with, many of the so-called sex novels were published by quality houses like Macmillan, Random House, and Julian Messner, and sold as hardbacks and paperback reprints in department stores and respectable bookshops rather than being confined to male-dominated spaces in train stations and drugstore news racks.[23] Indeed, it was their proliferation as much as their content that made them so explosive, provoking one astute critic to describe them as the "Literary H-Bombs" of the twentieth century.[24]

To be sure, *Peyton Place* had its sexy bits, and its opening lines are among the most erotic in the novel:

> Indian summer is like a woman. Ripe, hotly passionate, but fickle, she comes and goes as she pleases so that one is never sure whether she will come at all, nor for how long she will stay. . . . One year, early in October, Indian summer came to a town called Peyton Place. Like a laughing woman Indian summer came and spread herself over the country-side and made everything hurtfully beautiful to the eye. (1)

Metalious could write in a style that was "steamy, suggestive, and vague," and her dialogue ranged from the shy and reticent language of adolescence to the tough-guy candor of the hard-boiled detective.[25] "The most spiced-up story of all time," a teenager called it in a letter to the author. An older fan from Springfield, Oregon, was equally thrilled to find the book "liberally sprinkled with sex." Having read the novel twice, she wrote to thank "Grace," assuring the controversial author that her efforts had not been in vain. "I learned a few things from your book that I will not soon forget," she confided. "Oh, Grace, I salute you!" Self-styled sophisticates wrote to congratulate Metalious on getting sex right. "American women are beautiful," a French-born reader conceded, but when it comes to the "art of love," they disappointed. "In this country," he complained, "there is too much conformity, no imagination, every thing is done with a monotonous sameness." Scorning the "hacks" who wrote of "sex without the slightest idea of what it's all about," the letter writer rejoiced in Metalious's mastery of the subject, begging her to meet with him to discuss his own efforts to remedy the situation, a "fast story" called "The Vanishing Lover." Still, not everyone was satisfied: "If you ever launch another book, go a little stronger," an ex-preacher from Oklahoma City advised. "Include some Spanking Episodes also Oral scenes. Yours truly, C. O. Collins."

In the recesses of rural libraries, dusty used bookstores, and collectors' shelves, yellowed dog-eared pages fall open to reveal the underlining and marginalia left by fervent readers from the past. "Ask Katie about THIS!" the bold hand of Robert S. inked beside the much-memorized line "Your nipples are as hard as diamonds." Page 203 of his copy took an especially hard pounding as Rodney Harrington, teenage son of *Peyton Place*'s wealthy mill owner, found the "V" of Betty Anderson's crotch. And then there was the beach scene Peter W. circled in red ink three times:

> "Untie the top of your bathing suit," he said harshly. "I want to feel your breast against me when I kiss you."
> She had stood like a statue, one hand on the back of her neck where she had put it to fluff out her hair, when he spoke. He did not speak again, but when she did not move he stepped in front of her and untied the top strap of her bathing suit." (149)

"Mark! Try it out!" he scribbled in the margin of his copy.

The faded enthusiasms readers left behind, earmarked in its pages, evoke the charged atmosphere that hovered over sexual expression at the time and the tensions the novel ignited. "Sex," Rose Feld declared in the *New York Herald Tribune*, "is the dominant accent of the book, and Mrs. Metalious, in her effort to be realistic, spares neither detail or language in high-lightening her scenes in bed, car or on the beach."[26] *Peyton Place* was "shocking." Even the future mother of God first found Eros in its pages: "I was lying down on the bed, reading a book called *Peyton Place*," rock and roller Grace Slick told interviewers. "It was resting on my crotch and I was reading along and all of a sudden it got me off. For the next two weeks," she confessed, "I went bananas with it." Women weren't the only ones going bananas over the book. Metalious's biographer Emily Toth tells the story of Michael True who while stationed at Fort Chaffee, Arkansas, in the late 1950s, "could walk down the center aisle of any barracks and see forty men lying on their bunks, all still in army boots, reading the paperback version of *Peyton Place*."[27] Like an Indian summer in New England, the men, too, waited for an erotic return.

Still. Yet. When readers talk of *Peyton Place* or when we read extant letters from fans, an odd quality seeps out. Even in the anger and malevolence of critics, there is an aperçu of desire and longing that seems quite out of proportion to anything contained in even the most sexually charged scenes of the novel. In the fan mail that swamped Grace Metalious, there was little that surprised or outraged letter writers, who, on the whole, seem to have picked up their pens more to confess a certain uneasiness with the novel's astute rendering of the world than to comment on the licentiousness of the author's fiction. "The reason it struck people," the writer John Michael Hayes observed, "was that it was so real. They felt it. It didn't read like fiction."[28]

Peyton Place was oddly familiar and yet jarringly strange not only because the novel shocked but also because in the minds of many readers the distinction between the imaginary realm of fiction and the reality of their lives was surprisingly effaced—a reality at best vaguely articulated and at times described as quite "unreal," there being no words to express certain experiences, and thus no way to mark them off as such. Reading *Peyton Place* provoked an uncanny recognition, a glimpse into a somewhat frightening realm readers knew existed but could express in only a vague, inarticulate way, a taboo landscape, out of the public eye, that spoke to the silent fears and ambiguous emotions fans struggled to describe.[29] As we shall see, they wrote as if suddenly exposed, expressing both surprise and uneasiness at the range of emotions the novel called forth.

Almost always, their stories begin with subterfuge:

"It was the kind of book mothers would hide under the bed," a professor of English recalled.[30]

"It was the first time I remember hiding anything from my husband. I kept it in the ice box, behind his beer."

"I kept it hidden in the basement and used to sneak down there to read it."

"I always carried it inside a brown paper wrapper. But that became pretty obvious, so my girlfriend and I slipped the dust jacket of *Gone With the Wind*—they were about the same size—over *Peyton Place*. But we still got yelled at—my teacher hated *Gone With the Wind*."

"Dear Diary," Ruth Forero wrote in a 2008 letter to the *New York Times'* "Metropolitan Diary." "A few weeks ago on my way to work aboard the downtown No. 4 train, I noticed, across from me, a young woman oblivious to the comings and goings of her fellow straphangers, her face buried in her brand-new copy of Grace Metalious's *Peyton Place*. The scene transported me back to my early teens and the forbidden pleasure of reading the book at night with a flashlight under the covers in defiance of my mother's direct orders that I return the book to the library without reading it because of her strong objections to its supposed lurid content. My," Mrs. Forero concluded, "what a difference 45 years makes."[31]

"I kept it under the mattress. It was the only place close to me at night."

"Oh, I had this big sock I'd use at Christmas. I'd shove *Peyton Place* down its long leg when my mother came in to say good night. It looked like a snake had eaten it."

"In the toilet tank. We had one of those old-fashioned water closets, you know. The top had a little shelf where I hid stuff. *Peyton Place* sat there next to my *Playboy* magazines."

"Under my pillow."

"In a bag. A very deep bag."

"Way up on the top shelf. My husband was short so he never much looked up there."

"Under the lower bunk beds in the dorm. The nuns found it anyway and gave us hell. Then they took it back to the convent. We know they read it 'cause the sister who did the cleaning told us she had found it open on a table and what a disgrace it was to see it there. And I think they knew that we knew 'cause nothing was ever said about it and my folks were never notified, which was totally surprising!"

The Irish literary critic Patricia Craig was not so lucky, her expulsion from the convent school in Belfast executed in the wake of *Peyton Place*. "What has happened?" she asks.

> Someone, it appears, has identified me as the owner of a dirty book which went the rounds of Form 5A, and provoked some previously chaste girls to assume an uncharacteristic licentiousness in the back end of Donegal. So the whole rumpus can, after all, be laid at my door. Never mind that I, myself, found the book in question—the lethal *Peyton Place*—so dispiriting that I couldn't read it to the end, and had warned would-be borrowers that it wasn't enjoyable, only bringing it into school under extreme pressure, and then washing my hands of it. (It disappeared; and I never saw it again.)[32]

Virginia Alexander lost her copy going to work. "I read *Peyton Place* several times," she told Metalious. "Then I loaned it to the girl on the elevator in my apartment and that was the last of that!"

Peyton Place raced around.

"Almost fifty years ago PEYTON PLACE opened a whole new world for me," Sarah Goss remembered. "I was a freshman in high school when the book made its rounds through the school. Fellow students exulted in wrestling out the juicy parts of the paperback they kept hidden in their lockers. The best thing you could share with your fellow students was, 'Read page 187!' or whatever. As this became more common, it finally occurred to me. Why I should read the whole book! What a story. I hated for it to end. It's funny—I can't find the nasty stuff anymore. Anyway, I give that book total credit for my love of reading."[33]

In such ways did readers advance their education, but it was the furtive nature of their reading that initiated many into the pleasures of subterfuge and the useful arts of daydreaming, fantasy, and transgression. "I was always alone in the library," the writer Alberto Manguel recalled. "I was twelve or thirteen; I was curled up in one of the big armchairs, engrossed in an article on the devastating effects of gonorrhoea, when my father came in and settled himself at his desk. For a moment I was terrified that he would notice what it was I was reading, but then I realized that no one—not even my father, sitting barely a few steps away—could enter my reading-space, could make out what I was being lewdly told by the book I held in my hands, and that nothing except my own will could enable anyone else to know." In the wake of this "small miracle," silent and known only to himself, Manguel "breathlessly and without stopping" tore through Alberto Moravia's *The Conformist*, Guy Des Cars's *The Impure*, Sinclair Lewis's *Main Street*, Vladimir Nabokov's *Lolita*, and Grace Metalious's *Peyton Place*.[34]

The filmmaker John Waters was ten years old when he discovered *Peyton Place* on his grandfather's bookshelf. "I was so shocked, I would sneak and look at it every time." The first "dirty" book the film director ever read, *Peyton Place* "electrified" him. "I never got over it."[35] As if to preserve this moment of profound emotion and transformation, Waters framed a small patch of wallpaper a friend had scraped off the study wall of Grace Metalious's New Hampshire home. Displayed in the privacy of his workspace, the patch emits something of the aura of a purloined treasure which distinguishes it from the mass-produced memento or souvenir. Fans often seek out material remnants of celebrities, yet as Susan Stewart reminds us, it is not the relic or souvenir that is meaningful but rather the narratives of longing and desire that such objects represent. Like any souvenir, Waters's patch of wallpaper will not function without "the supplementary narrative discourse that both attaches it to its origins and creates a myth with regard to those origins."[36] Here, in other words, we can find in Waters's fragment of wallpaper a way to understand something of the power of *Peyton Place* as a work of personal transgression and transformation. Sought out on a pilgrimage to Gilmanton, delicately removed, hung and framed, the patch takes on the quality of a rare heirloom whose narrative history literally weaves Waters into Metalious's genealogy and the emboldened terrain her legacy afforded. With each look, the story is reclaimed; with each telling his inheritance secured.

"She put me on the wrong road early on," said John Waters with a smile, "and I am better for it."[37]

Not surprisingly, perhaps, it was the publisher of the French edition, Hachette Livre, that most explicitly placed *Peyton Place* within the domains of transgression and dissidence, of insurgent desire and danger. Retitled *Les Plaisirs de l'Enfer*, or "The Pleasures of Hell," the novel was linked not to the fiery home of Lucifer, as American readers might suspect, but rather to the secret archives of the French National Library. On these storied underground shelves, over 350 works of erotic art and writing ranging from the frantic pages confiscated from the Marquis de Sade to early pornographic photography sat cloaked in darkness and under lock and key. Almost every monastery and convent in France held such materials, guarded through the ages in their silent abbeys until claimed by the state. Then, in the 1830s, the National Library decided to isolate all works deemed "contrary to good morals" and tossed thousands of collections into the secret vaults of "Hell." Few readers ever gained access, and over time, Hell became the stuff of fantasy and legend, "the very place for forbidden thoughts."[38] A place of mystery, L'Enfer conjured a world of "pseudonyms, wrong addresses and dates, illegal publishing, closed places, convents, boudoirs, jails, but also the world of libraries."[39] *Les Plaisirs de l'Enfer* conveyed what many American readers often felt but struggled to express: the promise of secrets unveiled, a drifting away from the known world toward the heart-pounding revelations and forbidden nooks and crannies whispered beneath *Peyton Place*. "I can't explain it," the photographer Robert Monroe confided; "it just seemed to haunt me for a long, long time, like a shadow."[40]

In his famous 1956 study *The Organization Man*, the sociologist William H. Whyte argued that popular novels in the postwar period greatly distorted the realities of American life, often avoiding conflict and increasingly advising readers "to adjust to the system." Even when domestic squabbles came into view, Whyte charged, their purpose was "merely [to] highlight how lovable and conflict-less is the status quo beneath." Whyte's point, often missed in more recent critiques of his work, was not only that the Organization Man was growing uncomfortably conformist but also that realism in popular culture was becoming increasingly fake, a new kind of American fairy tale, an *unreal* realism. From *The Caine Mutiny* to the "slick fiction in the *Saturday Evening Post*," Whyte found a literature of solace and deception. These "tales are not presented as make-believe; by the use of detail, by the flagrant plainness of their characters, they proclaim themselves realistic slices of life. . . . But it is all sheer romance nonetheless." Even nonfiction, Whyte believed, was busy mythologizing the placidity of American life, and whether readers believed it or not, realism was becoming hard to find.[41]

Whyte completely failed to mention or honor the many efforts of progressive writers like Arthur Miller, Paddy Chayefsky, Reginald Rose,

Richard Wright, Lillian Smith, and others who sought to recast the meanings and boundaries of who and what constituted the typical and ordinary American with a social realism that harkened back to the cultural activism of the Great Depression.[42] But as Cold Warriors increasingly moved to depoliticize popular culture by repudiating the "socially committed representations of the 1930s" and by condemning the so-called affective fallacy of proletarian and ethnic narratives, consumers were increasingly eased into narrowed visions of life along with more benign representations of the system that produced them. Mobilizing against the entertainment industry and exerting increasing control over the airwaves, anticommunist and right-wing forces slowly but steadily seized control over defining the kinds of families that would be represented in visual culture.

As part of a chilling backlash against the liberalizing effects of the war, alternatives to supposedly "traditional" gender relations and "normal" families gave way to benign productions like *Father Knows Best* (1954–1963), *Leave It to Beaver* (1957–1963), and *The Donna Reed Show* (1958–1966), along with older favorites like *I Remember Mama* (1948–1956), *I Love Lucy* (1952), *The Adventures of Ozzie and Harriet* (1952–1966), and *The Danny Thomas Show* (1953–1971), all of which emphasized a child-centered home where male breadwinning, female nurture, and domesticity went comfortably unchallenged. Economic hardship, prejudice, and troubled race relations faded from the picture, while class, ethnic, racial, and sexual difference all but vanished from view.

Perhaps no TV show more dramatically illustrated this shift than the enormously popular working-class *I Remember Mama*, whose immigrant narrative onstage and in print had stood for wartime pluralism and ethnic struggle. In the years that followed the war, however, the show presented a more materialist and maternal Mama ready to defer to the men in a family presented as more contented and less rocked by the economic and social choppiness of the mainstream. Shows that once asked audiences to deal with complex issues morphed into easy confirmations and celebrations of the status quo. New *Mama* star Irene Dunne endorsed the changes downplaying the role of working-class women in juggling budgets, negotiating with landlords, and maneuvering families through hard times and social conflict. Both onstage and off, Dunne stressed instead women's role as supporting cast members. "Our main responsibility—also interest," Dunne told an interviewer, "always will be taking care of the man of the house because the man of the house needs to be taken care of—in more ways than you can shake a stick at." The Perfect Housewife Institute named her one of the "ten most perfect housewives in Hollywood."[43]

Like the character she portrayed, Dunne reflected the sharp conceptual retreat described by Elaine Tyler May as "domestic containment," a politics forged in the wake of postwar changes in women's attitudes and expectations and by the insecurities they unleashed.[44] As the hydrogen bomb fueled Cold War fears of chaos and decay, family stability and female domesticity became patriotic goals intended to unnerve dissenters as well as dry up funds and opportunities for entertainers and creators of popular culture who pushed for more realistic treatments of contemporary issues. To be sure, undercurrents of discontent flowed. Yet as late as 1957, 80 percent of Americans polled said that people who chose not to marry were "sick," "neurotic," and "immoral." Throughout the 1950s couples married younger and younger, with men taking vows at the average age of twenty-two by the end of the decade, their wives at twenty. "Young people were not taught to say 'no,'" writes Stephanie Coontz. "They just handed out wedding rings." The "essentially benevolent society" that Whyte saw in popular culture might have been a fiction, but it was one that gained surefooted traction as the decade reached its midpoint.[45]

In the struggle to mold society's "truths" and map its moral certainties, popular culture has been shown to be a fierce weapon used by weak and strong alike. Though it is remembered as a scandalous book, we forget that *Peyton Place* was also about a working mother, class injustice, social hypocrisy, religious dogma, and a cast of characters who pushed the boundaries of what Americans were beginning to call "normality."[46] "Dirty" books kept doubt alive. At their best, they extended the more cosmopolitan visions of the 1930s into postwar narratives that encouraged a rethinking of what constituted both "ordinary family life" and the borders of national belonging. Bringing into public view the "truth" about outsider identities, sexual candor, and social inequity, lesbian novels, pulps, and sex novels in general allowed readers to trespass, if only for a few hundred pages, across the boundaries of the normative and conventional.

Like melodrama and romance, "their art or politics veering dangerously close to a feminized world of commercial soap operas, especially if attention was directed to female rather than male disappointments,"[47] sex novels flew under the progressive radar as lightweight and frivolous, but the unfairness their stories revealed, the landscapes of difference they unearthed, and the erotic possibilities they conjured were seldom without political effect. If nothing else, they kept alternative roads from closing over and disappearing from popular view. Like a hot current under the Cold War, *Peyton Place* kept conversations flowing. What was normal? What was real? What was true?

In a landscape of social erasure and sexual opacity, fiction, as Jean Cocteau well understood, is often the lie that tells the truth.

2

The Sheep Pen Murder

Selena stood very still and looked down at the hand on her arm. Her dark,
gypsy eyes seemed to grow darker and to narrow slightly.

"Take your hand off me, Pa," she said at last, so softly that Allison could
barely hear the words.

Peyton Place

In the village of Gilmanton, New Hampshire, the story of the sheep pen
murder often begins with the concealed remains of Sylvester Roberts and
how they came to be discovered on the night of September 5, 1947. People
are apt to tell you how, the year before, he was shot dead and buried a few
days before Christmas, his body dragged to the barn then stuffed beneath
a sheep pen, where the earth remained warm and easy to dig. "They found
him the following autumn," old-time resident Laurie Wilkins recalled.
"There wasn't much left of him by then, just bones." That fall, newspapers
described the somber late-night procession as county officials drove out to
the remote farmstead and "there by the light of torches" discovered the
body where his daughter Barbara "had directed it would be."[1]

Like all "true" stories, the sheep pen murder found traction in the grip-
ping promise of veracity. Even as the truth shifted from speaker to speaker,
the story gained weight and heft by the fact of its having happened: "It
really did." Like the tactile quality of a fine wine, the sheep pen murder
had legs; it circulated as family legend, local gossip, newspaper articles,

court depositions, rural folklore, personal testimony, eyewitness accounts, memory, and small talk. Long before Grace Metalious set it in print, it had its many storytellers and as many uses.

But first, it is Barbara Roberts's story as told under the constraints of arrest and prosecution. It is at once confession and defense, the kind of "pardon tale" cobbled together by those who suddenly find themselves in need of narrative explanation: reluctant storytellers whose interests unexpectedly depend on knowing how to tell a good story.[2]

At 6:15 p.m. I heard my father raving as he came up the walk. I remembered that he had often warned me that if I failed to meet him at the train, he would kill me. I was in the pantry just finishing some ironing when he came in. He lunged for me, put his hands on my throat. I broke away. His back was turned, I think to put on the light in the kitchen. I picked up the gun and shot him. I think he was dead right away. I had a great fear of him. I killed him to defend myself.[3]

At nineteen years old, Barbara was what townsmen called "a looker." Dark-complexioned with blue Bette Davis eyes, she wore her long sandy-brown hair draped over her cheek, where it fell to her slightly padded shoulders. Photos show endless silky legs. Barbara was well liked, a quiet sort of girl of average means, people said, not well off or especially well educated, but a nice kid, a good girl, the kind other parents would welcome into their home. The farmstead she and her younger brother Billy managed together was weather-beaten but solid with a warren of rooms stuck onto its body at odd angles. Two big fireplaces stood at either end of a large, comfortable living room which faced the road and the main entryway. A small den poked into the room, and a smaller living area that was itself attached to a downstairs bedroom stood beside it. A long kitchen pushed up against a square, low-ceilinged dining room big enough to accommodate a ten-foot mahogany table. In the December light the house was cold and dark; the lifeless fireplaces could only have added to Barbara's sense of gloom. Billy, whom she had helped raise since their mother died in 1937, was down at Gilmanton Iron Works, a once industrious section of town whose stores, post office, church, and a half-dozen homes had burned to the ground in the fire of 1915, along with much of its livestock. Now it was just another bend in a remote New Hampshire road, its dozen or so mills abandoned forever, and the reddish-brown iron or "bog ore" that gave the tiny village its name oozed undisturbed beneath the rusty, swampy plain that hugged the banks of the Suncook River.

Located in the high foothills of the White Mountains, a range of towering spruce and granite-tipped peaks that P. T. Barnum once described as "the second greatest show on earth," Gilmanton had been a prosperous farming and academic community with a thriving theological school and a respected academy that sent many of its graduates to nearby Dartmouth College. More recently the town had trafficked in the picturesque, becoming in the late 1880s a summer destination for the world-weary businessman and his family who suffered in varying degrees from "overcivilization," a nervous condition Victorians seemed to acquire as they confronted the frenzied pace of the turbulent modern world. "Gilmanton is not gay or fashionable," the world-renowned travel lecturer John L. Stoddard told his enervated audiences, "but for complete rest, wonderfully pure air, and views which leave an impression on the mind as calm, inspiring and lasting as themselves, I know of no place in this country which I deem its equal."[4]

Sylvester Roberts moved his family to the Iron Works in 1927, a time when farmers throughout the state were struggling to hang on to their land. Even before the depression hit, abandoned farms, especially in the hill country, recalled the "austere New England landscape" Edith Wharton had found decades earlier as she motored across the desolate fields "enclosed in somber hills, and so remote, uninhabited and tragic under the dark sky."[5] Roberts, a big, handsome man not given to temperate rural ways, purchased the old Elkins place for reasons he alone seemed to grasp. A hardscrabble farmstead sited in dense woodland more than two hundred feet off the old town road, it was more than a mile from the nearest neighbor. Since the Revolutionary War it had been a working farm, and like many of the subsistence farms tucked along the Suncook, it depended on the cobbling together of wage labor with agricultural production. Each season laid its claims upon the family: berry picking and gardening in summer, woodcutting in autumn, slaughtering in winter, sheep raising and haying in the spring, and always the odd jobs for quick cash in the village shops or at Packard's Woolen Mill over in Ashland. When his wife died, Sylvester took the opportunity to pursue a less sequestered life, eventually joining his oldest son, Charles, in the Merchant Marine and leaving his oldest daughter, Marjorie, along with Barbara to raise Billy and work the grudging farm. When Marjorie married, Barbara became the primary caretaker for Billy, an undersized ten-year-old. Forced to quit school in the ninth grade, she kept the farm going by raising sheep, gardening, picking fruit, and working as a clerk at the village store in order to supplement the money her father and older brother sent home from their wages. In the spring of 1947, she found work in the local textile mill.

When the call came through that bleak day just before Christmas 1946, Barbara knew that trouble was ahead. Calling from the Laconia train station, her father, home from the sea, demanded a lift, and she knew that he wasn't going to get it. The family car remained crumpled in the repair shop, and if the bus wasn't running to nearby Alton, he would have to walk the entire twenty-eight miles from the station to the Iron Works. Even if the buses were running, it would still mean a chilling seven-mile hike down the road on a dark, wintry evening. His daughter had good reason to worry, for the mercurial rages of her father had often landed on his youngest children in the form of beatings and brawls. She pulled at her hair as the phone rang like buckshot through the farmhouse kitchen.

Since joining the Merchant Marine, Sylvester traveled when and where he could. It was his custom to sign up for trips at the mariners' union hall in New York City, where he would hang out, play cards, then catch whatever freighter came along. His returns were sporadic and unscheduled. He would simply notify his daughter by telegram a few days before his return to Gilmanton. This gave Barbara a brief day or two to prepare herself for his arrival. Still, it surprised her when she found the telegram waiting for her at the village store a few days before Christmas. The trip seemed too short. But for Barbara and Billy they were always too short. Anxiously she pocketed the telegram and struggled "to think her way out." By Saturday, however, her nerves were shot. It was the twenty-second of December and he was due to call at any moment. Too anxious to eat lunch, she bundled up against the cold and headed toward Poverty Corner and then over to Gilmanton to look for Frank Dowst, who doubled as the town's police chief and its school janitor. It was Dowst who had found Barbara in tears the year before as he entered Nockles' store where she worked as a clerk. "You have no idea of the kind of life I lead when my father is home," she confided to Dowst. When the beatings and "improper abuses" became public a year later, Dowst would come to Barbara's defense, but at the time there seemed little that he could do. He advised her to leave home, but

Billy, she told him, would then be left alone with Sylvester, who periodically threatened to shoot him, too. Still, Dowst had been firm in his support and told her to call him "if her father ever threatened to molest her again." That afternoon, however, Dowst was out of town, and so Barbara made her way back to the lonely farmhouse, "her great fear" more numbing than the icy wind that whipped up the hill.[6]

When William Keller heard the girl's confession some eight months later, his first thought was that her story was a hoax. Keller had practiced law in Belknap County for more than ten years and was known locally as the last defense attorney to lose a client on the gallows. Despite this, he was much admired for his legal acumen and easily won election as county solicitor, later serving as chief justice of the New Hampshire Superior Count. Tall, quiet, and distinguished with prematurely graying hair, Keller was responsible for coordinating all murder investigations in the county. True, no one had seen Sylvester, but it seemed most likely to Keller that he had simply missed his ship or maybe gone off somewhere.[7] Despite the part-time status of his county job, his caseload that fall was already bulging, as if the decrepitude of autumn had the power to drag human lives into its decay. He still couldn't shake off the "pepper death" of three-year-old William Burns, who had died the week before when his mother poured black pepper down his protesting throat in order to teach him obedience. If Barbara's story turned out to be true, they would both be arraigned in a week, when the grand jury was scheduled to convene.

Slow and deliberate, Keller prided himself on his patience, building a case carefully, like a dog not ready to deposit his bone until he was sure of its safety. He had been called to the Laconia police station just after supper, but the spreading darkness had brought little relief to the unseasonable heat. It was by now the first week in September, but still only a drizzle was predicted, and the warm, close air made it seem like high summer. All over northern New England forests were drying out. Wildfires had already destroyed more than twenty thousand acres in the state, with worse predicted. In the stuffy room it was hard to concentrate on what Barbara was saying, harder still to believe it was true. Like the others in the sticky interrogation room, Keller hoped the story was only the "hallucination of a girl left alone too much on the farm."[8]

Barbara had been brought to the police station on the evening of September 5 by her brother Charles, a lieutenant commander in the

Merchant Marine, and their brother-in-law Paul Richards, who now lived on the farm with Barbara's older sister Marjorie. In April, Barbara had unexpectedly left the farm, taking a job at the woolen mill in nearby Ashland and moving in with her boyfriend's parents. William Keller had known the Roberts family for many years. Barbara's uncle Charles, known locally as "Uncle Charley," had been a famous "boy orator," and another uncle, Ernest Roberts, operated a poultry farm in Gilmanton, just up the road from the Iron Works. Like everyone else in town, he liked Barbara but knew less about the seafaring father, Sylvester. Charles admitted that his father was "a man of high temper, but that he was apt to be over anger shortly." As Keller listened to the story, he noted Barbara's cultured voice, her stylish black dress, and her calm, ladylike demeanor. Barbara sat with her long legs crossed, occasionally shifting her weight and looking up at Keller and then at Homer Crockett. Crockett, a slim, fair-haired man, had been the county's High Sheriff for as long as anyone could remember. He and Keller had worked together on the "pepper death" case, and they worried about another sensational murder popping up in the newspapers. "In the war I have seen so much," Charles blurted out. "This is my own sister who has done this and I had to bring her in. What else is there to do?" No one spoke. Until the body was found, Keller cautioned everyone in the room to refrain from jumping to conclusions.[9]

At eight o'clock, Crockett and two officers left the station and followed Barbara's brother-in-law to the now deserted farmstead, a good half hour's drive. Barbara's older sister Marjorie, too "nervous" to join her husband at the police station and afraid to remain at the farm, had gone to her husband's parents' house. Without any woman friend to keep her company, Barbara resigned herself to the long wait at the station, her only movement the anxious opening and closing of a black handbag she held in her lap with the initials BER embossed in gold. Keller and Charles held vigil with her. Charles fidgeted in the closeness of the room, then rose from his chair and paced up and down the shadowy hallway. By nine o'clock there was still no word. Barbara smoked a cigarette. A half hour later Crockett called. "Which pen? What floor boards, exactly?" Finally, at ten o'clock their torches picked up the pale gleam of fleshless bones.

When the interview began, Barbara's voice was calm but whispery. Even in the hushed room the men strained to hear. "As he came up the walk, he was raving." It was too soon. She glanced at the clock: 6:15. He must have hitched a ride. The pantry was cozy from the hot iron and still warm clothes she was folding. When she turned, he was already in the doorway. Suddenly he lunged and put his cold hands around her throat. She hit him hard and broke away. Still ranting, he strode into the kitchen to turn on the light. She remembered picking up a gun, then a rifle. She aimed at his uniformed back. "I think he was dead right away," she told them. Later, friends would testify to her great physical strength. Clerks at Nockles' recalled their amazement "at the ease with which she handled large quarters of beef and pork." She was able to do a man's work, they attested. "She would even slaughter animals." Her muscles, they reasoned, "were apparently hardened by work on the farm." So at first no one doubted that she worked alone that night, pulling and pushing her father's body like a sack of feed the short distance across the frozen dooryard and into the barn, where livestock kept the ground soft and warm. Underneath the empty sheep pen she jiggled a few boards loose, exposing a narrow space about eighteen inches deep between the floorboards and hard ground below. Whether Billy helped her wedge the body down below is a question townspeople still debate, but down below is where Sylvester went three days before Christmas 1946.

In postwar America, incest was a hushed and guarded secret, a shadow act described by Louisa May Alcott as "that spectral whisper in the dark."[10] Conceived by many as something "rare and alien," well into the 1950s incest was viewed by experts as a one-in-a-million occurrence.[11] Modern anthropology held that cultures from around the world shunned abusers, thus recognizing incestuous acts as universally tabooed behavior. From this perspective incest appeared simultaneously "unnatural" and unlikely. Almost all forms of domestic violence were officially ignored, as family service workers, researchers, and counselors preferred to view complaints as "family matters" or look to the victims for root causes. Even when researchers in Colorado discovered 302 battered-child cases in the Rocky Mountain State alone, professional journals remained silent. Between 1939 and 1969 not one article on family violence appeared in the major journals of American family sociology.[12] Readers of the raw 1941 best-seller *Whistle Stop* had difficulty naming the incestuous relationship between the siblings Kenny and Mary. "We in Barracks No. 2," wrote one GI in 1945 to the novel's author, Maritta Wolff, "have examined the situation from all angles—and I do mean all angles—and we can reach no satisfactory solution."[13] Wolff had been subtle, but the incredulousness of readers paralleled the rhetoric of social workers, politicians, and sex experts who increasingly ignored incest even as they continued to investigate serious cases of child abuse.

Such widespread neglect on the part of authorities was a fairly recent development, however. If Barbara Roberts had reported her father's abuse in the decades before the First World War, public officials would have had a very different perspective on things. Throughout the late nineteenth century, charity volunteers and child rescue workers accepted the arguments of women's rights advocates who, as early as 1870, maintained that sexual abuse, especially among working-class and immigrant populations, was an everyday occurrence, the result of both male brutality and the lack of male sexual self-control, particularly on the part of those from "inferior stock."[14] In 1896 the young alienist Sigmund Freud believed he had discovered through the seduction stories of his female patients the "caput Nili" of human suffering, although he would later refine his arguments, claiming that it was difficult to distinguish between fantasy and reality in these disclosures. In America, his seeming dismissal of these stories encouraged many "Freudians" to reject them as improbable fantasy, the result of "hysterical mendacity."[15] Turn-of-the-century caseworkers, however, spoke of intra-family "carnal abuse" in casual, unembarrassed terms, while temperance advocates employed admittedly racist and class-bound attacks on alcohol use to publicize and prevent male violence against women and children. An acknowledged fact in rescue work, incest, like wife beating and corporal punishment, was blamed on male culpability and aggression. Courts and the public alike held fathers and husbands responsible for acts of violence, including incest, prompting, as Linda Gordon argues, "the identification of problems unmentionable by standards of Victorian propriety." In the decades before World War I, she points out, feminist advocates redefined incest and wife beating as social problems that challenged both the "sanctity of the Victorian home and authority of the paterfamilias."[16]

By the time Sylvester Roberts began to abuse his younger daughter, however, child sexual abuse had been radically reinterpreted. New challenges to the sexual order by an array of "sex rebels," along with highly publicized campaigns by the military against the "disease-ridden prostitute," helped shift images of the passive and "pure" child in need of protection into post-war portraits of wayward girls and loose women in need of correction. By the 1920s, public concerns over "the girl problem" and the female "sex delinquent" combined with a new pro-family campaign that pushed incest into the far corners of public discourse, while Freudian concepts of the psychopathic personality shifted attention away from the father and other male relatives of child victims to a colorful cast of perverted outsiders: the dirty old man, the sex fiend, or, in the newly crafted language of the clinic, the sexual psychopath. The rape or molestation of children, experts now agreed, was a crime of the streets, not of the home.

This did not mean that incest disappeared from case records; but in place of Victorian concerns over male violence and abuse, professional social workers, psychiatrists, and many academics increasingly attacked "unfit" mothers for "moral neglect" while blaming the "wanton" behavior of abused girls for their situation. In northern New England a diagnosis of "in danger of falling into habits of vice and immorality," whether made by town officials, judges, social workers, or parents, could land a girl in a state's industrial school until she turned twenty-one. Well liked in Gilmanton, Barbara Roberts would nevertheless be clearly at risk if put on trial. At the time of her arrest, she had left home to live with her boyfriend's family. Although the local newspaper was careful to mention that she was a "lady in every way," reporters also noted that, as "demonstrated by her looks," it was clear "that the girl from the tiny village farm and her counterpart in the city can no longer be told apart." To prove it, they printed a large photograph of a sultry, stylish Barbara, her legs casually crossed, her right hand seductively touching her lips. Her only jailhouse request the papers reported: a cup of coffee and a cigarette. Readers couldn't fail to notice that this "20-year-old motherless girl" looked very much the sexy woman whose calm, demure image seemed to contradict her plight as a longtime victim of incest, a crime many people thought implausible anyway, if not impossible.[17]

Far more dangerous to New Hampshire's children, state authorities argued, was the "sexual psychopath." In the years preceding and the decade that followed the Second World War, national concern over the sexual abuse of children focused sharply on the sex offender, whose "emotional instability or impulsiveness of behavior" was believed to be responsible for the majority of serious sex crimes committed against women and children. Despite the heavy press generated by the Roberts case (Concord, the state capital, was just eight miles from Gilmanton), New Hampshire civic leaders turned to the brutal murder of a seven-year-old Massachusetts girl two days after Barbara's confession, and the apparent "sex slaying" of another young girl not long after, to justify the creation of a commission to study the cause and prevention of "serious" sex crimes. It proposed legislation directed at "curbing the vicious tendencies of the sex offender who might someday entice your little girl or boy into a dark corner."[18]

The term the commission employed to describe such an offender—the "sexual psychopath"—had a long and complicated history, but as historian Estelle Freeman points out, its use took on new meaning during the revived sex crime panics between roughly 1949 and 1955. The sensational arrest in January 1948 of Caryl Chessman, known as the "Red-Light Bandit," offered opportunities for conservative politicians and religious leaders to claim a rise in sexually motivated crimes. Chessman, who would eventually be put to death in California's gas chamber, was accused and later convicted of robbing people along a lovers' lane and then forcing his female victims to perform sexual acts with him. Because in one case he lured his victim more than one hundred yards from her car, prosecutors were able to bring kidnapping charges so that the death penalty would apply. Signaling the beginning of a new sex panic, the Chessman case turned national attention to the dangers posed by strangers, sexual predators external to homes, communities, and "normal" social relationships. Readers of popular magazines such as *Time, Newsweek*, and *Parents* magazine consumed hundreds of articles with titles like "Queer People," "Sex Psychopaths," and "What Shall We Do about Sex Offenders?"

So taken were New Hampshire commissioners with this last article that they corresponded with its author, David Wittels, who recommended the passage of laws that would keep "such monsters" and "moral cripples" away from New Hampshire's women and children. Central to this approach was the shared assumption that strangers constituted the most dangerous and common group of child abusers. "The victim," the commissioners explained, "is attacked in a lonely location, the assault is accompanied by force, brutality or violence, even sufficient to cause death. Elaborate plans are usually made for a quick escape and against the possibility of recognition. This cunning is invariably present and marks the sexual psychopath."[19]

Strangers, of course, do commit sex crimes, and at times girls were more or less willing participants, many bribed into silence "with a nickel, an orange, a pail of coal." But as most studies reveal today, even unrelated molesters are seldom unknown to their victims or their families. More typically they are kin, neighbors, or close friends. And the home remains today, just as it was in Barbara Roberts's time, "the most dangerous place for children"; their most likely assailant is still their father.[20]

While New Hampshire's commissioners admitted that serious sex crimes occurred within their borders, they continued to assume that sex offenders tended to come from urbanized areas out of state, especially from ethnically diverse regions like Massachusetts, where, they charged, authorities "directed" moral offenders northward, at times even providing bus tickets.[21] Still, they insisted, the state remained vulnerable to "perverts," "sexual psychopaths," and "dangerous sexual criminals"—terms best understood today as arguments over what constituted the borders of normal sexuality rather than as definitions of any particular criminal behavior. The commission recommended, however, that anyone charged with attempting or committing rape, "unnatural and lascivious acts," bestiality, sodomy, or enticing a child be legally mandated to undergo psychological evaluation. Incest, by contrast, dramatically receded in importance among their concerns and was now ranked together with nonviolent acts such as lewdness and indecent exposure. Furthermore, the commissioners agreed, the examination of accused perpetrators was to be "discretionary," so that no county solicitor was "compelled to accept these alleged 'facts'" but rather could "reject them as mere gossip if he feels that such is the case."[22] Eager to scrutinize the activities of strangers and define the borders of sexual normality and deviance, authorities retreated from the home and the kinds of rumors delinquent daughters and problem girls were thought to spread.

In the fall of 1947, however, the "spectral whisper" of incest traveled around Gilmanton in the impolite and shielded exchanges of local gossip. For some it lacked the ring of truth, and they refused to believe the rumors about Sylvester Roberts. But for others the crime was as much in the telling as in the doing. "People talked about the dark things that went on in Gilmanton," longtime resident Roger Clark recalled. "They talked about them all the time, but not *publicly*."[23] Still, in its ability to dig out the hidden but suspected, town gossip pulled incest out of the shadows and away from the imaginary setting of tarpaper shacks and drunken lowlifes: the Robertses had been a respectable, even a locally well-known family. The printed word remained less candid. Only once did newspapers describe Sylvester's actions as incestuous. Reporters simply noted that Barbara "had been forced to submit to improper abuses by her father since she was 13 years old," often at gunpoint.[24]

But as the trial approached, the unspoken and the unspeakable found expression. While the woods burned around them, Barbara's story ignited the underbrush of village life and spread across the region. Papers noted the "talk" about Barbara's sister, Marjorie, who also had left home abruptly. Some in town took umbrage and heatedly spoke of Sylvester's "good reputation," while others wove old suspicions into the fast-moving narrative of murder, rape, and small-town indifference. Party lines hummed as people recounted Sylvester's tyrannical behavior toward his children, his possessiveness toward his daughter, his flashes of temper and his drunkenness during his occasional visits home. "He had two faces," a villager told reporters. "One he showed the neighbors, the other he showed at home."[25] Charles remained emotionally torn, admitting that his father was "a man of high temper," but also claiming that his anger blew over quickly.[26] Some expressed little surprise, having accepted sexual deviance and violence—"dirt and desire"—as the authentic underside of abandoned New England.[27] "I suppose we always kind of knew these things happened," a summer resident confided, "but no one talked about anything like that, not back then anyway." Full-time residents agreed. "Of course people knew," Laurie Wilkins insisted. "How couldn't they know? The way he looked at her, everything! No one I knew seemed too surprised by what happened."[28] But the word stuck in many people's throats: Sylvester was no shack dweller, nor was he one of the region's itinerant "queer folk" whose strange ways and warped behavior lingered in the region's cultural imaginary. How, townspeople wondered, could a father like this commit such a crime?

By December 1947, however, there would be little else to say. Just as the trial began, Barbara grew increasingly reluctant to discuss publicly the "sordid details of an unhappy childhood."[29] Facing a legal world of men (New Hampshire women had received the right to serve on juries that year, but only if they volunteered in writing), she had to consider her chances.[30] As the jurors shuffled in, a black-coated doctor gave the

defendant a sedative. A kindly minister and his wife from Acton offered
their support and testified to her good character. Then, hoping to protect
her younger brother, who had by now also been indicted for the murder,
and to prevent further scandal for her family, Barbara quietly pleaded
guilty to manslaughter and was sentenced to a term of three to five years
in prison. Because New Hampshire had yet to build a facility for women,
she would serve out her time in Vermont. Her brother Billy, who was fifteen at the time of the murder, was placed on probation for four years and
remanded to a state institution "consistent with his welfare."[31] They would
never return to Gilmanton.

When the publishers of *Peyton Place* told Grace Metalious to make Lucas
Cross Selena's stepfather rather than her father, the author thought
her book was ruined. "Now it's trash rather than tragedy," she told her
friends. Yet no one familiar with the horror of child sexual abuse would
ever dismiss *Peyton Place* as trash. A rare portrait of incest in the fifties,
Metalious's description of child sexual abuse remains vividly realistic
today. In almost every detail, the story of Selena Cross conforms to recent
clinical and historical studies that have revealed the discrepancies between
the myth and reality of girlhood sexual assault. In the novel Selena is raped
by an older male relative, her stepfather; the assault is heterosexual; the
younger brother is left untouched; she is isolated, humiliated, and terrified, turned into a second wife to perform household tasks and care for
a younger sibling. Her mother, Nellie, is ineffectual, disbelieving of and
oblivious to her daughter's signals of distress; town authorities look the
other way, noting that Lucas "paid his bills." Besides, "I was drunk," re-
peats Lucas in his own defense. "Honest Doc," he tells the town physician.
"I was drunk. I didn't know what I was doin'. . . . I don't know what got
into me" (159).

   That Lucas Cross is a shack dweller rather than the owner of a comfortable farmstead like the one owned by the Roberts family confirmed many
of the prejudices prosperous New Englanders had against the poor of their
towns. Yet Metalious holds the entire community responsible for Selena's
situation through their long indifference to the needs of working people:
social workers who "turned away from the misery of the woodsman's
family" (29), mill owners who bullied their daughters and underpaid their

employees, schools that moved the "shackers" along. In *Peyton Place*, incest, domestic violence, and unwed motherhood are not simply put on display; they are linked to social indifference and economic injustice, simultaneously political and private acts.

While describing Lucas as a drunk and an abuser, Metalious is also sensitive to the kinds of pain workingmen like Lucas suffered under the boot heel of local class hierarchies and social hypocrisy. "Good cabinet-makers the Crosses, said the people of the town. 'When they're sober,' they amended" (30). Like many of Metalious's disfigured and twisted characters, Lucas once had the dreams of youth. "When we hear talk of 'social consciousness' in American novels," the respected journalist Otto Friedrich sarcastically wrote in 1971, "we generally assume the celebrated discriminations of Manhattan's East Side, or, ultimately, the unhappiness of a John O'Hara on being blackballed at one of the more elegant country clubs. But the real class system, the one that young Grace Metalious came to know, is simply the system of the rich against the poor, and of the insiders against the outsiders."[32] In this telling, incest was not only a sexual crime but also a collective social failure.

And how to protect oneself against the effects of rape? What choices were available for the girl who got pregnant? Contraceptives were illegal in most states, abortion was dangerous as well as illegal, and in some states it was a crime for a doctor to discuss contraception with an unmarried woman. Crestfallen when told that Lucas had to be Selena's stepfather, Metalious worried that the abortion scene would not get a sympathetic reading. Why would a doctor risk losing his career to help a girl impregnated by someone other than her father? Even then a doctor risked prison. How could the abortion make sense to readers?

From the beginning, Metalious wanted her story to prick the moral skin of abortion opponents, and Doc Matthew Swain was exactly the right type of small-town doctor to do it: crusty and kind, much beloved and a bit of a rogue, a straight shooter with high principles. He hates three things: death, venereal disease, and organized religion. He is Metalious's truth teller. When he discovers Selena is pregnant by her "Pa," he treats it as what it is: rape. What matters, he believes, is the girl in front of him. As he wrestles with his conscience over breaking the law as well as violating his own code of ethics, the reader is skillfully pulled into the drama, becoming, even if only for a moment, a fellow outlaw willing the Doc to save Selena. Through Swain's "silent voice" Metalious asks, "What is life?"

> You've lost, Matthew Swain, it said. You've lost. Death, venereal disease and organized religion, in that order, eh? Don't ever let me hear you open your mouth again. You are setting out deliberately this night to inflict death, rather than to protect the life as you are sworn to do.
>
> "Feeling better, Selena?" asked the doctor, stepping into the darkened bedroom.
>
> "Oh, Doc," she said, starring at him with violet-circled eyes.
>
> "Oh, Doc. I wish I were dead."
>
> "Come on now," he said cheerfully. "We'll take care of everything and fix you up as good as new."
>
> And to hell with you, he told the silent voice. I *am* protecting Life, *this* life, the one already being lived by Selena Cross.
>
> "Listen to me, Selena," said Dr. Swain. "Listen to me carefully. This is what we are going to do." (145)

It's difficult to assess the impact of Swain's action upon readers, but Selena's abortion contributed to the novel's reputation as "shocking," confirming its "wickedness" among critics. As with so much of *Peyton Place*, it blasted open silent topics and propelled secrets like incest and abortion into the public domain. Through the characters it was possible to talk about behaviors that were otherwise difficult to discuss. "I used the characters to talk about my neighbors," said one reader. "You know, there goes Mrs. Partridge, the local gossip. But we all used the book to talk about things we never felt able to discuss before, certainly not with my neighbors. When you mentioned *Peyton Place*, well, it meant it was ok to talk about abortion or incest, I mean it was there in print!" Another reader explained that "it was the first book I read that didn't make me feel guilty over what I had done. We were middle class yet I had to sneak out into the night, risk getting arrested or, worse, infected or butchered by some doctor I didn't know. There were no choices here. To have another baby would have killed me. I remembered that line. 'I was protecting life, the one that was already depending on me.' "[33]

In the end, Barbara Roberts decided not to meet with me. The notoriety of her case divided first the family, then the town. The reissue of *Peyton Place* in 1999 further splintered the town between summer people, older folks who knew the Robertses, and locals who united once more against *Peyton Place* and the author "from away." Having been turned into Selena Cross, Barbara slipped out of public view, the spectral whisper that came to her in the night having taken on a new reality in a fiction others would use to help them come to terms with their own experiences and make of them what they could.

3

SCENES OF WRITING

I think all sorrows can be borne if you put them into a story.

ISAK DINESEN

Let me describe the scene as it was so often described to me: It is autumn 1954, the holidays not far away. The weather is raw and unusually bitter for late fall in New Hampshire. Two women sit in front of a large brick fireplace "talking and reading, reading and talking." The dark-haired one in the rocking chair is Grace Metalious, the young schoolteacher's wife whose penchant for wearing flannel shirts, jeans, and moccasins has not gone unnoticed in the small towns that make up the Lake District surrounding Laconia. Her hair is pulled back in a severe ponytail as she listens to her friend Laurie Wilkins read from the chapter Grace has just completed. Then she describes the next chapter and sketches out ideas. Her friend listens—she laughs, cries, frowns, and hoots as Grace's considerable imagination takes flight. Then they turn to other things. Laurie tells Grace about what she heard today down at the newspaper office, where she is a reporter of local "chit-chat." The phone rings; they wait to see if it is for the Wilkinses—five rings on a ten-party line—yes, it's for Laurie, a story she might be interested in. Grace picks up a magazine; she reads something to Laurie; Laurie tells her about the phone call, a call nine other people plus

Mrs. Knowles, the switchboard operator, now probably all know about too. They grab a beer and talk about Christmas, the bitter cold, and about the troublesome woodsmen—many of them now dead drunk down at the local store. Then Laurie tells Grace about the time the daughter of one of the local woodsmen killed her father just before Christmas and, with the help of her younger brother, buried his body in the sheep pen just off the barn where the earth was still soft. Grace felt the hairs on her neck begin to tingle.[1]

Laurie Wilkins was thirty-four years old when she came to live in New Hampshire: a handsome, athletic woman with sun-bleached hair, blue eyes, and an infectious laugh. She and her husband had long been seduced by the region. They had honeymooned in the White Mountains and, like many urbanites before them, found in the landscape a sublime grandeur missing from the world they inhabited. But Laurie was also aware that the north woods were not just a way to get closer to nature; they were also a way to get farther away from the social constraints and conformity of New York. A self-described "bohemian" and free spirit, Laurie never felt quite at ease with her family's wealth and social connections. Her father imported essential oils, the aromatic foundation for making fine perfumes and essences, and he provided a gracious home for his wife and daughter. Laurie's mother, whose elegant portrait towered over the farmhouse dining room, was an accomplished opera singer, and their house in Forest Hills was well tended by servants who catered to the needs of visiting writers, artists, and business leaders. But when Laurie entered Barnard College, the Great Depression was beginning to deepen, and like many of her classmates, she found in the progressive politics of the era a way to refashion her gender and class identity and the unease and restlessness they concealed. After graduation she set out on a career in journalism, taking a job as a reporter for the Scholastic Press Association, where she eventually met and married Bill Wilkins.

In 1947 the Wilkinses represented a tiny but significant trickle of middle-class urbanites whose search for what Helen and Scott Nearing famously described as "the Good Life" took them into the depopulated farmlands and sagging towns along the northern rim of New England. Even before the depression hit, New Hampshire farmers had struggled to make a go of it, but by 1940 their ranks had dropped to just over 10 percent of the state's working population. Manufacturing fared no better as textile mills continued to close in the wake of the Amoskeag Mills' devastating petition for bankruptcy in 1935. By the time the Wilkinses arrived in Gilmanton, the population level hadn't increased since 1900 and the town still carried the marks of discouraged farmers letting go—"the one steady pull more" no longer possible.[2] In a place dense with history, the landscape conjured a poetics of cultural longing—of unpainted barns slipping to the ground, of superfluous foundations now thick with raspberries and fireweed, of old wells, their caps rotten and dangerous. Elsewhere in the region, this defection of sons and daughters gradually slowed after World War II, but along the northern tier of New Hampshire, which extended west into Vermont and east into Maine, farm abandonment continued unabated well into the 1950s, setting off a real estate bonanza for urbanites in search of summer homes.[3] Writing from his recently purchased farm in Vermont ("an ideal spot to avoid the harsh facts of farm economics he teaches at Harvard"), John Kenneth Galbraith wryly noted: "It is the peculiar good fortune of the New Yorker . . . that he is close to a decadent agricultural region. Poor land makes good scenery."[4]

The arrival of the Wilkinses, however, was a sign of the glacial changes that were already subtly but profoundly altering the region as state planners and entrepreneurs shifted investment away from agriculture and dairy farming and toward tourism and defense-related industries. By 1948 the electrical industry was growing rapidly enough to offer Bill Wilkins a high-paying job, while Laurie eventually joined the *Laconia Evening Citizen* as its social reporter. Images of Edith Wharton's turn-of-the-century Massachusetts town of Starkfield were gradually replaced in the national imaginary with appealing, picturesque visions of birches bending to "left and right" and of horses "stopping by woods on a snowy evening," the complex images Robert Frost created and magazines like *Yankee, Reader's Digest*, and *Life* simplified and mass marketed along with lobsters, maple syrup, and baked beans. Leaving the city behind, the Wilkinses purchased a two-hundred-acre farmstead, enrolled their children in the town's only school, and, like Frost before them, bought a flock of Wyandotte fowl.[5]

Located in the high foothills of the White Mountains, just south and east of the Ossipee and Belknap ranges and about eighteen miles north of Concord, Gilmanton, like most places in northern New England, was far more remote on the mental maps of urban travelers than in its geographic distance from the modern metropolis. Frost, of course, was neither the first nor the last homesteader "from away" to transform the harsh and awesome landscape "North of Boston" into a lyrical, ruminative poetics of separation and escape from American materialism—just one of the more gifted. But as recent scholars have shown, the "invention of New England," to borrow a phrase from Dona Brown, had been an ongoing process almost from the beginning of its colonization by the English. It was the governor of New Hampshire, Frank Rollins, who in 1899 established Old Home Week as a way to plug the hole in the region's population drain and bring back, albeit temporarily, former residents and their purses. But far more important than this goal was the commodification of nostalgia which Old Home Week nourished, as those who had left for southern New England heaved sighs of longing for a rural past they remembered and reimagined in contradistinction to the industrialized environs they now inhabited.[6] A new Country Life movement thrived along with an expanded tourist trade of farm boarders, summer homes, and rustic camps. If southern New England signaled the capitalist future, northern New England trumpeted the past, turning its mountains and lakes into scenic views and healthful escapes from the hectic pace and smoke-filled skies of Boston, Providence, New York, Philadelphia, and Chicago. "Gilmanton's air is pure and wonderfully invigorating," the Mountain View Hotel promised its Victorian-era guests. "Situated far above ponds and rivers, malaria and typhoid fevers are there unknown. Physicians have stated that it has all the natural requisites for a health resort of the highest value."[7] Travel writer John Stoddard concurred: "I know of no place in this country which I deem its equal." A frequent and rejuvenated visitor, Stoddard joined a chorus of expert voices that extolled the restful, quiet pockets of northern New England as places "in which to recuperate from past dissipations, and to provide a store of energy for the coming season of social duties and pleasures."[8] His words echoed down the years as rusticators, tourists, and neo-Yankees sought out the Good Life in northern New England. Here, the transplanted Californian Robert Frost quipped, one got "Yankier and Yankier."

In the 1930s and again in the 1950s, regional planners picked up on all of these themes, launching huge advertising campaigns aimed at spreading the word and drawing more outsiders into the area. If Stoddard's lectures and Frost's poems helped urbanites conceptually uncouple northern New England from the rising turmoil of immigration, race riots, pollution, and union unrest that characterized an industrializing nation, regional policymakers worked hard to keep them physically well linked with miles of steel tracks and, later, with improved roads and superhighways. In 1880 a train trip from New York City to Tilton, New Hampshire, in a luxury parlor car took two hours and forty minutes. It was then a short hop on a branch line to Belmont, and another four miles to Gilmanton Center. The automobile wouldn't match this time even after the Federal Highway Act of 1956, but by then, motor traffic itself had became a major irritant driving urbanites northward. "Local real estate men," quipped Galbraith from his farm in 1953, "realize that their fortunes are tied up with New York City's traffic congestion and the state of its transit system. In line of duty they read the New York papers and view the future with confidence."[9] By 1948 the New Hampshire Planning Commission could boast that sales of summer homes to people from other states numbered over twenty thousand residences.[10]

The Wilkinses, however, were not simply summer people, and so they moved in a social world that was somewhat muddled: it included neo-Yankees, mostly other urban escapees as well as local professionals; but because they were year-round residents they also had contact with many "locals," a category that was itself always in flux as newcomers from previous decades took root and became natives to more recent arrivals. Still, to the many woodsmen, farmers, and millworkers who made up much of the town's population, Laurie and her husband were simply "from away." Educated, unconventional, the working mother of four, Laurie never felt "laced into the town."[11] Their farmstead also set them apart from many of the resident farmers whose economy depended on the labor of every family member as husbands, wives, and children juggled wage work in the woods, tanneries, and mills with berry picking, apple harvesting, sheep raising, and the cultivation of crops. Later, when Laurie's own life began to unravel, she would name her farmstead "Shaky Acres," but in the early years it was prosperous and solid. Two miles southeast of Gilmanton Corner, where the "quality" lived, the farmstead quietly meanders over a series of rising pastures smoothly carved out of the encroaching forest. Northern New Englanders call such places "big house, little house, backhouse, barn," finding in the cobbled-together structures easy passage out of the snow and ice of winter months. From the Corner, the Wilkinses' place marked the way to Lower Gilmanton, their bright red silo a fiery signpost to those headed down the Province Road. But if you drove northwest to Gilmanton Corner and turned right onto the old Ironworks Road, you would come instead to Poverty Corner, where a scattering of tarpaper shacks tumbled down the scrubby hills like abandoned slag. A few miles below this in the swampy plain that hugged the Suncook River, the road, unpaved in parts, came upon the remains of Gilmanton Iron Works, then turned sharply north toward the Roberts farm, and then on to the hamlet of Alton.

When the Wilkinses moved to town, Sylvester Roberts and his family had all but given up on farming. Only Barbara and Billy remained to run the farm while their father and older brother were at sea, and together they worked the garden, picked berries and apples, and raised sheep. Forced to drop out of school in ninth grade, Barbara also earned cash as a clerk in a local store, but when she met a young man who worked over at Ashland in the woolen mill, she too found a job there as an operative. In the spring of 1947, when Laurie went to buy some sheep to start her own farm, Barbara was twenty years old, neat and well dressed but hesitant and abrupt. "She gave me a creepy feeling," Laurie told a neighbor.[12] The sheep, Laurie discovered, had been sold. A few days later it was reported that Barbara had suddenly left town.

Nothing about the sheep pen murder shocked Grace Metalious, who regularly used her friend Laurie as a sounding board for a number of sexually explicit and decidedly "kinky" episodes from her work in progress. Laurie's kitchen was a place of literary experimentation. As a reporter, Laurie gathered all that was fit to print; as a writer of fiction, Grace turned what she had heard into imaginary experiences for those who listened to her stories. What Grace Metalious found in the farmhouse kitchen, besides friendship and a cold beer, was a site where writing was revealed as local and particular—the stuff not of universal truths and timeless ideas but of petty everyday struggles and problems that cut close to the bone no matter how routine. As Cold War arbiters of literary authority debated the state of American "Literature," Grace found in the kitchen newsroom a mode of writing inseparable from everyday conversations and the emotional and psychic underbrush they revealed. By sniffing out local gossip, Grace positioned herself as "one in the know," authorizing both a practiced distance from a painful personal life and a writerly sensibility as the observing Other. "Why," her husband would ask when she returned home from Laurie's, "can't you be like everyone else?"

Yet Grace had always been something of an outsider, even to those who knew her best. Like Laurie Wilkins, she was new to the Gilmanton area, but her status as a foreigner was more a product of ethnic than regional difference. Born Marie Grace DeRepentigny in the aging textile center of Manchester, New Hampshire, Grace grew up amidst the peeling gray tenements that housed the city's aging labor force. Her grandparents on both sides had joined the pioneering exodus of Quebec farmers, selling off depleted land in the 1870s and 1880s to purchase new lives in the prosperous American "Amoskeag"—a corporate net of labor-hungry mills that spread out over 8 million square feet, a work space equal in area to the former World Trade Center in New York City.[13] By 1910 the Amoskeag had drawn in seventeen thousand workers, including women like Grace's two grandmothers, Aglae Royer and Florence DeRepentigny, who found themselves uprooted, transplanted in foreign soil, and unexpectedly pressed into alien roles as heads of young households. Both joined an invisible army of immigrant wives suddenly deserted by men no longer bound as husbands and fathers by the regulating forces of church, community, and kin. When the fathers of their children left Manchester, Aglae and Florence entered the mills, where as a skilled spinner or weaver they could expect to earn a "man's wage."

By 1922, however, not even a male operative would have that chance. Demobilization, aging machinery, poor management, overproduction, and just plain greed overtook the Amoskeag, forcing layoffs for thousands, and for those who remained, an increased workday at a 20 percent cut in pay. The strike that came was both inevitable and doomed as management shrugged off its Yankee roots and looked southward. It was a pattern already rolling down New England's north country, slowly and steadily transforming the region from manufacturing outposts in search of ethnic labor to "invented" retreats in search of tourist dollars. Grace was born in the long wake of the strike, and her childhood moved in tandem with New England's rusting experiment in industrial capitalism. Manchester would always be "that wreck of a town," her neighborhood and her schoolhouse places to leave behind, and her Québécois ancestry an uncertain, ambiguous heritage, complicated by the insistence of her mother that the DeRepentigny genealogy, unlike that of her own parents, traveled a direct path from Paris, France. Her father's marriage to Laurette Royer meant escaping both the mills and the ethnic culture that marked them.

Fleeing Manchester's "Petit Canada," Laurette jettisoned her French, mastered an accentless English, and moved her husband and baby daughter to the borderline neighborhood wedged between the French west side of Manchester and the Anglo north. Grace grew up moving from one peeling apartment to the next; her homes, ten in all, were established in unkempt flats in "dirty, brown-shingled tenement houses" on the fringes of Petit Canada. A reflection of the city's general deterioration, they instilled in Grace an iron determination to "hack her way" out of poverty. "I don't go along with all the claptrap about poverty being good for the soul and trouble and struggle being great strengtheners of character," Grace wrote in the wake of *Peyton Place*'s financial success. Rather, "it has been my experience that being poor makes people mean and grabby, and trouble makes them tight-lipped and whiny." To escape her surroundings and the "big scale desires" of her grabby and whiny mother Laurette, Grace made the town library a second home. With the help of an "unusually kind librarian," she found solace from "poverty, drunkenness, and violent fights" in reading books. Soon she was making up her own stories, scribbling down descriptions and tall tales about friends, favorite places, and men who, unlike her vanished father, would never divorce or desert the family. Her characters, Grace later confided, "were far more real to me than the humans who surrounded me."[14]

Writing thus entered the life of Grace DeRepentigny less as a specific kind of wage labor leading, as it had for Laurie Wilkins, to self-support than as a vague creative urge and a doggedly practical way to escape momentarily the world she had been born into. Years later, when a reporter asked her what was the happiest thing she remembered as a child, Grace quietly replied: "I wouldn't say 'happiest' was the word—more like relieved. And that was when I realized I could leave home."[15] But at the time, neither the personal nor the social conditions for literary self-construction existed to provide Grace with the means to convert her sense of confinement into art that paid. Far more available were culturally sanctioned conceptions of marriage and motherhood, and in 1943 they offered Grace, as they did many women of her generation, a more specific means to escape the past and creatively imagine a different future. This is not to say that Grace stopped writing when she married her childhood friend George Metalious, now a struggling first-year student at the University of New Hampshire. George, a tall, dark-complexioned, somewhat passive and insecure young man (Grace called him gentle and kind, and later taciturn and sullen), encouraged Grace's writing, but the birth of three children and the couple's grinding poverty inexorably and discouragingly pushed her work to the margins of their life together. Nevertheless, by 1952, when they moved to the Gilmanton area so that George could begin his first teaching job, Grace had completed several short stories and a 312-page novel, which she called "The Quiet Place." Many in the small town of Belmont, where the Metaliouses occupied a small upstairs apartment, believed that Grace was writing a novel about them, and when rumors spread that a New York publisher wanted to buy the book, Laurie Wilkins scheduled an interview with the much-discussed schoolteacher's wife. "It did not take long," Laurie wrote in the *Laconia Evening Citizen*, "to realize that Grace Metalious was an extraordinary woman of brilliant intellect."[16]

Few people in town, however, shared Laurie's enthusiasm. In her lumberman's jackets and jeans, Grace ruffled the feathers of gender expectations in small-town postwar America. An ardent opponent of the "back-to-the-kitchen-movement," Grace honed a practiced distain for housewifery, and neighbors were quick to notice her "relaxed" methods of child rearing and housekeeping. Grace especially chafed under the pressures of respectability associated with being a teacher's wife and also bitterly resented the paltry salary a New Hampshire teacher could command. In many working-class homes, wives managed the family economy, and it was Grace's responsibility twice a month to stretch $92 to cover all their expenses. "I am trapped in a cage of poverty and mediocrity," she later wrote of those years, "and if I don't get out, I'll die." For Grace, "The Quiet Place" represented a major step toward turning "oceans of words" into an imaginary and actual escape.[17] Based in part on the suicide of a University of New Hampshire music professor who was rumored to be homosexual, it was a solid piece of writing and remained the favorite of her four books. "It took only a short perusal of the script," wrote Laurie, "to know that here was a real novel, written by a gifted person."[18] But publication would not come until much later, when, in the wake of *Peyton Place*, it appeared to mixed reviews as *The Tight White Collar*. Grace and Laurie, however, found in each other a kindred spirit. Eleven years older than Grace, the New York bohemian and free spirit became the writer's first mentor and the only woman Grace would ever trust.[19] In turn, Grace offered Laurie excitement, camaraderie, an infectious laugh, and in all their years together only one piece of advice: "Get rid of those chickens!"[20]

Together they picked the regional grapevine. But as a would-be novelist, Grace represented a new kind of threat to local residents. With Laurie's help, Grace turned an intense curiosity—"my nose trouble," she called it—and a storyteller's ear toward the small-town "sneaks" and "ax mouths" she blamed for making her life as "Mrs. Schoolteacher" miserable and lonely. The local journalist pointed the way, letting Grace in on gossip and town lore and helping her Franco-American friend mimic the speech patterns and local patois of the "shellback Yankees." When the Metaliouses' Belmont landlord evicted them because of Grace's blossoming reputation as a "wild" woman, Laurie found the family a new place to live.[21] Class privilege protected Laurie from similar insults, but in those years the two women were sisters under the skin; ebulliently unconventional, curious, bookish, mischievous, irreverent, and endowed with a generosity of spirit, Grace and Laurie occupied a private world always a little apart. "I have never gotten over missing her," Laurie recalled some forty years after Grace's death. "To me she was a wonder."[22]

The move out of Belmont put the Metaliouses on the unpaved fringes of Gilmanton Corner, where they moved into a "glorified shack" optimistically called "It'll Do." With its "pitched roof and little rooms stuck on to its body at various places," it sat deep in the woods not far from Laurie's own farm. On good days the Metaliouses thought of it as a "Hansel-and-Gretel-type house," but mostly Grace remembered it as one of the "cold horrors" that made up those years. Back teaching, this time at the Laconia State School, George settled into a familiar routine while Grace worked on a new novel she tentatively called "The Tree and the Blossom." When not at her typewriter, she was at Laurie's farmhouse, and when not there, she was usually out and about, taking the pulse of the town. Grace, people said, got around. At times she would hang out with the unemployed woodsmen who lined up at the country store "drinking away" the day. Other times she'd pile the kids into the old rusty Plymouth and drive over to Laconia, or when they were at school, listen to the old-timers at the rod and gun club. But to town officials, Grace's behavior had the rough, kicked-up feel of an unpaved road. "Everything about Grace turned into a scandal," Laurie recalled. "She had a knack for making people pay attention." Olive Bessie, a member of the Gilmanton school board, was secretly shocked and publicly "concerned." Some in town began to talk of Grace as "Mrs. Crazy."[23]

Yet even the skeptics agreed that she was a gifted storyteller, a bawdy raconteur in the French Canadian tradition. Throughout 1954, as the book moved toward completion, Laurie discovered that, as she put it years later, "Wow, Grace knew things."[24] When the book, retitled, became the most "sexsational novel of the century," reporters would inevitably seem dumbstruck that a wife and mother could have written such a story. "Golly," Grace would modestly reply, "Sex is something everyone lives with." Did sex ever seem repulsive to her? a reporter from *Look* asked. Grace was clear and unequivocal. "Far worse to me than any sex act is unattractive food," she calmly replied, "and I'm no gourmet."[25]

Married at seventeen, Grace regretted that she never had the chance to go to college, but she had always been a voracious reader, and when her husband, George, went to the University of New Hampshire under the GI Bill, she read over his course materials and shared in discussions with other students. When a particularly arrogant co-ed confided her admiration for "those two fellows, Krafft-Ebing," Grace smugly informed the woman that the famous sexologist with the double last name was one person. Like the writings of European sex researchers Havelock Ellis and Magnus Hirschfeld, the texts of Richard von Krafft-Ebing were widely available in the United States during the twenties and thirties, but they became standard fare for postwar youth who shared with researchers a growing interest in the serious study of human sexuality. The arrest in January 1948 of Caryl Chessman also escalated public interest in Freudian concepts of psychosexual development, especially as they might explain what appeared to be an increase in sexually motivated crimes. Signaling the beginning of a new sex panic, the Chessman case brought intense scrutiny to vague, unexamined definitions and measurements of sexual normalcy and deviance, while the sex panic itself worked "to heighten the importance of sexuality as a component of modern identity."[26]

Grace was not only familiar with these discussions but also often used her fiction as a way to explore the boundaries between normal and abnormal sexuality. She read Krafft-Ebing, she skimmed Freud, and she "devoured" the notorious reports by Indiana University professor Alfred Kinsey, whose controversial studies on white male and female sexuality became surprising best-sellers in 1948 and 1953. While Grace's own emotional life went largely unexamined ("I have often thought that Freud would have had a field day with me," she once said), popular concepts like libido, projection, and repression opened up new writerly possibilities for those "in the know." Sexual knowledge could be big business. Striking a modest, understated pose, Grace—cigarette in hand—would reply to interviewers' questions, "Well, you can get quite Freudian about that."[27] In the privacy of the farmhouse kitchen Grace and Laurie did just that, reinterpreting local gossip in the language of modern sexual needs. Laurie told Grace about drunken winter binges in abandoned cellars, about the misbehavior of school board members, and about the sheep pen murder. Grace shared with Laurie a couple of short stories that dealt with socially taboo subjects like homosexuality and sadomasochism. At times she and Laurie spoke about erotic love between women, and as Grace read from her novel in progress, which would become *Peyton Place*, she treated Laurie to steamy scenes of frigid, repressed heterosexual men and women whose carnal denial led them to aberrant acts of physical abuse and bizarre behavior. They talked about the need for safe, legal abortions, the hypocrisy of the Catholic Church, and the open secret of incest. "Was it shocking?" a reporter later asked Laurie about Grace's imaginative life. "No, no, no. . . . I'm an old hen, and it takes a lot to shock me." To her friend's delight and the town's horror, "Grace wrote what people were thinking. She had the courage to write about those things nobody else would write about."[28]

Come winter, however, "It'll Do" would no longer do. Windows periodically fell out of their frames, the asbestos siding slipped off in great chucks during storms, and the woods that glowed in Indian summer seemed now to tower over the desolate, shaky house. The only other dwelling on the isolated dirt road was a tarpaper shack occupied by the brother of Bert McClary, a local farmhand who rented one of Grace and George's upstairs bedrooms. Downstairs the kitchen overflowed with the discarded remains of meals past. "Dirty dishes," a visitor recalled, "were everywhere." The house became an adversary. "Nothing worked."[29] The coffeepot was always cold. Chairs lost their stuffing. Dirt refused to budge, and dog hair blanketed the furniture like coal soot. "Everything in arms," is how the eighteenth-century midwife Martha Ballard described her own rebellious house, left alone by a working wife and ignored by servants.[30] Modern voices did not recognize uncooperative houses or overworked women: the fault rested in the personal failures of wives and mothers. Grace, people whispered, "was a slob." She "only had to be in a room for five minutes to make it look like a pigsty," a neighbor told reporters. Less noticed but very much part of the daily scene at "It'll Do," however, was "one spotless corner" tucked away just off the living room, where Grace kept her well-oiled Remington typewriter.[31]

As the cold and dark pressed in, Grace used the isolation to concentrate on her book, often writing in ten-hour blocks without stopping. What little time she could spare for housekeeping would have to suffice. She preferred instead the sights and sounds of winter: "the soft sift of snow" against the small-paned windows, the snap of tree limbs "broken off by the sly snow's weight," and the howling power of winter storms. Attuned to the aural landscape of an urban childhood, Grace found in the Gilmanton countryside a profound contentment, taking pleasure when she could in nature walks with her children or excursions to the lake. But that year winter was ungentle, the winds "like living things, breathing unceasingly and mightily, with breaths as cold as death" (89). Nettled by confinement indoors, Grace found that her writing increasingly put her on a collision course with her responsibilities as a mother and wife. Grace and George were unhappy with each other; both recognized that the marriage had grown stale, the best parts now past. Fights were frequent and painful, turning the cluttered house into a minefield of recrimination and accusation. "Nights were filled with discussions after a dreary meal," George later wrote about that sour winter. "Dreary and thrown together."[32] Grace withdrew to the world of fiction, to another man's bed, to the laughter of Laurie's kitchen. George sputtered and kept to himself. To the kids, all seemed normal. When the New England spring finally came with its oozing mud and false promises of summer, Grace understood that something had changed forever. But what, exactly? "I don't know," she later mused. "I don't suppose anyone ever does. What day is it when you wake up and realize that what you have is not what you want at all?"[33]

Retreat. Take cover. Get lost in stories. Take flight in the fantasy scenarios fiction can invoke. Take comfort in the imaginative, fantastic reorientations of self and place they stimulate. Take hold of characters that were, in Grace's words, "more real to me than the humans who surround me."[34]

It was a familiar strategy honed over the years. As a child, Grace read compulsively and aimlessly, finding in words the pleasure of being "carried away." When Manchester's guardians of Literature echoed national concerns over the corruption of American letters, including the vulgar use of books by advertisers to tout products from Milk of Magnesia to Cream of Wheat, Grace quietly scoured the town for Literature's castoffs: adventure, detection, romance, and "when nothing else was around, the telephone directory."[35] When her father deserted the family, she turned to Somerset Maugham, F. Scott Fitzgerald, and Nancy Drew mysteries, inventing a female sleuth of her own and writing her into a storied life. Teased at school because of her "Canuck" accent, her Catholicism, her plain looks, Grace used storytelling and story reading to explain her exile, to cultivate her differentness, to claim for herself the privacy that loneliness imposed on her. "Did I read because I was lonely, or was I lonely because I started to read?" Grace would later ask herself.[36] Her fictive friends came into her life through what Michel de Certeau famously described as the "silent production of reading."[37] They waited for her in the family bookcase, the town library, even the bathroom of Grace's grandmother's house, where a plank of wood over her knees served as her first desk. From here Grace would silently enact her writerly dreams.

And those dreams were all around her. In the front room her mother proudly displayed "The World's Great Books," the hand-tooled bindings of works by Charles Dickens, Guy de Maupaussant, and Alexandre Dumas ("fils et père"), lined up like cultural sentinels holding vulgarity at bay. Questionable books and magazines, like Nancy Drew mysteries and *Screen Magazine*, Grace borrowed on the sly from the town library or purchased at the local drugstore. Like appreciating "sterling silver, fine table linen, and Beethoven," understanding the difference between "quality" books and cheap novels was for mother Laurette an act of cultural emulation and social differentiation. Born into the mills, Laurette wanted "Paris trips and a Colonial house with a fanlight over the door and a chauffeured limousine and she never got any of them." Book ownership and display became a way to distinguish the DeRepentigny household from their ethnic working-class neighbors and so supported Laurette's often sagging belief that the family was culturally, if not economically, superior to them. "All the years I was growing up," Grace recalled, "I heard every cliché ever invented by people with little wants applied to my mother and her big-scale desires. She tried to make others believe that she was better than other people, but she was never able to make herself believe it, nor did she convince my sister, nor me."[38] Like cosmetics, stylish clothes, and high heeled shoes, books were for Laurette the cultural steppingstones on which to escape Petit Canada and make up for the unfairness of things in a materialist world that had passed her by.[39] But the only thing she ever really owned, or passed on her daughter, was a palpable envy.

A culture of longing shaped Grace's childhood and infused her writing. From the ache of her mother's desire, Grace learned the social and psychological implications of being female in a household isolated and estranged from the ethnic mill hand communities that became for so many other working-class families a source of mutual aid and collectivity. Taught to lie about her heritage, speak of clothes that came from the "very nicest shops," tell of easy money in her house, and act as "if gentility had been bred into her," she learned as well the rules of an unforgiving social structure that pressed upon her family. Grace's earliest storytelling abilities were honed in the retold dreams and ambitions of a mother's empty grasp. "I led strangers to believe that I was a lady of Background," Grace recalled, "that I had been to college, and that I was married to the most fabulous man in the world. He wasn't. And I was what I came to discover myself to be. A phony."[40]

Deployed as family weapons to explain their particular situation as exiles in a world that had let them down, Grace's stories increased her own sense of inadequacy and falsehood while pushing her more deeply into a writerly self. At the age of ten she wrote dozens of stories about Prince Charming, then drew from her own prolific reading to create a "who-done-it," complete with a girl detective; then at age twelve she wrote a sprawling historical novel not unlike the wildly successful *Anthony Adverse*. Escape, fantasy, self-delusion, but also self-invention—borrowing, appropriating, crossing the bounds of this life, this self, into other lives, other ethnicities, other genders, other subjectivities to fashion *something different*. Writing, to borrow a phrase from Robert Frost, as "a stay against confusion."[41] She recalled: "I made up stories about my relationship with my father in which he was the shining prince and I the only object of his affection. . . . I made up stories about family heirlooms which were pieces of junk . . . and I lied my head off about my family background."[42] From this dis-location, Grace oriented herself as a writer. Nurtured by her mother's longing—"beaten out of her" long ago—Grace pieced together an understanding of what it meant to live in New England as an ethnic woman and in consumerist America as a woman without means. "I think I began *Peyton Place* the day I was born," she once remarked.[43]

But her mother's dreams were not without effect. In the New England that Grace came to know as her world and her heritage, writing came into a young woman's life as something of a strange idea. There was no such thing as French Canadian literature, nor was women's writing an enfranchised genre capable of liberating a lower-middle-class woman like Grace. Marriage was a more immediate way out, but Laurette willed her daughter an outsider's edginess that pushed Grace to forge a better future for herself, to organize her life around the idea that difference might just be something worth having. Poised expectantly at her typewriter, Grace gave birth to her "fourth baby," renamed *Peyton Place*, in the late spring of 1955. To the chagrin of almost everyone in town, the story of the sheep pen murder was about to travel beyond the discretionary ears of local gossips and into the hands of unquiet readers. "Run for your life," Grace was fond of saying. "There's trouble coming."[44]

4

The Other Side of Writing

"Someday," said Allison, "I'll write a very famous book. As famous as *Anthony Adverse*, and then I'll be a celebrity."

"Not me." Norman replied. "I'm going to write thin, slim volumes of poetry. Not many people will know me, but the few who will will say that I am a young genius."

PEYTON PLACE

Ink. Paper. A typewriter in need of a fresh ribbon. How to imagine authorship? "How does a person of will and imagination," the literary historian Richard Brodhead asks, move into "that more specialized human self that is an author?"[1] Certainly we can picture the personal side of writing at "It'll Do," where Grace's will and imagination elbowed their way into the center of things, organizing scenes, plots, and characters, she would later write, "more real to me than the humans who surrounded me."[2] A winter of horrors: gray, icy days, a rattling wind raising doubt and fear, a writer's eagerness, a spouse's edginess: "Why can't you be like everyone else?" Signs of Grace's differentness piling up like a New Hampshire snowfall; difference chilling domestic life, seeping through the town, making a spectacle of itself. A literary life played out in the pecking sounds of an old Remington keyboard. Words lined up, scratched out, inked in. Words in a constant struggle for order and sequence, for some place on the page. Characters cropping up in the middle of the night, their names, personalities, bodies taking shape while potatoes get peeled, bills paid, children dressed, washed, taken to school.

Allison MacKenzie—like her creator, restless, eager for success, hungry for something else. Young, out-of-place, an awkward girl except when walking the woods of Road's End, where a natural gracefulness emerges from her feeling safe and at peace among the old-growth trees and flower-infused meadows. At home, her nose always in a book, her body all wrong: "too long in the legs and too round in the face," and worse still, "too plump with residual babyhood" (11). And, yes, different. A small-town girl without a father but whose mother carries on in arch solitude, protecting her past by keeping a social and emotional distance from others. A restless girl, bright, resentful, hating at times this mother called Constance "for her differentness, for making her different" (19). With her friend Selena Cross, "a peculiar pair, those two, Selena with her dark, gypsy beauty, her thirteen-year-old eyes as old as time[,] and Allison MacKenzie . . . her eyes wide open, guileless and questioning, above that painfully sensitive mouth" (7). And "little" Norman Page, "constructed entirely of angles": a mama's boy; nothing really wrong with him but not quite right, either (7). All day long, Grace decanting her story, filtering out the unpleasantness of the present, dropping herself, bit by bit, into alternative material and emotional landscapes, constructing, confirming, fantasizing a self. Grace authoring a life; picturing a way, picturing her way out of poverty.

Imagine, too, the intense kneading of a story, the mimetic acting out of every detail, each scene performed once, twice: first for George at night, and then, whenever the ice-rutted roads allowed, for Laurie over at Shaky Acres. Here we can imagine the marital give-and-take and the rowdy scenes of female friendship amidst a gaggle of kids, the bouts of joyously absurd gossip, girl talk, tall tales and wild stories, and plenty of beer, at least as long as the fire lasts in the kitchen hearth. And always that deep, hollow pit of desire and need; feeling oneself trapped in a narrative of poverty and mediocrity. And then the grocery check bounces, the rusted old Pontiac slides off the road and into the freezing darkness. *The sheer effort of it all.* "Snowbound in my obscurity," Grace writes of Allison in *Return to Peyton Place.*[3] Stories always at the ready, always there to ward off the emptiness, the loneliness, the everyday exhaustions of life on a food budget of $20 a week, the hope that, unlike her rattle-trap house, her novel *will* do. Imagine, too, the longing for a different story, a different kind of life—feeling "gypped" as Grace approaches her thirtieth birthday and the knowledge of things denied takes on specificity: a university education, travel to Europe, a house by the sea. Even the "little wants" remain out of reach—books, a season ticket to the civic music concerts—and not for the lack of money alone, but for her having come to believe that such things were out of bounds, meant for the others of this earth. Imagine Grace seeing her mother's life unfolding again as her own. Grace Metalious: smart, generous, restless, emotionally volatile, needy, strong; a harried wife and mother tiger; a woman from America's unpaved places. How does authorship enter into such a life?

There is a photograph of Grace Metalious that invites viewers to imagine this difficult-to-envision journey. It is a glossy black-and-white photograph taken for a Hollywood publicity agency. Dressed in a tailored tweed jacket and crisp white blouse—a Peter Pan collar fastened at the neck—Grace sits behind a large desk, its dark wooden top almost hidden by the tools of her trade: pencils, a stack of paper (a new manuscript perhaps), a cut-glass ashtray at the ready. An arm rests lightly on a polished Underwood typewriter as a small hand extends out to touch the carriage—a gesture that reminds one of a musician cradling a beloved and ancient instrument. Grace's head is slightly turned so that her gaze drifts offstage to the left of the camera, where the light accentuates a youthful and unassuming face. Her smile is shy and warm, her eyes kind and slightly bemused. There is something slightly familiar here. Perhaps it is the pose that resonates, turns the unknown figure into a person one should know. She is captured at work, a page of unfinished text braced underneath the roller bar of the typewriter as if waiting patiently for the photographer to leave so that the writer may return to her work. You can tell at a glance that this is the real thing: the writer alone in a room of her own.

Grace was always hard-pressed to explain how she became a writer. Not given to introspection—more likely to act out than to scrutinize her emotions—she tended to see her new novel as an extension of her motherhood: "my fourth baby," she would tell people, as if to erase the unconventionality of her other grand passion. "I don't think I can explain my feelings about writing," she told reporters in 1957. "I don't know how I write or why I write any more than I know why I breathe. It has always come easily to me. I have the feeling that anybody could write if they only tried. I don't suppose this is true. The only rule I ever heard about writing that made

Figure 3. Images of the "writer-writes-alone" flooded popular culture, offering a form of subjectivity that contrasted sharply with the rationalization and standardization of modern labor in the twentieth century. This photograph of Grace Metalious was taken by 20th Century–Fox Productions to publicize the film version of *Peyton Place*.

any sense is: 'apply the seat of the pants to the seat of the chair.'"[4] Echoing Metalious's isolation as a young and hopeful writer, Allison MacKenzie "locked herself in her bedroom," where, despite the infertile literary soil of Peyton Place, a strong will and youthful imagination take hold as authorship evolves in private acts of self-invention, her success propelled by a talent seemingly undenied and undeniable (48).

This was the side of writing Grace grew up with, read about, and dreamed of: the writer in private moments of creativity when authorship takes shape as an exercise in individuation, the "innocently imperial self" so at odds with the world.[5] Pasted within the "album of modernism," Linda Brodkey observes, is the enduring image of the lonely genius whose focus and solitude give to writing a marked seriousness (both sacred and profane) and to writing's artifacts—the poem, the novel, the play, the essay—an exclusivity that precludes examination of those particularized things that bring writing to public life.[6] A product of the "anti-individualizing effect" of mass culture and the commercialization of Literature, the "writer-writes-alone" motif increasingly provided to American audiences a public subjectivity that contrasted with more rationalized portraits of work and production from the Fordist assembly lines of the 1920s and 1930s to the "Organization Man" and the "gray flannel suit" of the postwar period.[7] Made possible by new forms of journalism—human interest stories, popular magazine biography, and the gossip column—it circulated in films, plays, television, and magazines, compiling a visual archive of rustic garrets and "owl's nests," tweedy jackets and pipes, individual autonomy and unconventional swagger. This was a seemingly timeless tale of authenticity and solitary endeavor free and apart from the means of its own production.

Still, Grace understood the limits of this cultural imaginary, and we pick up in her heroine a strong echo of her own struggle to comprehend the literary and to insert herself within it. This is especially true in the wake of the unexpected success of *Peyton Place* and the emerging images of the author as both "promising first novelist" and scandalous housewife/writer. Pressed hard to write a sequel, Metalious has Allison return to her hometown not just as a famous author but as a sensational "hack," for "in New York," the now notorious author of *Peyton Place* tells readers, "certain wheels had been set in motion" that no writer could control. Writing had ghostly accomplices, and Grace found it to be something of a strange and evil enterprise: a "nebulous trade" dominated by greedy publishers, unscrupulous agents, wily public relations firms, and overbearing editors.[8] But this commercial side was only part of a larger renegotiation under way between writing, mass consumption, and celebrity that would provide to the young, unknown housewife the conditions under which her authorship would be made possible.

The problem, in other words, is not that the image of the inspired, secluded writer ("seat of pants to seat of chair") is false—Grace knew many moments like this—but rather that it banishes to the margins of discussion and analysis alternative moments of writing, moments that call into question the cloistered world of authorship and expose its social and material side, moments gathered and empowered on "the other side of writing."[9] Richard Brodhead puts it this way: "Writing has no general existence, no existence merely as 'writing.'" It cannot exist outside the means of its own production. Rather, he argues, it emerges "in differently organized (if adjacent) literary-social worlds, in differently structured cultural settings composed around writing and regulating its social life." In what he describes as "different cultures of letters," every literary attempt involves a kind of imagining—an ability to envision writerly self-realization and so position oneself within its social life.[10] But the will to literary expression is also and always a negotiated desire that is inextricably bound up with the cultural-historical settings that are grounds for its creation and the regulator of writing's existence.

When Grace Metalious decided to make the heroine of her new book an aspiring young author, she had also to decide what kind of writer Allison MacKenzie would strive to become and how she might succeed. And in so doing, she must also have sorted out in some way within her own desiring self a scheme of writing that would accomplish a similar metamorphosis. Her husband, George, saw his wife as a grand storyteller, a gifted raconteur who took the French Canadian tradition of oral storytelling and humorous entertainment to new and spicier heights. Her friend Laurie embraced her as a writer of "genius and enormous talent," a "painter with words" who could bring to life "the beauty of nature and the ugliness of people."[11] This in effect was the extent of Grace's literary circle, such as it was in the remote environs of lived experience. Far more "real" to her, and far more useful as a scheme of self-fashioning, was the invented realm of her life, wherein the literary unfolded in and through a set of public personalities: individuals celebrated for their difference yet made oddly familiar by the innumerable images embedded in newspaper supplements, magazine covers, radio, and eventually television talk shows. Authoritative yet reachable, a plethora of outsider identities empowered by fame was made possible in a rapidly expanding world of celebrity reproduction and appropriation.[12]

A compelling social narrative, celebrity authorship invoked powerful fantasies coalescing around the "glamour, freedom, and money" writing could provide in mass-market book publishing, where the overnight success of previously unknown men and women spawned what critics began to call the "jackpot" author and the "would-be-writer industry," which promoted the former and profited from the latter.[13] What Grace had to orient herself, in other words, was not much: two unpublished typescripts, a hundred or so unpublished short stories (most of them destroyed after her death), a library copy of *The Writer's Handbook*, and a fantastic notion of herself as a famous author. As a scheme of writing, it wasn't much. But if we think of authorship not only as an outsider identity but also as a cultural commodity, then we can begin to understand its many meanings for those who, like Grace, saw in writing their one best shot at that "something more" in a materialist world that was passing them by.

In the fall of 1955, the *Saturday Review* magazine offered its readers a breezy "how to" guide for women tempted by the literary life. Titled "Eight Ways to Become an Authoress," it sketched out short biographies of recently published female writers whose books were meant to illustrate the wide range of topics available to "lady authors" as well as the uneven talent they represented. Jane Dolinger, known to fans for her cheesecake "pinups" as much as for her globetrotting adventure stories, shared the spotlight with Rinehart Publishing's hot new prospect, the stout Mrs. Thyra Ferré Björn, whose book *Papa's Wife* promised readers the same "golden haze of spiritual light" they found in the hugely popular *I Remember Mama*. Also included were Michaela Denis, whose *Leopard in My Lap* marked the beginnings of a distinguished career in wildlife writing and management; Carol Grace (twice wed to and doubly divorced from playwright William Saroyan); fashion model Pati Hill; successful magazine writers Gladys Taber and Charlotte Paul; and dilettante socialite Gloria Vanderbilt, whose slim volume *Love Poems*, the article suggested, was produced as much for the society columns as for the literary pages. "The whole country, it seems," gushed the editor, "is alive and well with young things who would like nothing better than to turn themselves into real live lady authors."[14]

The *Saturday Review* was not the only magazine to draw attention to the rising success of women writers. In both England and America, reviewers, journalists, and editors took increasing notice of the "emancipated modern authoress," the female "comer" who showed "real" literary skill or who, with a "modicum of talent" or the spectral help of a literary ghost, managed to hit the jackpot. At times condescending and dismissive—"Little Women at Work," *Time* magazine cooed as it introduced readers to "teen age sophisticates" Françoise Sagan, Anne Bodart, and Lucy Daniels—stories about women whose books "now steal the headlines" signaled not just the survival of the novel in the new era of television, but the seemingly endless possibilities for the housewife who aspired to write, the "authoress in an apron."[15]

It was easy to imagine the would-be writer finding a place at such an expanded literary table. The abundant variety of ages, subjects, and talents lent a certain air of democratic possibility appropriate to a Consumers' Republic where all things seemed obtainable, at least rhetorically.[16] Even the superior tone of certain reporters—that whiff of literary unease that seemed to trouble them like the pea under the princess's mattress—was easily drowned out in the flood of writing tips and sensational stories that heralded the "unknown" author whose best-selling novel became itself a literary phenomenon, "a one-shot bonanza" like the 1933 sensation *Anthony Adverse*, or three years later *Gone With the Wind*.[17]

In recent years, however, the history of female authorship in postwar America has most often been told as a story of gender, in which women writers are measured according to their complicity with, or resistance to, a "feminine mystique" famously identified and named half a century ago by Betty Friedan. Writers like Betty MacDonald, Jean Kerr, and Shirley Jackson, for example, have taken on new scholarly interest in so far as their work exemplifies or contradicts the "domestically contained" ideologies of 1950s womanhood.[18] The "housewife writers," who Friedan blamed for perpetuating the feminine mystique even as writing careers released them from it, become either a sign of the limits placed on women writers who might otherwise have been included in the broader canon of postwar fiction, or part of a broader discourse of discontent that subverted idealized visions of home and family and women's subordinated position within them.

Important as these studies have been to revising stereotypes of postwar domesticity, arguments like these rest on a much-disputed assumption that authorship operates on some general level of aestheticism whereby the female writer finds herself historically at a disadvantage vis-à-vis her location in domestic life. But if we accept the notion of writing as maintaining a social as well as a cultural life, then we can see in the postwar discourse of domesticity and gender differentiation a perch from which the housewife writer might launch an authorial self and market her literary wares. Whether as challenge, endorsement, or comic entertainment, stories of domesticity expanded with the postwar culture industry, spilling into consumers' lives from Henry Luce's domestically grounded *Life* magazine to television shows like the popular daytime program *Home*, hosted by Arlene Francis. Whatever meaning viewers and readers gave to these stories, they provided to those most intimately connected to the terrains of home and hearth a fixed point from which to set their literary compass. In many ways, it was an old story.

Trumpeted in mid-century news accounts as a new type of author, the literary housewife actually held a venerable place in American letters and in the history of both print culture and laboring women. Aspiring to join the "scribbling women" so famously bemoaned by Nathaniel Hawthorne, nineteenth-century wives and mothers turned to the literary marketplace to supplement other forms of employment considered more suitable for their gender and class. "No happy woman ever writes," the popular Fanny Fern told her Civil War–era readers, because as Mary Kelley so perceptively shows, writing by women was often understood to be a function of necessity rather than solely a form of aesthetic pursuit.[19] At times these "literary domestics" wrote anonymously or adopted a pseudonym to bridge the gap that divided the nineteenth-century female voice from the public stage of literary fame. But down through that long nineteenth century of true womanhood, writers like Mary Jane Holmes, Sara Parton, Catherine Maria Sedgwick, E. D. E. N. Southworth, Harriet Beecher Stowe, and Susan Warner found unexpected commercial success.

They did not launch a great revolution in American publishing, but their stunning successes spurred profitable innovations in cheap paperback production, eventually pulling into writing's orbit Victorian scribblers like Laura Sheldon, Carolyn Wells, Laura Jean Libbey, Charlotte M. Yonge, and Rhoda Broughton. After the Great War, Doris Nigessee, Montange Sieyes, and Peggy Gaddis produced dime novels and popular romances, sufficiently purged of the piety and moralistic sentiment of the "domestics" that they could be found in every cheap lending library shelved under such headings as "Action," "Adventure," or "*Romance*" ("always with the accent on the *o*").[20] In parallel with the mechanization of book production, "women novelists" like these became ambivalent cultural figures, easy targets of critics who happily applauded when Gilbert and Sullivan included them on the *Mikado*'s executioner's list: "They'll none of them be missed; they'll none of them be missed."

Word merchants knew better. In an age known for its excess and avarice, storytelling turned as cutthroat an enterprise as any that gave the late nineteenth century its "Gilded Age" reputation. "The American eagle," one genteel critic observed, "has become a bird of prey, with a goatish taste for paper and printer's ink."[21] *Publishers Weekly* summarized the problem: "That the majority of [popular novels] were characterized by the feeblest indications of talent—not to mention genius—and that many, especially from our women writers, were inspired by a motive so base, and illustrated with details so gross, as to put the blush to many famous French offenders in this line, is putting the case mildly."[22]

Cultural anxiety swelled exponentially as cheap reading materials (including paperback books and inexpensive hardcover novels) expanded writing's publics and challenged traditional notions of both "Literature" and authorship.[23] The invention of groundwood paper, the rotary press, and composing machines, combined with improvements in photogravure and distribution (including rural free delivery), made available to ever-expanding audiences ten-cent to fifty-cent novels (both those pirated from abroad and the "new" American types), "cheap Libraries" (generally reprints offered in the form of collections), newspapers, periodicals, journals of all stripes, storybook supplements, mail order lists, and by the 1920s pulp and "slicks"—magazines known for their glossy print and mass distribution—that catered to readers of diverse economic means and wide-ranging tastes. Almost a quarter of all books published in 1885 were in paper form, a "tidal wave," as Kenneth Davis puts it, that would recede as copyright laws increasingly disrupted the illegal trafficking of pirated novels and stories. Not until the late 1930s would the industry ignite a third revolution in paperback publishing. But the "commercialization of literature," spawned by low-priced books and magazines in the Gilded Age, had done its work by pulling into the literary world those who, worthy or not, sought to make a profit from words in print.[24]

And it was the success of certain authors, mostly women, in these new mass markets, especially in magazine publishing, that marked them and their popular confessional tales and true *ro*mances as outside of and in contrast to what academics, editors, critics, and certain authors, mostly men, came to call the "Literary."[25] The much-studied response to this "feminization" of mass culture was a strategic movement toward the muscular: a hypermasculine authorial image promoted by writers who sought both to establish elite literary credentials and to enter the lucrative sphere of mass-production publishing. "Starting with London," Loren Glass writes, "and reaching an apogee with Hemingway, a virile masculinity bordering on caricature became central to the public image of celebrity authors in modern America."[26] For the modern female authoress this was not always a problem, but it did have the effect of conceptually uncoupling the genre in which she excelled—heterosexual romantic love—from the logics of serious literary labor. Enabled by an expanded and democratized "Republic of Letters," the female author signaled as well its enervated state and lack of "authenticity." Deeply gendered, the "transcendent self" of authorship emerged in the modernist imaginary as a function of the interiority of masculine endeavor, epitomized by the boy geniuses whose "thin, slim volumes" of poems, experimental novels, and learned essays took on a marked seriousness in an otherwise frivolous and feminized marketplace.

But the cheap book business of the nineteenth century did not simply open up outlets for new kinds of literary labor; it reconfigured cultural production in ways that continued to alter notions of authorship and the relation of writing to it. Central to this transformation was what Janice Radway describes as the "growing prominence of the circulating book," the idea that a book, especially a novel, was an exchangeable commodity with a particular use associated with readerly desire and need rather than with the identifiable labors of "serious," usually established and well-known individual authors. "Regularly associated with the pleasures of leisure time or with the particular objectives of specific interests and occupations, this book," Radway argues, "was viewed as a utilitarian object, as a tool for accomplishing a concrete goal."[27] To Victorian literary elites, such books were nothing but a "promiscuous eatable," like an apple or a bonbon, "to be consumed on the spot."[28] Books like this were talked about and passed around, their titles duly noted, even if their authors were not. "A novel with every cake of soap purchased," one enterprising book-man announced.[29] The "mob novel" had come into its own.

In its wake, competition soared for new supplies of raw materials. Word merchants, after all, needed words, millions of them, organized and packaged in forms and styles that would meet the needs of their mob read-ers. Could authors be invented? Julian Hawthorne feared as much when in 1906 he warned book lovers against "inspiration 'ex machine,'" whereby books were not just made by machinery but were conceived by machinery as well. "The ease with which they are produced in material form, and the cheapness of their price, causes them to be read by everyone, and the famil-iarity with methods of literary composition thus acquired enables anyone, almost, to write books that publishers will print and the public will read."[30] As early as the 1850s the financial success of the serialized short story and the novel altered in small ways the autonomy of the singular author, whose imagination was increasingly reined in by editorial limits on length, num-ber of installments, deadlines, and even content.[31] "With capital," Mary Noel astutely noted a century later, "came the 'hack,' who was as much a product of the Industrial Revolution as was the Hoe printing press."[32] Paid a flat fee to write stories from precut plots conceived by editors and pub-lishers, wordsmiths underwent alterations in the work process not unlike those experienced earlier by their artisan counterparts. Known in the trade as "penny-a-word-formula-fiction," mass-circulated stories tended to be assembled like so many component parts, creating what Michael Denning described as "unauthored discourse," materials completely detached from the voice of an individual author and marked by a brand-like collectivity or corporate structure.[33]

Culturally suspect because of their popularity and their at times "unsa-vory" content, dime novels, confessional stories, and romances joined forces with girls' and boys' adventure books as problematic cultural prod-ucts made by unknown hired hands. Aimed at immigrants and young readers, early series titles like *Baseball Joe, The Khaki Girls, Automobile Girls*, and *Rover Boys*, as well as the more respectable Bobbsey Twins, Tom Swift, and Nancy Drew series, underscored the intensification of the commercializing of literature as books increasingly competed with other commodities. "Books," Henry Holt famously declared in 1905, "are not bricks." But "the more they are treated as bricks," he warned, "the more they tend to become bricks."[34] Detached from the "singularity of individual

imagination," books like these smacked of wage schedules and storytelling schemes made up in "fiction factories."[35] They were "not written, but
manufactured," the head librarian of the Boy Scouts of America, Franklin
Mathews, complained.[36] Not art but commodities.

Not quite bricks, but just as cheap. In 1920 the *Saturday Evening Post*
cost just a nickel, while almost all the nation's magazines, many of them
between 60 and 130 pages long, remained well below fifteen cents until
World War II, when paper rationing drove prices up. Sold in drugstores,
and in chain stores like Woolworth's, McCrory, McLellan, and S. H.
Kress, magazines such as *Crime Mysteries, Modern Screen, Snappy Stories,
Five Novels*, and *I Confess* were also sold at every Union News Stand in
train stations across the country. For magazine publishers, access to venues
like this put them at a competitive advantage when marketing paperback
books, but for their audience it solidified reading as a popular form of leisure and an important marker of cultural status. Between the wars, book
readership rose dramatically and steadily. In 1939, when Pocket Books
launched its famous series of best-sellers in soft, brightly colored cardboard
covers for only twenty-five cents, they discovered that readers increased
their book purchases from two- to twentyfold. "Wherever people worked
or played," historian John Tebbel notes, "Pocket Books were carried about
and read—very often transported literally in pockets."[37]

This tsunami of books, magazines, and newspapers not only reduced
the physical distance between print culture and geographically remote
readers but also blunted the psychic and emotional barriers that tended to
separate ordinary readers from the lofty aerie of authorship. For writers
of all kinds, pseudonymous authorship in pulps, slicks, and series books
encouraged experimentation, while for nontraditional writers, especially
housewives, it opened up new ways to supplement income as freelance
news reporters, magazine writers, or storytellers. Mildred Wirt Benson,
who wrote over fifty novels for the Stratemeyer Syndicate (including the
earliest Nancy Drew mysteries under the brand name Caroline Keene),
typically wrote her stories from outlines the company sent to her home
in Iowa (later Ohio). This allowed her, like many other hopeful novelists,
to juggle writing schedules with household demands. The finished product would then be sent to New York, where it would be edited, handed
off to the publisher, and then returned to Benson for minor revisions.[38]
Because many cheap publications used literary pseudonyms, writers were

also able to neutralize gender differences between themselves and their readers simply by matching their nom de plume to the gender of their intended audience (a strategy of "rhetorical drag" that actually had a long if hidden history in American letters).[39] Josephine Chase, who had written the popular Marjorie Dean series as Pauline Lester and the Patsy Carroll and June Allen books as Grace Gordon, enlarged both her readership and her bank account by penning the Long Trail Boys and the Adventure Boys series under the more androgynous name Ames Thompson.[40]

Bemoaned by the apostles of culture, blacklisted in many public libraries, the series books were nevertheless enormously popular. By 1931 the fifty-cent books accounted for almost 15 percent of all book sales, or more than 22 million copies.[41] The characters these hired pens created quickly became fixtures of popular culture in the 1920s and 1930s, while both their real names and the practices they pioneered remained deeply guarded secrets. "The only time people will ever know I am a writer," the prolific but pseudonymous Josephine Chase quipped, "will be when I die and they write my obituary."[42]

She was not alone. Anonymity encouraged invention, allowed for different voices, and pushed into print controversial subjects that authors might not want attached to their real names. Mass-market magazines, journals, publishers, and Pocket Books in turn encouraged an image of writing as a marketable commodity, something that could be learned in "ten easy lessons," a cliché that readers of "Eight Ways to Become an Authoress" had been hearing for years. Publishers of guidebooks like *The Writer's Handbook*, *The Power of Words*, and *Short Story Craft*, as well as popular magazines such as *The Writer, Writer's Digest, Author & Journalist, Writer's Yearbook, Coronet, Saturday Review, Confidential, Reader's Digest, Ladies' Home Journal, Good Housekeeping, Keyhole, Inside Story, True Stories, Weird Tales*, and *Women's Day*, encouraged readers to try their hand at writing. Articles and advertisements invited readers to test their skills through an assortment of "quizzes," surveys, prizes, and contests supervised by "famous writers" who stood ready to guide the hopeful "dead-in-earnest" amateur. "Find out the reasons behind rejection slips," Macmillan promised readers who, for $3.75, could also "learn the craft and techniques of writing salable short stories."[43] "If you can write plain English," Charles Meredith boasted, "I'll show you how to sell it for as high as 30 cents a word!"[44] Even groups at odds with mass culture labored within it. The Judson Press, a Philadelphia firm long specializing in Christian books, increasingly published manuals and advertised workshops to teach inspired postwar readers "how to write and sell Christian publications." But the spiritually motivated were not discouraged from pursuing more sinful outlets. For a small fee they too could purchase an additional "ten inclusive chapters" that would get them into the slicks and pulps.[45]

"Reaching the masses" took on new urgency throughout the depression as political forces from all persuasions sought to win over faceless constituencies. The Left, which gained a large readership in the thirties, sought to bring those on the outer edges of American life into what Michael Denning calls the "cultural front." Radical bookshops, experimental paperback firms (such as Modern Age Books), leftist lending book clubs (including George Braziller's Book Find Club), and pro-labor pulps were joined by the League of American Writers in the hope of bringing proletarian and ethnic writing into popular cultural venues. An active cadre of intellectuals and writers offered courses in "radio scriptwriting, women's pulps and confessions, detective stories and thrillers, writing popular articles, and labor journalism." Rejecting the association of writing with the leisured and privileged, a League pamphlet assured its subscribers that "writing is a job and a craft."[46]

This too was the new motto of writing entrepreneurs who launched a network of for-profit correspondence schools and writing programs such as the Magazine Institute, the Shepard School, the Hollywood School of Comedy Writing, and the Famous Writers School, all of which promised success after "a short course of study."[47] Smelling profits, the slicks teamed up with these dream merchants, advertising both their schools and newly invented writing contests to readers who showed "promise and talent." Universities entered the business at much-reduced rates, while publishers from Macmillan to *Mademoiselle* magazine offered substantial prizes to college co-eds. Universities and intellectuals also developed writers' conferences, fellowships, retreats, workshops, and postgraduate degrees as a way to protect the burgeoning business from unscrupulous hucksters while capturing a piece of an increasingly lucrative market.[48] In the age of the jackpot author, literary capital was running out, for when it came to writing, "anything goes," declared Edwin Seaver. "As last the Dodo said, Everybody has won and all must have prizes."[49]

Throughout the twentieth century, the "serious" writer, who was believed to be under assault by these changes, was arguably undergoing a sort of rebirth as an emblem of anti-commercialism. Books increasingly circulated among a consuming public informed by both the promises of mass consumption and the concomitant anxieties they called forth. In the wake of the cheap book business, contemporary observers feared that American culture, even civilization, was in danger, cheapened as it were by the "barbarism" of both "too many [bad] books" and the indiscriminate buying habits of unpredictable readers.[50] Many old-line publishers put the blame on the literary agent, whom they saw as a disruptive figure in an otherwise "easy" relationship between publisher and author. "Now," Henry Holt complained, "the connection is mainly a question of which publisher would bid highest." Imported from England, the literary agent was accused by publisher Robert Sterling Yard of introducing sharp "business methods," including book advances—"as unwelcome as the English sparrow."[51] Agents demanded higher royalties for authors, too, sometimes drumming up business by soliciting established authors and offering them to publishers for more money. At other times they sold stories that were written for and promised to mass-market periodicals and newspapers for serialization, a practice Holt believed to be responsible for turning the literary world into "a new Eldorado."[52]

The problem for publishers like Yard, Frank Dodd, and Holt, in other words, was not only that agents introduced "business methods" into the writing profession but also that in doing so, they encouraged a renegotiation of the Literary whereby the economic potential of writing was emphasized over aesthetic concerns. The literary agent, Holt accurately observed, enfranchised the "worthy" and "unworthy" author alike, shackling the publisher's ability to control either.[53]

What emerged amidst the increasing deluge of word merchants and fiction factories "churning it out," however, was not just a new arena of consumerist activity but a new standard against which the Literary was weighed and measured. Organized in opposition to the hack and the popular writer, modern authorship accrued cultural capital as a protected zone of authenticity and autonomy, a sign of an aesthetic rejection of Fordist economics, mass production, and the consumerist culture it spawned. In this symbolic landscape, the female author called attention to the paradoxes and confusions that lurked beneath those promises as gender relations were increasingly reconfigured within the expanding orbit of mass culture and consumption. Anxieties over woman's rights, sexual radicalism, and feminism took shape within the literary field as "a form of deep distaste for the purported feminization of culture and the emasculation of otherwise assertive artists and aggressively discriminating readers."[54] Less out of step with their culture than the "literary domestics" who preceded them, "emancipated modern authoresses" nevertheless echoed their predecessors' "peculiar circumstances" as women defined by social norms that their success as writers disrupted and made uneasy.

That the term "authoress" continued in popular culture well into the 1950s attests as well to the long shadow cast by a generation of literary critics who emerged in the wake of first-wave feminism. Mobilizing a "modernist" position against which to challenge the popular and "sentimentalist" style of the nineteenth and early twentieth centuries, critics in the thirties called for a more muscular Literature to help define modernist sensibilities. "There has been no woman novelist since Miss Cather's death," one observer quipped, while others busily expunged Willa Cather from the literary canon altogether.[55] Still others saw commercial forms of writing as unmanly, equating serious authorship with virile masculinity. "What will happen when we stop this dreadful round of meaningless 'writing,'" a distraught author asked his fellow "prisoners"? Speaking on behalf of "writers who once were men," he saw no escape from the "piffle" demanded by a market dominated by "advertising agencies and the public relations departments of power and light corporations."[56] Commercialism emasculated the authorial voice by rendering it anonymous and formulaic: a standardized "stir simple" product of a crass consumerism. "We have all come of literary age," complained another writer, "at a time when the machine-made cultural product has pushed the 'hand-made' book or play out of the market."[57] Here was the terrain of the low, cheap, and slick, the mass-produced claptrap of unmanly hacks against which modernist narratives of "real" authors and good books would find critical traction.

Yet the same everyday operations of consumer culture that encouraged the suspect reading habits of the masses also made it possible for the "literary" to enter into the lives of those traditionally beyond its scope. At times this came about in unexpected ways as new areas of readerly interest called forth new kinds of authorial voices. Brodhead makes this point in his perceptive study of regionalist writing, in which popular stories of old salts, remote landscapes, picturesque manners, odd dialects, and quaint folkways turned unknown and variously skilled storytellers into some of the most celebrated authors of the late nineteenth and early twentieth centuries.[58] In this scheme of writing, ordinary men and especially women who lived in the remote hinterlands of America and who had scant access to the literary could conceivably become authors by turning their marginality and exotic Otherness into tales of "local color." Their sketches were serialized in mass-market magazines and circulated to an armchair audience of genteel readers itching for adventure and rustic relief from the burdens and trappings of urbanization and modern life. "Regionalism," Brodhead wryly notes, "produced the opportunity it offered."[59]

Inviting readers to imagine themselves as writers, advertisements for schools and contests conceptually flattened hierarchies of talent and effectively tethered authorship to the consumerist fantasies of the era. In the 1940s, publishers candidly enlisted newsmagazines, newspapers, and literary agencies not just to advertise their books but to turn top-selling books and their authors into dramatic news stories for the general, nonreading public. Like the mythical Hollywood starlet whose "discovery" fed the desires of young girls to escape their hometowns, stories of the "jackpot author," the "Million Dollar Class of Writers," and "Big Money Writing" operated as powerful wish images for ordinary readers, especially for those who found in the "true life" story of wordsmiths and dream merchants a realized version of the fictional heroines whose trials and triumphs had been for decades a staple of romance magazines and the female-oriented slicks. Such news stories encouraged the fetishization of the best-seller, making it appear as if these books and their authors emerged out of thin air—a stroke of magic not unlike hitting the lottery. Big books, it seemed, were the stuff of luck and pluck, and perhaps a correspondence course or two.

Wildly successful novels like *Anthony Adverse* (1933) and *Gone With the Wind* (1936) further leveled hierarchies of talent as unknown authors with ordinary-sounding names like Hervey Allen and Mrs. John Marsh (Margaret Mitchell) increasingly shaped images of best-sellerdom. Working in tandem with the processes of cheap bookmaking and mass story production, images like these remapped the demographics of authorship and enfranchised a generation of nontraditional writers, many of them from ethnic and working-class backgrounds. Speaking of the rapid increase in the numbers of such authors during the thirties, Michael Denning points out that storytelling "allowed them to represent—to speak for and to depict—their families, their neighborhoods, their aspirations, and their nightmares."[60] By extending authorship to include the dreams and fantasies of ordinary readers, cheap book production offered as well a scene of writing that housewives could imagine as their own: a literary landscape in which readers could place themselves no matter how cut off from the world they understood themselves to be.

Public fascination with authorship, of course, was hardly new to the twentieth century. Coined in the 1850s, the term "celebrity" coincided with the new phenomenon of the "literary personality" which had earned a cult-like status in both America and Europe.[61] Mass-circulated magazines and the lecture circuit conjoined to market writers in new ways, turning authors as diverse as Charles Dickens, Oscar Wilde, Louisa May Alcott, and Mark Twain into transatlantic stars whose tours have been compared with those of the Beatles in the 1960s, complete with "overnight queues, packed theaters, huge box office receipts, ticket tours, and the use of police to control crowds."[62] Modernist writers—one immediately thinks of Hemingway, Fitzgerald, even Stein—were no less pulled into this circuit of commerce and celebrity even as they defined their writing in opposition to it.

Some have argued that the aim of twentieth-century interest in the literary celebrity was, at least in part, to find an interpretive "key" that would shed light on the author's texts. Thus, in the decades between the world wars, both cultural authority and authorial personality tended to accrue value over time, based on a body of work rather than any single literary achievement. In his pioneering study of public personalities, the sociologist Leo Lowenthal found that in the first four decades of the twentieth century, popular biographies published in mass-circulated magazines like *Collier's* and the *Saturday Evening Post* focused on "politics, captains of industry and people from the serious arts," what Lowenthal came to see as "idols of production."[63] By the 1930s, however, he detected a marked shift, one propelled by newer forms of leisure that featured "idols of consumption"—sports, film, and television stars—whose fame and appeal revolved around sudden success and whose biographies emphasized "luck and circumstance."[64] Studies of celebrity authorship argue for a similar transformation, although scholars tend to see the collapse of the "modernist model" as happening much later—in the last three decades of the twentieth century—as "books become mere adjuncts to the world of mass media" and publishing becomes more of a corporate enterprise than a cottage industry.[65] Idealized in magazines like *Time* and *Life*, the figure of the writer in the 1950s assumed a special place within mythic Cold War narratives of conformity; an individualist's individual "set apart from other men," with "whiskey and ink" the fluids needed to survive in a world plagued by mediocrity and artificiality.[66] But as creative figures celebrated for their difference and remove from crass commercialism, authors were also exposed as "real" people doing ordinary things: they shopped, traveled, had families, got married and divorced. The paradox of literary celebrity was that it was simultaneously different and familiar, "a pull between hierarchy and equality" that gave writers a heightened place in the American imaginary well into the 1960s.[67]

Such momentous but subtle transformations in culture are difficult to pinpoint, but certainly we can see in Grace Metalious's authorship the workings of this metamorphosis. Embracing the mass market against which modernists defined themselves, Metalious used images of literary celebrity to differentiate and mark herself as other than what she was "supposed to be." Yet in the wake of the publishing success of *Peyton Place*, she found in her celebrity status an unexpected fame as an "ordinary housewife and mother." Public interest in her was propelled, at least in part, by readers seeking to understand neither her text nor her writing style but rather her fantastic migration from average (but lucky) housewife to best-selling author. "I wish there was a key," Grace would quietly reply over and over again to talk show hosts, reporters, and fans. "But I don't know how these things happen."[68]

In the highly commodified culture of mass-produced letters, authorship offered to readers far more than the stories confined within their texts. Like many other, more tangible products, authorship held out to consumers the possibility of personal transformation while at the same time opening up new kinds of collectivities organized around the authorial personality. In the postwar period, the housewife writer piqued the imagination of ordinary women with aprons draped over kitchen typewriters. In the highly segmented marketplace of publishing, the writer manqué emerged across a dreamscape of consumerist longing and desire.

The celebrity status accorded the female author of a certain type marked a point of entrance and possibility for those with average and unexceptional backgrounds. "It cannot be overstressed," Richard Dyer argues of the 1950s cultural imaginary, "the degree to which ordinariness was offered as the ultimate moral attribute of the American way of life, rather than the ideals of piety, charity, heroism, and so on, whose very idealness makes them not ordinary."[69] As we shall see, part of the imaginative labor of both *Peyton Place* and Grace Metalious's highly publicized life was to conceptually render access to the literary "ordinary" and plausible to women "just like her." Her celebrity status, in turn, was part of a larger movement away from merit and ability and toward what David Marshall describes as "a language of character and the personal history of the star."[70] As a celebrity writer, Metalious herself would quickly become a discursive battleground that centered as much on the norms of individual womanhood and personality as on the writing of books.

In the circulating images of the "would-be writer" and celebrated authoress, Grace began to see her way out. "It's not always going to be like this," she whispers over and over again to her oldest daughter, Marsha. "I promise that someday everything is going to be beautiful and you're going to have everything you've ever wanted."[71] Amidst the consumerist politics of postwar America, Grace set her literary scheme against the thin, slim volumes of the boy geniuses living out impoverished lives in small circles of lofty fame. She would instead insert herself within the narrative fantasies of mass-circulated magazines and the "jackpot" best-selling authors they set afloat. She wrote and wrote, and she "lied her head off," but always to hack her way out of poverty. In the postwar explosion of the emancipated female authoress, Grace would seek the lineaments of an authorial self and hitch her wagon to that star. And from the writerly aspirations of readers like herself she began to weave her tales and conjure her heroine Allison, who, like her creator, used stories to remedy the terrible unfairness of things.

Grace knew her audience. In Allison, readers saw themselves plunking down dimes and quarters to buy *Photoplay* and *Silver Screen* or books covered in paper jackets that pictured slave girls "naked from the waist up." Clipping coupons, Allison celebrated a generation of fashion-starved women who sent away for cosmetic samples like "Oriental #2" or for free booklets, "always wrapped in plain paper," that explained the mysteries of menstruation, sex, and modern words like "adolescence." What readers might not know, Allison, Norman, Betty, Mike, Selena, and Constance taught them: that "all women have erotic areas around their breasts," that when aroused, nipples became "as hard as diamonds," and that there were such things in this world as incest, rape, abortion, and "bachelor girls in apartments in Greenwich Village."[72] In Allison, readers saw as well the fabled "Eldorado" Holt feared: cheap book production made possible, celebrity culture glamorized, and the "would-be writer's industry" marketed. "You're a genius," Allison tells her gifted but starving boyfriend. "I'm not. I'm a hack and very pleased with myself." Although "she was young," Metalious wrote in her sequel *Return to Peyton Place*, she was "not so young that she still believed that art could be found only in a cold-water flat."[73]

There was, Otto Friedrich wrote in a sensitive portrait, a "fierce vitality" to Grace Metalious that upended popular images of the "lady novelist," and happily so. If she had gone to college, he suggests, and become "one of those elegant creatures who write so tirelessly about the sensitive and the misunderstood," her literary sins might have been forgiven. He suspected, too, that a preference for "blended whiskey rather than vodka martinis" fueled more than a few of her critics. But in the end it was a cookie-cutter prose style "like something created in one of those fluorescent-lighted high-school classrooms where salesmen and discontented housewives gather for night-time courses in creative writing" that put him (and others) off Grace Metalious as a writer, if not as a woman he otherwise respected and admired.[74]

Grace, of course, never asked for nor received any writing lessons in the mail, she paid no agent to read her work, and she never returned any talent surveys to the Famous Writers School. But she was not untutored. In stories of the literary celebrity she saw what she wanted to be. In novels, Grace reread her life and spun alternate narratives to what was; with borrowed words she then invented a writerly self and set her difference into creative motion. In short, she "poached" from others, inserting herself into their stories and using them to make up her own. Reading, Michel de Certeau reminds us, is a "silent production," best understood as part of the "arts of making" and "making do."[75]

We speak of people getting "lost" in books, but we can see too that, rather than an erosion of time, this constitutes as well a creative space of activity. And Grace fashioned there not just a self but a voice and a writing style that readers quickly embraced. "A real page-turner," people would say; prose packed more with "store-bought fancies" than with the "home-made goods" Sherwood Anderson famously described as a modernist's "kitchen of words."[76] But if this was true, it was because Grace was simply making do: a consumer enfranchised by mass culture to produce it as well. Reading becomes autobiography.

In the late summer of 1954, Grace Metalious opened *The Writer's Handbook* to page 557 and glanced thoughtfully at the names of forty-one literary agents listed there. Then she made her choice: M. Jacques Chambrun.[77] Exactly one year later, Monsieur Chambrun would escort Grace Metalious to the '21' Club—"the fanciest saloon in New York"—to celebrate her book contract with Kathryn "Kitty" Messner, president of the respectable hardback publishing firm of Julian Messner, Inc. "I was an author," Grace wrote, "with a contract that said so. I had a French agent and a lady publisher. I was in '21.'" As her eye took in the warm red wood room with its soft, low-hanging lights and old-school knickknacks casually tucked into nooks and crannies at the bar, Grace sipped a pale green daiquiri— "so cold it hurt my teeth." By the end of lunch, Monsieur Chambrun had asked her to call him Jacques. "I had arrived," she remembered thinking. "It was the greatest day of my life."[78]

5

The Gendered Eye

If reading trash makes you unhappy, don't go into publishing.
The Lady Editor

Jacques Chambrun entered Grace Metalious's life in the spring of 1955 and exited it six years later, a much richer man. "I just picked your name cold out of a book," Grace wrote to him from her chrysalis at "It'll Do." "It is the same system I use playing horses and I often win."[1] There seemed no reason to consider her pick much of a gamble. Chambrun was one of forty or so New York literary agents whose names regularly appeared in the "how to" guides and writers' handbooks that catered to the popular market in would-be authors. Besides, his French name lent him a certain worldliness that Grace attached to book publishing. Moreover, his Frenchness, Paris-hatched rather than Québécois, bolstered his appeal, feeding the considered opinion of Grace's mother, now her own, that Culture and things French must certainly go hand in hand. "It was something," Grace wrote of those intoxicating early years, "to go to a famous place and have the headwaiter greet your agent by name and discuss the weather with him in French."[2] Then, too, there was the list of authors' names attached to Chambrun's that brought the bet home: Sherwood Anderson, Jean Cocteau, Luigi Pirandello, Frances

Parkinson Keyes, Aldous Huxley, Ben Hecht, and Somerset Maugham, "the prince of cats among popular storytellers."[3]

"I shall be glad to read your novel and to handle it for you," Chambrun wrote back, "if it seems to be saleable."[4] Later, when she began to view Chambrun as a friend, Grace would dedicate her second novel to him. But it was to Monsieur Chambrun at 745 Fifth Avenue that Grace addressed her literary long shot and on him placed her greatest wager.

Manhattan in the 1950s was a patchwork of distinct territories, and although the Old New York society of Edith Wharton, with its elaborate "set of arbitrary signs," had been knocked flat by a certain leveling between the wars, the city remained a deeply coded landscape.[5] The most visible differences continued to be the geographical divides between people of disparate ethnicities and classes. With a population of just over 8 million people, "the City" at mid-decade remained more than 80 percent white, with discrete physical boundaries separating Jews from gentiles, whites from blacks, Italians from Hispanics. With the famous exception of bohemian Greenwich Village, "white and black people did not mingle," Anne Bernays and Justin Kaplan noted in their literary memoir.[6] In publishing circles, barriers of class and religion retained something of the hieratic world Wharton described so well. Old-line firms like Holt and Scribner signaled their lists and employment policies as much by their uptown addresses as by their listings in *Publishers Weekly*. Telephone exchanges such as BUtterfield, REgent, and RHinelander signified white Anglo-Saxon Protestants who lived on the restricted Upper East Side. A literary agent or upstart firm at MOnument, RIverside, or ACademy, by contrast, was probably Jewish, most likely a German Jew of means, or perhaps a Yiddish-speaking Jew moving up, but out of Russian soil. A publisher bearing the LAckawanna designation carried the whiff of newness, commercialism, and the potential threat of radicalism.[7]

Things like this still counted in the fifties and in book publishing. Even as the lines between Jew and gentile weakened somewhat after the war, they continued to convey meaning, at times as markers distinguishing old family-owned houses that published "serious" books from the newcomers, mostly Jews, who ushered in "fun" paperbacks directed at more popular audiences. "It was still something people thought about," the publisher

Michael Korda acknowledged, "even talked about from time to time, and it mattered."[8]

Publishing in the decades before and after World War II carried with it an aura of "class" and cultivation, unlike the more dubious appeal of Wall Street.[9] When Chambrun came to New York City during the Great Depression, many of the social and cultural patterns of modern publishing were already in place, remapping the terrain of its operation in radical ways. Like other businesses, book publishers were struggling to make ends meet, and up and down what was then called Fourth Avenue—"publishers' row"—the dust of hard times settled into the literary woodwork. But the expansion of mass-market publishing in the 1920s, including advances in distribution and innovations like the "slicks" (printed on glossy coated stock), series books, film magazines, confessionals, and book clubs, had opened up opportunities not just to Jews but to anyone who could afford an office and a telephone, and who could boast "a sharp eye for a book that would sell."[10]

Innovation in the twenties helped keep many publishing houses afloat in the thirties. George Delacorte was typical of this new generation of savvy young businessmen willing to test the boundaries of print culture and branch out with different kinds of literary wares. With the $20,000 he received in a buyout from the New Fiction Group, he formed Dell Publishing Company. His other assets included members of an equally new and different generation of editors: Elizabeth Sharpe, Anita Fairgrave, and Valdo Freeman, one of the few African Americans in the business. Together they launched with astonishing success *I Confess* (a tell-all humorously recalled by one staff member as a magazine of "personal experience for the intelligent people of the United States"), and would soon follow up with a fleet of comic books as well as romance, confessional, and pulp adventure books, and eventually paperback reprints and originals.[11] Others began firms with far less capital, "sometimes with as little cash as it took to buy a new car."[12] In 1933, as banks across the country crashed, Julian Messner and his new wife, Kathryn (Kitty), combined their savings of $3,000 and established Julian Messner, Inc., at an office a few blocks away from the fabled brownstone of Boni & Liveright, where for fifteen years Julian had worked as vice president and Kitty as a freelance editor.[13]

A "hatchery of talent," firms like Boni & Liveright, Alfred A. Knopf, Harcourt, Brace & Co., Messner, and Simon & Schuster had little patience with the conservative backlash against the Roaring Twenties that brought book burnings, a Clean Books bill, and the infamous Watch and Ward Society, which made "banned in Boston" a badge of pride to writers and publishers well into the 1950s.[14] Some, like the legendary Albert Boni and Horace Liveright, began their careers with deep roots in the bohemian atmosphere of prewar Greenwich Village, where they embraced the work of socialists and pacifists as well as "titles that exuded a scandalous air."[15] Julian and Kitty Messner were committed to keeping their firm small, specializing in children's books, light fiction, and novels that fostered progressive values. In 1946 they created the Julian Messner Award for the best book promoting racial or religious tolerance in America. During the depression they encouraged left-leaning writers who sympathized with progressive causes. In 1937 they published both Edward Seaver's proletarian novel *Between the Hammer and the Anvil* and Daphne Greenwood's *Apollo Sleeps*, one of several sympathetic renderings of homosexuality that Messner would bring into print.[16]

The publishers *sans argent*, in other words, could afford to take a few risks. They could gamble on unknown authors, take chances on experimental avant-garde writers, print new kinds of magazines, or publish questionable subject matter in ways that old-line firms, whose reputations and sales often depended on books and stories written by established authors, could not. Upstart firms were also more willing to take advantage of advertising, flamboyantly publicizing their books on Fifth Avenue buses, highway billboards, and automobile roof cards (painted by famous artists like John Held), making the legacy of these newer publishing houses as much commercial as literary.[17]

Indeed, it is this conjoining of marketing savvy and the commitment to "modern," even avant-garde literature that has, for some scholars, put Boni & Liveright at the center of *Peyton Place*'s success and its place in publishing history. In his 2005 study of mass culture and the marketing of books, Evan Brier makes the important point that *Peyton Place* should be understood as a text that emerged out of and not in opposition to the institutional apparatus that produced many of America's most celebrated "high culture" modernist works. Arguing against interpretations that tend to view *Peyton Place* as a turning point in either publishing history (the first blockbuster) or literary merit and taste (a symbol of cultural rupture and decline), Brier situates the novel as "an end, a culmination of a distinctly commercial success story that dates back to the twentieth century."[18]

To shore up his point, however, Brier takes a great many leaps of historical faith. Noting that both Julian Messner and Aaron Sussman worked under the innovative roof of Boni & Liveright (the former at one time in charge of sales and the latter the head of advertising), Brier creates a "genealogy" that charts a "clear" and "direct" line between *Peyton Place* and the marketing of modernist writers such as Eugene O'Neill, William Faulkner, and Sherwood Anderson. His implicit argument is that since Messner was "general factotum" at Boni & Liveright, he must have imbibed that firm's "recipe for commercial success," thereby pulling *Peyton Place* into Messner's future orbit. Brier links *Peyton Place's* importance to publishing history even more explicitly with Sussman, known in depression-era book circles for his 1934 "How to Enjoy James Joyce's Novel *Ulysses*" ad, which, Brier tells us, "was hailed as a landmark in the marketing of modernism to the general reading public."[19] Pulling this thread of advertising triumph into the 1950s, Brier loops it around *Peyton Place*. Hired by Messner's firm to help with advertising, Sussman gives Metalious's manuscript "The Tree and the Blossom" its more memorable title and so completes the "clear but as yet unnoted line connecting" the two "scandalous" novels. "The links between *Ulysses* and *Peyton Place*," Brier writes, "are institutional rather than literary, and what they suggest is that the commercial success of the one is not that different from the commercial success of the other—a truth obscured in the prevalent narratives of 1950's cultural decline that have dominated discussions of *Peyton Place*'s place in book history. Those narratives of decline notwithstanding, no great institutional divide separates *Ulysses* from *Peyton Place*; they are products of the same book trade."[20]

Fair enough. But in his effort to recast *Peyton Place* as part of a continuous family tree rooted in the selling of big books, Brier prunes from his tidy narrative those messy sprigs and saplings that give linear history its tarnished reputation and Whiggish inevitability. Most important for our purposes here is the snipped-off demographics of mass commercialized publishing, which for the first time in history began to match the highly gendered landscape of fiction reading and novel consumption. When Boni & Liveright opened up shop in 1915, women were as scarce in the publishing world (some firms even refused to allow female secretaries within their walls) as they were central to the mass consumption of the printed word. By 1950, however, a survey by the Book and Magazine Guild revealed that 80 percent of those employed in the publishing industry were women, and in book publishing specifically, just under that figure had been reached as early as 1940.[21] That *Peyton Place* has a role in publishing history is without doubt, and clearly much of that story rests on its links to the commercialized world of print culture as it unfolded in the decades after World War I. But if you want to locate *Peyton Place*'s specific site in publishing history, even from a genealogical perspective, first *cherchez les femmes*.

By 1930, few publishers needed Henry Holt to remind them that books were very much like bricks, but still, a publisher's product was simultaneously material and mercurial. This was especially true in the small, competitive, and unpredictable world of trade fiction, where a first novel could be expected to sell around two thousand copies at most. How to find just the right book? How to recognize that one book in a thousand that might hit the jackpot? Would one know it when one saw it? Careers were made on such decisions. With books, marketing was never enough. Before the advent of the blockbuster and the corporate takeovers of the 1960s (and even afterwards), the success of a first novel was wildly unpredictable, a storied landscape of missed chances and accidental triumphs. It was the ability of a firm to know not just the realm of "high" serious writing but of popular taste as well, to have not just a feeling for books but a feel for "a good read" that often made the greatest difference to small and big houses alike. To succeed, and initially for new firms to stay afloat, it was essential to know what readers wanted, to develop not only better methods of distribution but also sharper ways of reading; an eye for fiction must reflect not the arbitrary rules of literary taste but the interests, needs, and desires of the publics that publishers hoped to woo and in turn would help to create.

In theory this sometimes meant turning to new techniques in marketing research, and some firms, like Simon & Schuster, pioneered the use of polling and other research methods to try to track popular taste. But in practice, publishers either had this mysterious knack or depended on female staff, family, and friends to guide them. In *The Best of Everything*, Rona Jaffe's fictional account of a paperback house in early 1950s New York,[22] the college-educated heroine and would-be editor, Caroline Bender, finds that to get out of the typing pool, she needs more than a college education. "Here," the editor-in-chief of Derby Books, Mr. Shalimar, tells Caroline, handing her a stack of manuscripts. "Read these this week. I'm interested in a young girl's opinion."

"*Mine?*" says the incredulous secretary.

"Use your instinct. I'm not interested in your college education. Some of the people who buy our books regularly are college graduates, but most of them aren't." Later, when he takes her to a bar for the routine afternoon scotch whisky (which follows the ritual two-martini lunch), Shalimar further explains his methodology: "How do you think I know what every woman in America wants to read?" he boastfully asks. "Because I talk to women, find out what their secret dreams are, what they fear." Gaining access to the editor's chair required what Jaffe and many editors thought of as "instinct"; and it was the talented clerk, secretary, or "girl reader," college degree or no college degree, who knew how to read like the woman mass-market paperbacks appealed to. Getting out of the competitive typing pool, as Caroline Bender discovers, was recognized as a matter of both holding one's liquor and soaking up popular taste. "Don't ever tell an editor . . . that you want to write," a 1941 guidebook warns the aspiring "Lady Editor." "You are much more likely to get the job if you tell him or her you like to *read*."[23]

Like many who landed jobs in publishing, Jaffe was in the right place at the right time. But as a graduate of Radcliffe College, Jaffe entered Gold Medal Publishing in the early 1950s as a file clerk shortly after Gold Medal had turned the book world on its head by publishing not paperback reprints (the firm was inhibited here by other contract arrangements) but paperback originals, a daring move at the time. Created in 1950 by Fawcett Publications in an effort to enter the paper market, Gold Medal offered authors excellent terms and quickly proved that writers were quite willing to have new work published in paper form if offered favorable contracts.[24] Like her heroine, Jaffe found herself in a strategic position, using her role as "girl reader" to work her way into an associate editorship at Fawcett, where she stayed until 1958, when she left to write her novel.

Editors and publishers either read like their readers or tapped into secretaries, clerks, typists, assistant editors, or even wives and girlfriends who did. At times this meant creating formal positions, such as at Jaffe's fictionalized Derby Books, where "readers" like Caroline could eventually escape the typing pool. But the practice was also more casual, especially within smaller firms like Messner, or start-ups and mid-sized companies like David McKay, Dell, and Alfred Knopf in the years leading up to World War II. When Elizabeth Sharpe needed a sounding board for Dell's pulp confessionals, she turned to her fifteen-year-old clerk, Helen Konig Meyer, whose "feel" for a good story made her an invaluable member of the intimate Dell staff. Meyer quickly advanced, taking over circulation of the magazines in her twenties and eventually becoming president, then chairman of the board of Dell Publishing Company—one of the only female heads in the business and a legend in the publishing industry.[25] When Julian Messner died in 1948, Kitty took over as president, finding in her well-honed editorial gaze the readerly eyes necessary to keep Messner nicely stocked with saleable manuscripts. The director of sales was Doris Flowers, Lora Orrmont headed publicity, while Carolyn Weiss took over everyday operations as secretary and office manager. "When Kitty hired Arthur Ceppos in 1951 to head a new Messner line," Emily Toth writes in her biography of Grace Metalious, "his gender was considered noteworthy enough for mention in *Writer's Digest*."[26]

There is, of course, a long and important history of male editors and publishers discovering not only talented writers but also mediocre writers of best-selling sensations like *Gone With the Wind* and sexy potboilers like *Mandingo*. Readerly "instinct" was neither unique nor essentially female, but with the commercialization of Literature came opportunities for women, who often found themselves at the center of changes in the industry and the corresponding demographic shifts in authorship they engendered. While this was especially evident in the mass-market magazine and paperback book industry, trade publishers also found themselves increasingly dependent on female underlings in the wake of the famous Pocket Book revolution of 1939. Here the "sherry and biscuit boys"—artisan publishers and male editors of "serious" books, who tended to equate cheap paperbacked books with lowbrow mass-market magazines—happily left their paperback operations in the hands of female secretaries and assistant editors, who not only handled negotiations with new authors but often selected as well which authors their firms would publish.[27] As Kenneth Davis points out, "that strategy placed many women in key roles just as subsidiary rights flowered in importance to hardcover publishers." By the early fifties, trade publishers, who had "handled the reprinters like dead fish," found themselves eager to line up paperback guarantees, while others started their own paperback imprints.[28] And then Gold Medal raised the stakes. Almost by default, female secretaries and assistant editors found themselves pivotal players in the unsettling transition to paperback books.

Typically "compelled to begin their careers as secretaries," women in publishing, much like Rona Jaffe and Helen Meyer, found their opportunities growing in tandem with the great swelling tide of mass-marketed paperback books. As Muriel Fuller advised in her 1941 guide to careers for women in publishing, the way in was to "take good dictation"; the way up was to take over what you could, and in small firms this often meant negotiating paperback reprint rights and overseeing contracts and authors.[29] And like Jaffe, Meyer, and many, many others, they typically started as clerks, secretaries, and readers of manuscripts. They also made half what their male counterparts made, with some women earning as little as $50 a week. But for those whose "instincts" captured the reading habits of the public and who brokered the flow of reprint rights and subsidiaries, the job of "Lady Editor" at $100 per week was a real possibility. "You will not make money," Fuller cautioned readers of *The Lady Editor*. "If you have your eye on your old age, and a pension, be a policewoman, a school teacher, or an airplane hostess. Go into hardware or plumbing."[30]

Still, by any measure the reading of manuscripts was an arduous task no matter how many formal or informal readers a publishing house employed. In the increasingly expanding business of mass-market publishing, the "slush" pile grew in tandem with its notoriety, forcing more and more firms to turn to literary agents—"human reading machines"—who cast their nets widely in hopes of finding new talent on the streets and down on the farm. In the same ways that mass-marketed print ushered in new opportunities in publishing, the enfranchisement of authorship to those outside the realm of literary life opened up new possibilities for the representation of writers. Often left off the family tree of publishing history, the literary agent was in fact an increasingly key player in the business.

The bane of old-line publishers like Henry Holt, who blamed them for bringing into the gentlemanly world of Literature "sharp business practices," literary agents were also conduits between book publishing and mass-market magazines. Tainted by their close connection to magazine sales—the notion of representing book authors gained ground only slowly in the 1940s and 1950s—the author's agent was viewed for many years with an element of suspicion: "flesh peddlers," Helen Strauss, one of the most respectable among their numbers called them, men and women who "had collected such outlandish commissions and deductions as to place their clients in bondage."[31] The "genteel racket," it was agreed, was the product of some very un-genteel behavior. Carl Brandt, the son of the founders of one of the oldest and most renowned literary agencies in New York, recalled how his father, who, just before World War I, had been hired to sweep the floors of a literary agency, took over after the war and brought in Carl's uncle to help him run the firm. "The uncle," Brandt wryly explained, "was a very straight arrow and my father was not, so it was obvious my uncle wouldn't quite do as an agent, and he went off, quite rightly, to be an editor at the *Saturday Evening Post*."[32] But authors' agents quickly became critical factors in the making of the modern literary marketplace, not just improving the conditions of individual authors with better royalties, reprint rights, and expanding subsidiary rights, but fueling the rise of the literary celebrity. By connecting individual authors to magazines, newspapers, radio, and eventually television, agents put the collective life of authorship into the public realm.

To Grace Metalious, it was the literary agent who gave authorship a face. In the celebrity authoress she could imagine herself, and in Jacques Chambrun she could picture a way into the distant galaxy of literary life. But unlike Carl Brandt's honest uncle "who wouldn't quite do," Chambrun fit in nicely, finding in the "genteel racket" a way to make a very agreeable living.

Short, with wisps of hair held in place with black pomade, Chambrun exuded a clichéd suave Old World charm. It was rumored that he was a count. Most publishers knew that he was not, but he indulged the fantasy by dressing in what passed at the time as sophisticated "continental" style. Donning tailored double-breasted suits, he sported "the well-fleshed features of a gourmand." Despite an unlovely face, "pendulous and lumpy," there was a joie de vivre about him that made him popular with both clients and the bejeweled and lipsticked émigrés he joined for tea and tango amidst the fading Moorish décor of the Alhambra Room. Describing one such afternoon with Chambrun in 1959, Michael Korda, then a newcomer at Simon & Schuster, recalled the "grave courtesy," impressive French manner, and sartorial flair that made Chambrun somewhat of a character in publishing circles. "His shoes were unusual: narrow, expensive, and well polished, with high-buttoned tops to them in some kind of black stretch material, the sort of thing that Proust might have worn."[33]

From the beginning his command of the French language and his European connections gave him access to writers like Cocteau, Colette, and Mavis Gallant, as well as to Jewish authors from central Europe such as Ferenc Molnár and Lion Feuchtwanger (Hitler's "enemy of state number one"), while his ever-bending ethics landed him Nazi sympathizers like Knut Hamsun. To Julian and Kitty Messner he brought *Dinner at Antoine's* by Frances Parkinson Keyes, whose gothic tales of loveless marriage and noble struggles against convention made her one of the best-selling authors of the 1940s and gave the Messners their first big hit. Enterprising, intelligent, and well connected, Chambrun found his way around the publishing world by cloaking the business in a mystifying language of bussed hands, lunches at the '21' Club, and cultivated European style. He could be reached at the classy-sounding number PLaza 5–9464.

Maugham fired him in 1948. He had known for some years of his agent's habit of shorting him but found Chambrun a difficult scoundrel to hate. When Helen Strauss met with Maugham to see if she could improve the author's financial picture, Maugham declined her services "because," he confessed, "I have so much fun checking out his statement."[34] But then Maugham's friend and new editor in chief at Doubleday, Ken McCormick, tallied up the cost: "He ended up hiring a lawyer at 2½ per cent to watch over Chambrun's 10 per cent."[35] Most authors, however, proved much less amused and considerably less forgiving about their agent's sticky fingers. His impressive list became a revolving door, with celebrity authors walking in and then out sometimes after a year or less. Chambrun started to cheat new authors in order to pay back the earnings stolen from former clients now threatening to sue. So bad had Chambrun's habit become that Philip Wittenberg, a much-respected literary lawyer, accepted a case against him gratis, explaining to the author Chambrun had cheated, "This man is a menace to the literary profession."[36] In the clubby atmosphere of postwar publishing, the "count" circulated like a bad penny. When Maugham finally fired him, he estimated that a tidy $30,000 in royalties had gone missing, probably more. Publishers soon responded by sending royalty checks directly to Chambrun's puzzled authors, deducting the standard 10 percent for their impenitent agent.[37] Grace knew none of this. In the late spring of 1956 she knew only of the gamble he had taken on her behalf. "All the rest of my life," she later wrote, "I'll remember that he was the only person I knew who had faith in me at a time when we were all sure that it was not justified."[38]

It may be that Chambrun initially accepted Grace as a client because he was genuinely touched by the letter she sent him. In five "agonizing" pages Grace "poured out her dreams and hopes, and a long tale of her determination to become a writer someday."[39] Perhaps, too, the enterprising Chambrun gasped the possibilities of the story she had sent him. But this seems doubtful. Given the conservative, prudent nature of the houses to which he sent Grace's spicy story, it's not unreasonable to suspect that among the few Americans who failed to read *Peyton Place* was the author's own agent.

More likely Grace's desperation simply matched his own, for at the time she wrote him, Chambrun's client list was in a serious nosedive. *Publishers Weekly*, which had regularly listed his name in its directory, dropped him in 1953 with a cryptic notation explaining that "a new editorial prerogative has been exercised in the compilation of all the lists" whereby names of "author's agents" would now be published at the discretion of the journal. Whether or not this was due to his truncated business activity and soiled reputation, Chambrun's name would never again appear in publishing's most influential trade magazine. The sale of *Peyton Place* must have surprised him as much as it did his client, for if the truth be told, it happened quite accidentally. And once again the girl reader comes into view.

Leona Nevler was in her early twenties when she left Little, Brown and headed to New York City. A graduate of Boston University, Nevler entered the low-profile but distinguished Boston firm a secretary but soon found a mentor in the brilliant editor Angus Cameron, who elevated her to assistant editor before the year was out. Thin and smallish, a "woman who moved quickly," Nevler impressed with her ability to recognize and acquire talent. "I mean this in the very best way," a prominent publisher recalled. "She could read like a teenager, with that intensity, avidity, and suspension of disbelief; it served her very well. She was smart, of course, intelligent, but that isn't the part of her brain that she read with."[40] Hired by Fawcett World Library in 1955 as an associate editor, Nevler rose quickly through the ranks, becoming managing editor two years later and in 1964 head of Crest Books, Fawcett's new line of reprint paperbacks. At Crest, Nevler put her reading skills to work pulling into the firm such popular titles as *By Love Possessed, Lolita, The Ugly American*, and *Please Don't Eat the Daisies*. Like Helen Meyer at Dell, she would become one of the few women in publishing to rise into the upper levels on her own merits, eventually becoming publisher and vice president of Fawcett's swelling empire.

In 1951, however, Nevler lost her patron, who, in the midst of McCarthy-era red-baiting, was forced to resign from Little, Brown. Whether she left Boston because she was disgusted by the firm's handling of the Cameron affair or because her own position had grown increasingly tenuous is not clear, but in New York she made ends meet by freelancing as a reader of manuscripts for publishing houses up and down the East Coast. In between jobs she looked for a position as a fiction editor, and in the months before she was hired at Fawcett, she interviewed with Kitty Messner, then the president and editor in chief of Julian Messner, Inc.

The job opening at Messner, however, was not in the editing department, so Nevler decided to keep on looking while continuing to pick up a variety of editorial work along the way. But she liked Kitty, a fellow "reader with gusto," and enjoyed discussing books with her, including a manuscript she had recently read and rejected for J. B. Lippincott, a first-time novel called "The Tree and the Blossom." "I liked the book straightaway," Nevler recalled. "It was fun, a real page-turner, and it had the same feel as other best-sellers like *Kings Row*. But of course it was absolutely not the sort of thing Lippincott would ever consider publishing. It was absolutely wrong for them."[41]

But it was absolutely right for Messner. When the manuscript arrived from Chambrun's office the next afternoon, Kitty lit up a cigarette and sat down for a quick read before heading out to a dinner engagement. But like Nevler, she found herself irresistibly drawn into the story and so caught up with the fortunes of Peyton Place's denizens that she canceled her dinner plans, lit another cigarette, and continued reading long into the night. Then she called Chambrun and for $2,000 bought the rights to what would become mid-century America's most famous novel.

6

Sex Talk

Please, god, please, don't let me be normal.
THE FANTASTICKS, 1960

September. The air cracks and snarls with news of *Peyton Place*. Grace Metalious holds her breath. It is two weeks after her thirty-second birthday and *Peyton Place* is a gathering storm. In just ten days, sales reach 60,000 copies. By Halloween, the figure surges to 104,000 copies. By the time the New Year is rung in, *Peyton Place* sets a publishing record: the fastest-selling novel ever published, the most profitable first novel in publishing history.[1] In another year it will become the best-selling novel ever sold up to that date.

Kitty Messner watched in disbelief as orders raced in and printers struggled to keep up. Flying off shelves, *Peyton Place* reignited long-winded debates over pornography, the democratizing effects of cheap, accessible fiction, and the growing sexualization of American culture. Neutrality seemed impossible. The book was either an example of the "cultural tripe" that critics like Bernard DeVoto pilloried in the wake of the "two-bit revolution" or a "vital factor in the dynamic expansion of a free society," as Kurt Enoch declared in the *Library Quarterly*.[2] Words like "scorching," "shocking," "vulgar," "convulsive," and "explosive" were used to describe the combustible arc *Peyton Place* carved across the cultural landscape. A month after publication, 20th Century–Fox flew some of its people to New York, and in one dizzying morning Grace Metalious, New England housewife and mother, pocketed $125,000. "This book business," Grace wrote to friends, "is some evil form of insanity."[3]

Grace used the cash to shift gears, put her life on a new road. Saying farewell to "It'll Do," then, with more regrets, to her husband, George, she piled the kids into the car and moved down the road to the iconic New England Cape that had long tugged at her heart. She bought a used Cadillac, new bathing suits for her kids and their friends, and then, as if to shut the doors forever on a hungry past, bought the largest refrigerator she could find and stuffed it with as much food as it would hold. *Peyton Place* triumphantly climbed to number two on the *New York Times* best-seller list, turning the unknown author into a subject of escalating curiosity and wonder. "Wow!" exclaimed Floyd Major, owner of Charleston, West Virginia's, only bookstore in a comment card he returned to Messner: "John O'Hara move over—Grace is coming thru."[4]

To conservatives still reeling over the "great Kinsey hullabaloo," Grace's "coming thru" was greeted like any weather emergency: warnings and preparations were hastily put in place. In Indiana, Allen County prosecutor Glenn Beams ordered the state's booksellers to keep *Peyton Place* off their shelves or face prosecution. Boston retailers were "warned off" by the notorious Watch and Ward Society, whose members posed as buyers of "immoral" books and then reported to friendly prosecutors the names of dealers willing to sell them. Although the Supreme Court had substantially narrowed definitions of pornography, local actions like these remained effective tools of censorship, intimidating booksellers and librarians as well as publishers. Catholic readers faced excommunication, while schoolgirls of all faiths risked expulsion. In Providence, Rhode Island, the bookseller Harry Settle (who apparently didn't) was convicted of selling a copy to an underage reader and faced both a fine and a prison sentence despite questionable evidence. In quick succession, *Peyton Place* was banned in Canada; Fort Wayne, Indiana; Omaha, Nebraska; and countless county libraries. In upscale Beverly Farms, Massachusetts, a sign posted on the library's front lawn read, "This library does not carry *Peyton Place*. If you want it, go to Salem," the nearby town infamous in colonial days now seemingly infested by a working-class population bewitched by both bad books and the sorcery of sex.[5]

"We did not cotton to the obscenity or sexiness of the book," declared Fred Dobens, publisher of Nashua, New Hampshire's *Telegraph*. The book was "evil" some said, while others thought the "evil" was in the reading of the book. A man who'd been young at the time recalled, "My aunts would hover together in a knot outside our apartment, angrily discussing the perils of *Peyton Place* as we kids crept by."[6] For Cold Warriors in small towns and urban centers, *Peyton Place* confirmed their suspicions that American morals were under attack. Some saw the novel as a "literary H-Bomb" whose fallout threatened the stability of the family as it unleashed what one conservative described retrospectively as "fifty years of cultural terrorism."[7] The Catholic Church, Protestant ministers, evangelical preachers, school committees, parent-teacher organizations, and self-described guardians of morality like the National Citizens for Decent Literature (founded by Charles Keating Jr., himself later convicted of fraud, racketeering, and conspiracy in the savings and loan scandals of the 1980s) attacked *Peyton Place* as a sign of the unraveling of traditional American morality, a lethal weapon aimed at the purity of family life, the sanctity of (heterosexual) marriage, and good taste. "This sad situation," thundered the influential conservative William Loeb, editor of New Hampshire's *Manchester Union Leader*, "reveals a complete debasement of taste and a fascination with the filthy, rotten side of life that are the earmarks of the collapse of civilization."[8] When a North Carolina television station manager named Jesse Helms heard that *Peyton Place* was to become a TV series, he lobbied national network executives to black it out in his home state. When they refused, he decided to run for political office.[9]

While censorship made the distribution of controversial novels difficult, the mechanics of bookselling in mid-century America also contributed to readers' frustration as they sought out *Peyton Place*. Distribution problems had long plagued the industry, and most readers purchased books through direct mail or book clubs; bookstores accounted for less than a third of sales.[10] A vast majority of readers understandably depended on local libraries, whose funds were always vulnerable to the prevailing winds of politics. "I am so sorry that I can not say that I read your books," a Texas native wrote Metalious. "I cannot afford to buy them and I have no access to a library. My state is still in the hands of thieves and for that reason it is very backward." Bookstores remained scarce throughout the decade, with only about 1,500 large retail vendors in the entire nation. It was a "rare city under 50,000 population," the head of the American Book Council noted in 1956, "that has a good bookstore."[11]

Yet even in metropolitan areas, readers complained of the difficulty of locating *Peyton Place*. "I find it impossible," a distraught fan from a New York City suburb wrote the author, "to obtain my own personal copy of 'Peyton Place.'. . . I have tried in six different locations in Newark, N.J. (some of the largest department stores even) and find it impossible to get hold of my own copy." Even residents of Gilmanton had to drive out of town to get a copy of their neighbor's novel, although store owners grudgingly acknowledged its popularity. One shop in nearby Laconia, population fifteen thousand, reported selling a hundred copies a day despite a vigorous "I-hate-Grace campaign." Down the road in Meredith, a shop window proclaimed the owner's torn allegiance between profits and protest: "Peyton Place is here—I don't know why you want to read it, but we are selling it at $3.95."[12] No such luck awaited readers in Canada, Australia, South Africa, or the Soviet Union, where it was illegal to import *Peyton Place* through the mail.

No matter how controversial the novel, it no doubt came as a surprise to many American readers that the French, long decried as culturally risqué and their country scorned as the imaginative center of the avant-garde, felt their own discomfort with *Peyton Place*. "Such intimate and delicate subjects are rarely treated so explicitly in French," author Pierre Fisson informed American readers. Comparing the young literary sensation Françoise Sagan to Grace Metalious, Fisson, a winner of the Prix Renaudot, declared: "The American girl's book is much more daring. It would cause considerable tongue-clicking in Paris. Some of Mrs. Metalious's 'down-to-earth' descriptions would be 'eye-widening' to the average French reader."[13]

In the lexicon of the day, Grace Metalious had indeed dropped a "bombshell," and its fallout heightened the anxieties of an atomic age. Increasingly used to describe "sexy" women, terms like "knockout," "dynamite," and "bombshell" signaled the degree to which postwar female sexuality increasingly unnerved the nation. "Fears of sexual chaos," Elaine Tyler May points out, "tend to surface during times of crisis and rapid social change," and the dropping of the real atom bomb came in the midst of enormous alterations in the economic and sexual behaviors of women. "It was not just nuclear energy that had to be contained," May writes, "but the social and sexual fallout of the atomic age itself."[14] Exposing female sexual autonomy and expression as well as unconventional sexual behavior, Metalious's "H-Bomb" intensified those fears and turned *Peyton Place* into a heady symbol for the destructive power and disruptive force of out-of-control sexualities. Declaring the novel "wicked," "sordid," "cheap," "moral filth," "lewd and indecent," a "tabloid version of life," critics fought hard to keep the novel away from impressionable youth and undereducated adults.

Readership soared. *Peyton Place* planted itself on the mental map of America.

This is not to say that Grace Metalious failed to attract serious critical attention among reviewers. Writing for the *New York Times Book Review*, Princeton professor Carlos Baker linked *Peyton Place* to the "revolt of the village" tradition, putting the housewife and ingénue author into the same class as some of America's greatest writers, including Sherwood Anderson,

Figure 4. One year after the publication of the novel, *Peyton Place* was part of the mental mapping of American culture, another exotic place to visit. "Mid-Town Travel Bureau," *New York Times Book Review* August 4, 1957.

Edmund Wilson, Sinclair Lewis, and John O'Hara. The writing, he opined, was "pretty fair for a first novelist," and her "earthy words" were not untypical of the "emancipated modern authoress."[15] After declaring her writing "good of its kind," a critic in the Sunday *Chicago Tribune* warmed up, admitting in the end that Metalious displayed "great narrative skill."[16] At least a few with more highbrow tastes concurred. "She [Metalious] does have a style, and a manner of creating atmosphere and character," Julia Child wrote her friend Avis DeVoto after reading *Peyton Place*. Satisfied with her excursion into best-sellers, she returned to Goethe, "where I shall remain," she said, "until another bombshell appears."[17] Even the disapproving critic Phyllis Hogan admitted that Metalious showed "humor, heart, vigor, and a feeling for irony (as well as unblushing candor and a restless flow of profanity").[18] Whatever its faults, critics admitted it was a page-turner, impossible to put down and, as conservatives feared, encouraging not just what Child described as "reading-for-pure-self-indulgence" but "surreptitious reading" among millions of the "untutored and vulnerable."[19] The United States Office of Immigration and Naturalization used it for years to teach English to immigrants.[20]

To be fair, book reviewers took up *Peyton Place* at the very moment when many believed that American culture itself was falling apart. Narratives of decline—in literature, morality, and family life—ripped through postwar commentary in heated jeremiads against mass entertainment, mass competition, mass education, mass literacy, and mass publishing. Commercial interests and "proto–mass culture" threatened to standardize and commodify from above the realms of taste, values, and aesthetic virtue. With *Peyton Place*, such fears conjoined with images of the sexual chaos the novel supposedly represented, forming a perfect storm at the center of American cultural and social life. Wherever one looked—television, comic books, amusement parks, paperbacks—it seemed that the known world was under serious attack. How to explain not just the publication but the popularity of a novel in which patricide is condoned, female-headed households are normalized, bachelor girls with names like Steve live happily without men, oral sex and female lust are not just exposed but celebrated, abortion and divorce are recognized, and, as one critic put it, "suicide and murder are presented in a context of justification."[21] What is a best-seller, after all, if not the product of commercial forces operating outside the tutored realms of Literature? How to explain an author like Grace

Metalious, whose fame came instantly rather than as the culmination of effort honed over the course of many years? How, in an era when first novels written by unknown authors sold on average two thousand copies, tops, to explain *Peyton Place*, which in the first ten days of its official release sold sixty thousand? "The decline and fall of the American novel predicted by the pessimists," Fanny Butcher of *Publishers Weekly* noted in January, "had one corroboration in the sensation of the year, Grace Metalious's *Peyton Place*." Even the industry's major trade magazine was fretting.[22]

Still, it seems so excessive.

Peyton Place, after all, was published just eight years after the "great Kinsey hullabaloo," and was far less explicit about sexual matters than the famous studies on human sexuality published by the Indiana professor in 1948 and 1953. Published in English, rather than in the customary Latin or German often reserved for "scientific" sex research, the reports were a massive compilation of personal histories and interpretive statistics gathered over a decade. In surveys and interviews, sex boldly stepped up to the microphone and described itself in ways not commonly heard before: just under 40 percent of adult men, Kinsey reported, had experienced at least one homosexually related orgasm, while of the 5,940 white women interviewed, 26 percent admitted to having had sex with someone other than their husband. Among single women, half claimed they were no longer virgins, while similar numbers of married women reported having lost their virginity before marriage.

In the mythological history of sexuality, the Kinsey Reports mark the advent of sexual candor—a frankness newly embraced by a postwar generation seemingly freed of old constraints and eager to experiment. With these revelations and a string of Supreme Court decisions that narrowed definitions of obscenity, "the veil of nineteenth-century reticence," scholars John D'Emilio and Estelle B. Freedman argue, "was torn away, as sex was put on display." Selling for the high price of $6.50, the 804-page first volume sold 200,000 copies in the first two months after publication.[23]

Sex, it seemed, had found its voice. Explicit, detailed, and attentive to diverse sexual acts and behaviors, Kinsey's findings provoked interest, curiosity, shock, and outrage. "It is impossible," the evangelist Billy Graham roared, "to underestimate the damage this book will do to the already deteriorating morals of America."[24] Authorities and the public alike seemed compelled to comment, determined to ferret out what was being said about Kinsey, what could be testified against, commented upon, and repeated over and over. In the incitement to talk, the "great hullaba-loo" sent sex here, there, and everywhere.

So much talk. So painstaking the detail, so exact an accounting, as the French philosopher Michel Foucault would have it. So endless the need to speak about it, the insistence that it be spoken about, even as critics—with more words—sought to silence the discussion. Twenty thousand accumulated histories, eleven thousand intimate case studies. Yet what did all this talk add up to? And why, after all was said and done during the Kinsey hullabaloo, did *Peyton Place* have still more to say? "I don't know what all the screaming is about," a stunned Grace Metalious complained. "To me *Peyton Place* isn't sexy at all. Sex is something everybody lives with—why make such a big deal about it?"[25] Why indeed?

At first Kinsey and his researchers found their subjects reluctant to discuss their sex lives, but gradually, he wrote, as "our techniques were develop-ing" and "with an increasing understanding of [the study's] significance," people proved eager to contribute their histories.[26] Sex was uncorked. The timing seemed especially right, as the economic, demographic, and emotional upheavals of wartime expanded the realm of adventurous con-versation. Whereas before the war, everyday conversations had colluded with polite public discussion to deflect "delicate" and "sensitive" topics like racial and class exclusions or gender and sexual nonconformity, events dur-ing and after the war turned them into everyday talk.[27] When the Kinsey Reports came out, an audience was waiting.

It is difficult—perhaps impossible—for a reader so accustomed to the sexualized culture of today to imagine the linguistic onslaught occa-sioned by the Kinsey Reports. Sixteen thousand pages, just under 900,000 words, a riot of adventurous, bold vocabulary. Terms like "masturbation," "homosexual outlets," "petting to climax," "animal contacts," "mouth stimulation," "anal eroticism," "oral stimulation," "incest," "cunnilin-gus," and "extramarital coitus" broke out like goose bumps across the social landscape—words that shocked not simply because they waged war against traditional values and standards of morality, but because they rep-resented what can only be described as an "excess of language"; words that quickly outpaced a nation's ability to comprehend them.

Words, in other words, that demanded a story.[28]

(of

And the time was ripe. When Kinsey came along, the story of America was in flux and under revision. War had upended the apple cart. Haltingly and unevenly yet indisputably, tales of racial segregation, female dependence, gender codes, and conventional sexuality lost the uniformity of conviction as the drama of war altered the social and economic landscape. New plots emerged. Bold scenarios pecked through the shell of convention. Outsider voices rang out.

A key voice, to be sure, Kinsey buttressed the notion that sex had moved out of the Victorian recesses of reticence and into the bright light of modern science. Kinsey saw his work as an origin story—like evolution, inevitable, plotted, and purposeful—suited to a new generation "increasingly desirous of making [sexual] relations satisfactory."[29] He attributed his candid interviews to freer attitudes, the emergence of a new sexual frankness, and a new willingness among the younger generations to expect, even demand, satisfaction, even perhaps to experiment before marriage.

There is something quite hopeful in seeing the Reports this way—putting a triumphant end to Victorian narratives of sexual reticence and repression, its publication date a day to remember, the beginning of sex's outing. Yet in the end, this story falls short.

In his famous critique *The History of Sexuality*, Foucault warns the teleologist against confusing the sexualization of modern culture with the enfranchisement of its sexualities, "as if what was said . . . were immaterial, as if the fact of speaking about sex were of itself more important than the forms of imperatives that were imposed on it by speaking about it." Rather than situating the Kinsey Reports in opposition to those Victorian practices of reticence and repression, we might better understand their effects (and those of *Peyton Place*) as part of a long and steady "proliferation of discourses concerned with sex," their transformation into postwar discourse less a story of sexual candor and emancipation than one of new norms under which sex was organized, spoken about, and regulated.[30] If the public display of sex intensified in postwar culture, so too did the need for discretion; silence and the processes of silence are part of the story the Kinsey Reports had to tell, part of the guilty pleasures *Peyton Place* produced.

The words we still link to the Reports, after all, were grounded in and through the mediating narratives of what at the time was called normality; the meaning of sexual behaviors and gender identities was formulated in the powerful language of new "sex experts" who turned to Kinsey's findings for authorization and legitimacy. Far from tearing off the "veil of nineteenth-century reticence," the Reports moved in tandem with it. "There is not one but many silences," Foucault reminds us, "and they are an integral part of the strategies that underlie and permeate discourses."[31]

Like most scientists, Kinsey and his research team found terms like "average," "normal," and even "moral" useless and in fact damaging impediments to scientific explorations in medicine, biology, psychology, and social behavior. When the Reports came along, however, the ideal of a normal boy and girl, a normal man and woman, was rapidly gaining traction in American public life, their prototypes actually on display at the New York World's Fair.[32] In the vocabularies of social workers, sociologists, sex educators, and "anti-crime" advocates, scientific-sounding terms like "normal," "average," "deviant," and "abnormal" buttressed claims to credibility, professional expertise, and objective evidence.[33] And despite Kinsey's emphatic opposition to concepts like abnormal and normal, his methodologies suggested to others the possible measurability of both. Vague terms became more specific, the borders of behavior and personality more easily determined, described, and pronounced. As faith grew in the limitless ability of science to unlock the secrets of physical disease, Kinsey's methods suggested a way to uncover the social and mental ills of the nation, while his data empowered sex as a potent sign of social, mental, and national health. Sex seemed to lurk everywhere, its significance deep and mysterious, and in the wake of Kinsey's histories it could signify deep trouble, potential danger, even perversion. What was normal? Who was and who was not?

By mid-century, social science research itself, especially the survey and personal interview, were so identified in the popular imagination with sex research and efforts to uncover sexual averages, means, ranges, and norms that researchers often had a hard time getting informants to talk about anything else. While the Barnard sociologist Mira Komarovsky found Kinsey "eased [my] path" for her study of blue-collar marriage, others worried that it made informants *less willing* to talk about other subjects. Betty Friedan was thoroughly frustrated and annoyed by the situation. "I did not do a Kinsey Study," she tells readers in her feminist manifesto *The Feminine Mystique* in 1963. Yet when she tried to interview housewives in the years prior to publication, many of them assumed that it was sex that had brought her into their homes. "I would ask about their personal interests, ambitions, what they did, or would like to do, not necessarily as wives or mothers, but when they were not occupied with their husbands or their children or their housework." Instead, Friedan fumed, "they made mysterious allusions or broad hints; they were eager to be asked about sex; even if I did not ask, they often took pride in recounting the explicit details of some sexual adventure."[34] Sex mattered; it must mean something. Surely this was the point of so many knocks on the door?

If the social science survey represented in the minds of many the growing importance of sexuality in everyday life, so too did the term "normality" offer a simple way to differentiate between conventional and unconventional sexual practices and gender roles. By the mid-1950s the term haunted the cultural imagination, standing inescapably in relation to words like "psychosis," "neurosis," "pathology," and "deviance." Popular magazines and newspapers flooded the parent-oriented market. "Is Your Child Normal?" the National Parent-Teacher Association asked. "What Is Normal?" *Look* queried and then joined *Ladies' Home Journal, Life*, and *America* in providing a helpful set of guidelines.[35]

Amidst the insecurity and anxiety of the Cold War, discourses of normality spoke as well to the story of American exceptionalism. In mass-circulated magazines and newspapers, pictures of happy couples and healthy children conjoined with images of national belonging—the flag, church, the Fourth of July, Parents' Day, beauty pageants, backyard grills, military parades, civil defense drills—to open up a cultural conversation in which groups of geographically different, if not racially diverse, people could imagine themselves as a center in opposition to those abnormal others who hovered on the periphery. White, married, and child-centered, readers inserted themselves into a pictorial archive of photo-magazines, films, and television, where the "normal" and the "average" took on sharp and purposeful focus.[36] Unlike conservative campaigns that attacked sexually explicit materials and outsider groups directly, discourses of normality crept into popular culture imperceptibly, offering a vision of national unity that seemed rooted in common sense rather than exclusionary politics.[37]

The weight of criticism thrown against Kinsey worked to press these terms ever deeper into the seams of American life. Kinsey, critics charged, had caused people to confuse "normal" with "moral." "The whole bent of Dr. Kinsey's work," an editorialist from *America* wrote, "did incalculable harm by giving countenance and even 'scientific' respectability to an utter misuse of the word 'normal.'"[38] Even for a Christian critic who found in Kinsey a "plain truth"—that standards of morality were indeed in decline—it was the conflation of average behaviors with normal behaviors that offended. "[Kinsey cannot] grasp what for him must be a very subtle distinction between the idea of norm as a simple report of what people do and the idea of norm as what people ought to do."[39] Dismissing the counting of noses as a guarantee of normality, critics nonetheless confirmed their belief that "normal" existed, cementing the idea firmly into the American imagination.

Parameters narrowed. The essential ingredients in the making of the "normal" American, Kinsey's critics insisted, were sexuality within marriage, focused on reproduction within the family, and contained by female domesticity; numbers to the contrary mattered not at all. Just because millions of American men masturbated, committed homosexual acts, experienced orgasm outside of marriage, or had wives who worked outside the home did not make such behaviors normal. Reluctantly forced to speak of such things, critics spoke out again and again against them, confirming the legitimacy of the normal man and woman and the dangers of sexual and gender difference and unconventionality.

Almost everyone, it seemed, had something to say about American normality. No longer "inner-directed" by an innate sense of being good, as David Riesman famously observed, Americans were turning outward in the hope of discovering how to be normal.[40] "Keeping up appearances" not only became a national pastime; it also became a site of safety. Authorizing new experts to discover its secrets, the Reports buttressed assumptions that sex had secrets to tell. Both enormously important and little understood, its significance seemed to hover over every thought, quiver, urge, act, twitch, and wandering hand. With questionnaire at the ready, an army of social scientists and sex educators knocked on doors, took notes, testified before school boards and city councils, consulted with private citizens' groups, informed journalists, and lobbied politicians. There was no telling the damage that uncontrolled desires might cause.[41]

The injection of sex into discourses of normality gave human sexuality new descriptive and diagnostic power across a wide spectrum of American life. For Cold Warriors, it offered a way to construct norms of the civilized and moral against the communist and non-Western Other. For newly emerging social and mental health experts, it provided legitimacy and authorized the professional voice. For the mass media, it opened up new avenues of public investigation, concern, scandal, and outrage. Indeed, whatever information American readers picked up from the Kinsey histories, it's a good bet that it was not from flipping through the difficult prose and complex data contained in the studies. Most Americans read *about* Kinsey, his findings consumed from newspapers, supplements, and magazines where his work was often edited into more conventional narratives, his data modified and condensed with added disclaimers from publishers anxious not to offend readers or advertisers. It was, trade publishers admitted, "the least-read bestseller until the work of Masters and Johnson appeared."[42] Yet even for those rare readers who read the tome, the histories were never there for the taking. The data, facts, and stories all took on meaning through the mediating force of Cold War anxieties over the exact boundaries of gender and sexual normality and the efforts of "professionals" to locate and fix them. Sharpened by everything that was said or written about Kinsey and his Reports, normality moved to the center of interpretive life.[43]

Kinsey himself made no attempt to alter any impression in the public mind that he too was anything but a normal American male. Between the publication of his study and his death in 1956, his unusual domestic life and homosexual desires were carefully controlled by tweedy images of the professor as a conventional family man. Talk to the contrary might not have ruined his career but it would certainly have discredited his science. The mere extraction of his statistics also clouds the degree to which Kinsey and his associates actually complemented the social goals of conservatives who, like Billy Graham, feared sex outside of marriage. "They too [the Kinsey Report authors]," writes Carol Groneman, "hoped to strengthen the institution of marriage and to control promiscuity." The social value of the scientific approach to sex, in other words, was to support "normal" sexual relations within marriage, what Kinsey argued was "the cement of social organization."[44] The demystification of human sexuality, Kinsey argued, would lead to greater understanding and pleasure *within* the marital bed. Kinsey's facts may have shocked a nation, and gay people may have found support in his data, but the Reports unfolded within a reassuring narrative of heteronormativity, female domesticity, and the normality of the American nuclear family.

Kinsey, it's fair to say, "made sex talk," the Reports becoming part of what Foucault described as "the plurisecular injunction to talk about sex."[45]

Yet sex speaks, Foucault reminds us, in complex ways, its "speechifying" a means not merely to describe erotic desire nor simply to announce sexual diversity but also to make them up: to define their meanings and map their social, emotional, mental, even criminal boundaries, giving rise to new ways of speaking about sex, authorizing different voices to speak about it, and organizing new borders around what could and *could not* be said.

What Kinsey set in motion, in other words, was not simply the casual recounting of sexual adventures and personal experience that moved talk along the grapevines of the everyday. Nor was this long-winded hullabaloo a national voice for sexual candor, openness, and frank discussion. Sex talk here speaks rather to the productive idea of sexual behavior as an anchor to the normal as a measure of personal and national health. The Kinsey hullabaloo was powerful not because it gave voice to hidden desires trapped beneath a coherent regime of "no," but rather because it helped reorganize and reorder sexual meanings. The study and its critics, as Foucault famously argued, turned sexuality's timeless pleasures and casual practices into more specific and precise categories, problems, and roaming dangers, organizing the narrative terms by which desire could be grasped, understood, located, and even experienced. When sex spoke in the fifties, questions of normality hovered over every utterance, pressing its demands in the flow of talk, setting in motion the constraints of discretion, the wisdom of secrecy.

It is a mistake, in other words, to interpret the sexualization of postwar American culture in general, and the "revelations" of the Kinsey Reports in particular, as enfranchising the sexual behaviors and practices they put on display. Quite the opposite was true. Sexual behaviors once casually tolerated or merely ignored before World War II grew increasingly demonized in the years that followed, their expression seen as a threat not simply to morality but to the emotional and mental health of the nation at large.[46] Almost any kind of sexual and gender nonconformity became increasingly suspect. Ten years after the first Kinsey Report was published, 80 percent of Americans polled said that people who chose not to marry were "sick, neurotic, and immoral," while the term "pervert" was used to describe an increasingly wide range of individuals, from "adults who engaged in same-sex consensual relationships" to those who committed violent acts of rape, murder, and child sexual abuse.[47] Rather than tearing the veil off sexual reticence, Kinsey's findings were widely invoked to stigmatize and pathologize all manner of unconventional behavior, real or fictional. When the blue-blooded literary critic Sterling North sought to discredit the characters in *Peyton Place*, he turned to the Reports for proof: "Their sex habits are what the late Dr. Kinsey reported in people who have never progressed beyond the eighth grade."[48] Others agreed. "Characters like these," one critic wrote, "belong in an asylum, and, as a security measure, the town would be declared out-of-bounds by all civilized people."[49]

Even the bachelor and the spinster now joined divorced women, single men, and parentless couples as disturbed figures capable of harboring deep sexual depravities. "Neighbors shunned them as if they were dangerous," Elaine May writes. "The government investigated them as security risks. Their chances of living free of stigma or harassment were slim."[50] So too did transgressions of gender take on new and suspect sexual meanings. Whereas unmarried "career girls," feminists, and lesbians had been viewed before the war as "mannish women"—asexual traitors to gender—they emerged in the postwar era as dangerously hypersexual females, even as "sexual demons," in the words of historian Donna Penn. "By the second half of the twentieth century," Penn notes, "disseminators of expert opinion demonized the lesbian in order to position her, along with the prostitute, as the essence of female sexual degeneracy."[51]

One element of a larger "sex panic" that urged Americans to become more vigilant in recognizing and preventing "uncontrolled desires," the sexualized woman was placed alongside an array of "deviants" in need of treatment.[52] Between 1935 and 1965 the sex criminal loomed large on the national landscape, galvanizing campaigns to investigate, uncover, and diagnose erotic desires and behaviors that lurked beyond the sexually appropriate and socially normal. Across the country, new statutes and regulations marked the ascendancy of both the "sex crime" and the psychiatrist as city, state, and federal governments steadily transferred authority over sex offenders from the courts to the psychiatric treatment center.[53] The power and prestige of the mental health industry soared.[54]

For working-class and African American girls and women, sexuality took on especially ominous meanings as sexual nonconformity came to represent in the cultural imagination the kinds of social dangers that had been unleashed by war and the demographic shifts that pulled southern black migrants northward and rural working-class white women into urban areas. Both groups generated a set of "moral panics" that transformed the sexual behaviors of each into well-publicized social and political concerns, "a problem," the historian Hazel Carby argues, "that had to be rectified in order to restore a moral social order."[55] Discourses of "sexual delinquency" that once focused on working-class "problem girls," whose promiscuity was associated with "broken homes, bad companions, a disdain for authority, in addition to urban pleasures," underwent revision as concepts of sexual pathology and deviancy increasingly aligned improper sexual behavior with class and racial identity.[56]

As class and racial exclusion found new expression in American cultural life, anxieties over untamed female desire and excess accentuated the perceived dangers of working-class and African American sexual activity. Individual pathology among normally "good girls" could be contained; hypersexual "bad girls" could not. For African American girls and women, postwar sexual and gender discourses highlighted an already "visible deviancy" that sharpened their distance from American normality and stories of belonging. Sexuality had long been a contentious measure and mark of social identity within both black community life and mainstream culture. As Tricia Rose points out, "the association of black women with sexual deviance and excess has discouraged many from speaking openly about their sexual desires and experiences," a situation that would be compounded in the postwar period when first the civil rights movement and then black nationalism and welfare politics turned black women's sexual agency into a meaningful if conflict-ridden political statement. To be sexually "inappropriate" brought into question the reputation of the women involved, but in the context of the heightened racial tensions of the fifties, it became as well "an act against an already embattled and despised black community." To be female, black, and working class in the 1950s was more often than not to be "sexually misseen and misheard."[57]

Even as Kinsey's report on *Sexual Behavior in the Human Female* was published in 1953, progressive voices faced a fierce and silencing backlash. Among those best poised to talk back—union activists, civil rights workers, feminists, and well-known progressives—it was increasingly difficult and, at times, dangerous to break the silence surrounding what passed for conventional gender and sexual behaviors. Cultural producers, progressive writers, and media personalities became targets of intense anticommunist campaigns, and those who openly spoke out against racism, anti-Semitism, and intolerance increasingly did so at great personal and professional risk.[58] Campaigns for "free speech" reflected the politicized arena within which public expression increasingly operated, as words like "communism," "feminism," and even "peace" invited distrust and official scrutiny. Less dramatic and certainly less visible than the McCarthy hearings, the silence and silencing produced by discourses of normalcy were nonetheless a ubiquitous shaper of everyday life in the Cold War years.

For housewives and young unmarried women, sex increasingly constituted "an area of secrecy and self-doubt."[59] Whether confronting questions about an unwanted pregnancy, birth control, homosexual desire, or sexual intercourse, women experienced a sense of isolation that could keep even friends from voicing their concerns or anxieties about sexual matters with one another. When one upper-middle-class girl from the Midwest "got caught" by becoming pregnant while single and at college in Massachusetts, it was illegal not just to give out contraceptives to unmarried women but to provide any information about contraception at all. "I didn't even know Margaret Sanger existed in New York," she said. "How would I know? There wasn't anyone to tell me anything. We never talked about it." Even less likely to get the kinds of help they needed from largely middle-class professionals, working-class women and girls were especially vulnerable. Despite a rise in premarital sex and rates of illegitimacy, contraception was difficult to find in many blue-collar communities, white or black, for married as well as single women. One thirty-seven-year-old Protestant mother of seven children told researchers that she had "to go to the next town to get fitted with a pessary" because her doctor "was afraid to tell her [about contraception] because of all the neighboring Catholics in their community."[60]

In her fictional account of growing up in the 1950s, Alice McDermott depicts the paucity of communication between mothers and daughters and among friends at a time when intimate exchanges were painful and awkward. The narrator and her girlfriends "were of the generation who spelled the words they couldn't speak and followed strict rules regarding what could be discussed in mixed company." Talk between the generations proved no less difficult. Struggling to tell her daughter that their neighbor, an unmarried teenager, is pregnant, the narrator's mother can't bring herself to say the word, substituting instead the popular ornithological euphemism: "After a botched, embarrassed and only sporadically explicit attempt to explain what Sheryl had done, she told me, 'Let's say the stork missed our house and landed on hers.' "[61] How to talk of sex when sex meant so much, held so many hidden dangers? "They coped," Annie Dillard recalled. "They sighed, they permitted themselves a remark or two; they lived essentially alone."[62]

College men suffered from similar levels of ignorance, silence, and secrecy despite opportunities in fraternity houses and dormitories to share personal knowledge and experience with their peers. "As an unregulated, off-the-books activity," the oral historian Benita Eisler notes, "the erotic in the Age of Eisenhower could still be regarded as instinctual." A white man from a small town in the South confessed that as a college student, he "just wasn't very knowledgeable about how girls got pregnant. . . . You just never discussed it, except for the little bit of bragging typical of the male." He told Eisler, "The much-vaunted masculine bull sessions were just that: occasions for strutting your stuff, not for revealing innocence or asking for the real facts of life."[63]

It was an era obsessed with sex and committed to its public display, in which the word whispered beneath every action, dream, and twitch was "sex." Yet the "silence of sin" is what people remember most, and what has come to define the decade best. "Who I was becoming," gay activist John Preston reflected, "what I was becoming a part of, was not talked about in Medfield [Massachusetts], certainly not at the barbershop, not in my school, not in my family. I was becoming something that could not exist in a New England town."[64] Sex: Renounce thyself. "Thou shall not go near, thou shall not touch, thou shall not consume, thou shall not experience pleasure, thou shall not speak, thou shall not show thyself; ultimately thou shall not exist, except in darkness and secrecy."[65] And so it was. "We did not talk about such things," the town historian of Camden, Maine, recalled on the novel's fiftieth anniversary. "To speak of incest, rape, domestic violence, homosexuality was to admit they existed in town and so no one said anything. Of course, we knew these things happened. But it just wasn't something you could talk about. No one would."[66]

"Nobody talked about sex in the fifties," Benita Eisler concluded. "Nobody talked about anything."[67] The "great Kinsey hullabaloo" left a generation quite speechless. Even in *Peyton Place*, talk serves a regulatory function. When Constance MacKenzie sees that Allison has dimmed the living room lights, she fears the worst, picturing her teenage daughter lying there with a man. "SHE'LL GET HERSELF TALKED ABOUT!" the distressed

Constance exclaims to herself (50). A central character in the novel, talk lingers everywhere, and everyone fears the voices of Peyton Place. When Selena's boyfriend Ted tries to sort out his future with or without Selena, talk steps forward to remind him of its power: "The only other argument his folks had was that people were bound to talk if he kept on with Selena. People were bound to talk anyway, Ted had told them. Look at the way some people still talked about his mother's first husband. People always talked and they always would.... They could see, couldn't they, how little talk really amounted to in the long run?" (171).

But in the end, they could not. And neither could Ted, who jilts Selena when her secret is made public.

For readers, the silence of sin spawned a cartload of illicit pleasures. The sexually forbidden gained a firm toehold in social life even as constructions of the normal and deviant expanded their operations. "Silence," writes John Howard, "was not absence."[68] Transformed into discourses of normality, sex talk produced the pleasures it denounced. What people were telling oral historians, social scientists, and readers of memoirs were not false memories but rather stories of resistance, scandal, subterfuge, and the guilty pleasures such reticence opened up. "If all you wanted was homosexual sex," John Preston confirmed, "you were in pretty good shape in the sticks." Within the shadow of silence, sexual taboos forged intimacies all the more coveted because they were under cover. Speaking for many of her generation who had premarital sex in the fifties, a women informant told Preston: "Our sexual relations were entirely between us. That was our secret. I would never have told anyone. Not my sister or even my best friend. In those days, no one did."[69] At other times silence spawned erotic collusions while the "will-to-not-know" plowed new spaces for unconventional sex acts. "In a period when everyone talked incessantly but took care to say nothing," a young women recalled, "the 'sweet conversations of the flesh' were the more powerful."[70]

The reticence of the fifties was provoked not by bad memories or wrong stories but by the "power generated by what was said," by the "injunction," as Foucault identified it, "to *talk* about sex."[71] The guilty pleasures of illicit sex, gossip, fantasy, and the secret sharing of "dirty" books begin here, in the paradox of postwar discourses of sexuality and the silences they produced. Without them, *Peyton Place* might have been so much hot air. Instead, it put them to work.

"For heaven's sake, Tom. It's abnormal in a child that age. There's something wrong with a kid who thinks overmuch of sex," Constance declares. At least one reader heavily underlined the heated discussion in which Constance's lover Tom defends the amorous emotions of his students, especially those of Betty Anderson.

"What do you mean by overmuch?"

"By overmuch," she said crossly, "I mean just what I say. It is thinking overmuch of sex when a fifteen-year-old girl lets some boy like Harrington take her out and do whatever he wants with her. If Betty hadn't been thinking too much about sex for years, she wouldn't even know enough to realize that a boy wanted to take her out for what he could get. The idea would never enter her head."

"Wow," said Tom, lighting a cigarette. "Are you confused!"

"I am not! It's abnormal for a girl of fifteen to be as wise as Betty is. Well, she wasn't wise enough, apparently."

"I'd be inclined to think that if Betty, at fifteen, didn't think about sex she was abnormal. Much more so than because she obviously has thought about it. I think that any normal kid," he said, pointing his cigarette at her— "'normal' being your word, not mine—has thought plenty about sex." (216)

Quite suddenly, it seemed, normality was up for grabs.

7

The Women of *Peyton Place*

"We can't behave like people in novels, though, can we?"
"Why not—why not—why not?"
Edith Wharton, *The Age of Innocence*

It was the historian of paperbacks Kenneth Davis who first explored the connection between Alfred Kinsey's 1953 report *Sexual Behavior in the Human Female* and the novel *Peyton Place*. What shocked Americans about Kinsey, Davis argued, was not simply the explicit nature of his findings; rather it was the lack of remorse expressed by unmarried mothers, adulterous wives, and sexually active single women. "The chaste conceded only that they had lacked opportunity," he wrote. If Kinsey was right, women and girls not only enjoyed sex but also were enjoying lots of it, often on their own terms. "The news came as a major challenge to the polite notion that 'good girls don't.' What was important about *Peyton Place*'s women," Davis concludes, "is that they represented this unspoken reality."[1]

Peyton Place spilled the beans.

Certainly for those on the outskirts of political life, for those who seldom gave a thought to politics or political action, the Kinsey Reports materialized in useful ways a discourse of discontent, an articulation of things deeply felt but rarely discussed. Despite fierce counterattacks, Kinsey challenged long-standing notions that there was such a thing as "too much" sex or the "wrong kind" of sex. A nymphomaniac, the professor famously stated, was simply "someone who had more sex than you do."[2] Women, it seemed, were having not just more sex but apparently better sex, with Kinsey reporting a "distinct and steady increase in the number of females reaching orgasm."[3] Experimentation too was now viewed as part of the postwar legacy, as more and more women affirmed their willingness to engage in bedroom nudity, oral sex, and varied coital positions.

Yet if sexual satisfaction among women had gained new respect, married women remained the site of investigation and research. Women may have liked sex, but official talk of sexual pleasure revolved around the marital bed, the confirmed site of erotic pleasure. Single women, unwed mothers, and women who rejected the roles of wife and mother remained on the dangerous edges of polite conversation even as their growing numbers revolutionized American life. Only publishers, it seemed, took notice.

Between 1940 and 1945, the overall rate of mothers living without husbands increased by an astounding 40 percent. Remorseful or not, sexually active women were rapidly altering the American landscape. While Kinsey collated his data, rates of premarital sex continued their rise unabated, a scenario the professor had thought unlikely, arguing instead that sex before marriage had peaked between 1916 and 1930 with only "minor" increases after that.[4] Vital statistics, however, tell a different story. Between 1940 and 1960, the "frequency of single-motherhood among white women increased by more than two-and-one-half fold, rising from 3.6 newborns to 9.2 newborns per thousand unmarried white women of childbearing age," according to one study, rates that came to define a sexual revolution in the decade that followed.[5] Even in New England, a region notorious for its sober "blue laws," censorship, and prudery—"a land of frenzied moralists," H. L. Mencken famously quipped—single pregnancy wasn't just keeping pace with national rates; it often led the way.[6] When it came to single pregnant women and premarital sex, in other words, the difference between the 1940s and the 1950s was one of "word, not deed." Far from their being "an era of sexual candidness," the historian Alan Petigny makes clear, "it was precisely the absence of such candidness that helped obscure the exploding levels of premarital sex during the forties and fifties."[7]

By the time *Peyton Place* was published, characters like Betty Anderson, "knowledgeable beyond her years," Selena Cross, "dusky," sensuous, "gypsy-like," Constance MacKenzie, "well-built, blond, lusty," and Ginny Sterns, "a tramp and a trollop," were familiar figures in the social landscape (7, 4). The unwed mother was an open secret in every town, neighborhood, and suburb across America. Still, if unmarried girls and women were having sex in greater numbers than before the war, it was hardly on their own terms. Even *Esquire* mourned the passing of the "hearty, love-happy nymph of song and story," whom science, the magazine declared in 1954, had destroyed.[8] As the Cold War deepened, uncontrolled sexualities coiled into a menacing force, catapulting family life into the center of containment politics. Irregular and unconventional sexuality, critics charged, from homosexuality to out-of-wedlock pregnancy, endangered the health of the nation, increasing America's weakness in the face of communist aggression and signaling American vulnerability from within. In an unstable world, experts argued, safety resided in "traditional" morals nurtured in the home by submissive wives and protected by "family men" whose virility marked them as both normal and patriotic Americans.

In this Cold War version of the modern family, female sexuality was both acknowledged and desirable, but it was the wife's ability to channel her sexual energy into marriage that neutralized her danger to society and defined female normality. No longer the "sexless angel" who tamed "men's more insistent desires," the newly eroticized wife nevertheless walked a fine line between respectability and moral depravity. The "sexy" wife, like the oversexed woman, raised fears not only about the disruptive and destructive force of female sexuality but about "emasculated" husbands as well.[9] Husbands, the academic experts and health professionals agreed, should assume not just economic but sexual dominance. Kinsey idealized the husband as the "sexual athlete," demonstrating both a familiarity and a felicity with what people cryptically called "the facts of life." Sexy wives, daring single girls, divorced women, and even young widows all presented a potent threat to the social order because they disturbed the gendered and sexual foundations on which healthy families functioned.

Enter the women of *Peyton Place*.

Betty Anderson and Constance Standish MacKenzie represented a particularly troubling type of womanhood: women whose sexual pleasure and desire operated outside the confines of marriage. As wedlock gained new importance as society's principal bulwark against subversion, the dangers posed by widows, single girls, unwed mothers, and female heads of household grew proportionately more serious as the decade wore on. Betty at first sight is "an overdeveloped seventh grader," the daughter of an aspiring Peyton Place mill family whose hope for advancement had already been dashed by Betty's older sister, who, readers are cryptically informed, "had to move away" (8, 139). The town's "good girls" use her story as protection against the advances of their boyfriends. "She couldn't even get a job in town," Selena warns her clean-cut, respectable, but passionate boyfriend, Ted (139). "Bad girls" like Betty embrace it. In high school Betty flaunts her sexuality, dominating the sexual play of boys like Rodney Harrington, the mill owner's son, "a normal, healthy, good-looking boy," potentially entrapped by the girl from across the tracks (207).

In the hundreds of yellowed and tattered copies of *Peyton Place* my students and I thumbed through over the years, Betty earned the lion's share of excited scribbles. Bold, beautiful, and comfortable with her sexuality, Betty seems at first glance to be the girl everyone knows will come to no good, but her sexual frankness, honesty, and confident manner underscore the ambiguities of postwar girlhood and bring into view the contradictions so many oral historians have unearthed. She is intriguing and complicated, savvy but vulnerable, smart but without options. Betty discusses sex in the bold tough-guy language familiar to readers of Mickey Spillane, offering no apologies for the pleasure she takes in her body and in asserting her claim to sexual autonomy. "Listen, kid," she tongue-lashes Rodney. "I don't have to account to you or anybody like you for my time. Get it?" (199). Betty is a cold smack of reality that triggers both anxiety and sympathy.

"Betty was great," a female reader recalled. "So out there and in control. I think that was the thing that I remember most, her taking control of sex with Rodney and the others; she was the one who knew what was what—you wanted her to succeed."[10]

But Betty does not succeed. She becomes pregnant, is humiliated by her boyfriend and his wealthy father, is beaten by her own father, and is forced to leave town in disgrace, while Rodney blithely continues his amorous adolescence. In the promised glow of postwar consumerism, aspirations among working-class families like the Andersons and the Standishes grew rapidly. Almost 80 percent of Americans defined themselves as middle class by mid-century. Among working-class whites and African Americans, the route to middle-class respectability, always precarious, was made even more so by the potential for sexual impropriety among their daughters. Across class and racial divides, daughters who violated codes of sexual conduct risked a family's reputation, jeopardizing, perhaps forever, their families' claims to respectability and middle-class status.

Even as professionals redefined the white unwed mother as pathological—her pregnancy an expression of deep emotional trouble—her ability to damage the family heightened the need for secrecy. With the national spotlight on the problems of male youth and juvenile delinquency, millions of young girls moved under the radar, traveling out of town to maternity homes, distant relatives, or urban hospitals, where their babies were born and family reputations (somewhat) protected.[11] "For those families moving up," one author concluded, "whether white or black, there was a tremendous fear of losing the ground they had gained. Conforming to the middle-class values of the time was paramount. Many of the women I interviewed spoke about their parents' fear of being ruined if anyone learned they had an unmarried pregnant daughter."[12]

Like Betty, Constance also learned the bitter unfairness of female sexuality. Ambitious and bored, she saw early on "the limitations of Peyton Place" (15), and over the protests of her widowed mother, Elizabeth, took off for New York City. There she became the mistress of a wealthy man, Allison MacKenzie, whose wife and children are as vaguely sketched as the place where they live: somewhere "up in Scarsdale" (15). When a daughter is born, Connie's mother goes to the city, leaving behind elaborate excuses for friends and neighbors. For the rest of her life she will live with the fear that Peyton Place will find her out.

> "There goes Elizabeth Standish. Her daughter got into trouble with some feller down to New York."
> "Constance had a little girl."
> "Poor little bastard."
> "Bastard."
> "That whore Constance Standish and her dirty little bastard." (16)

Connie, in turn, cuts off all ties to her hometown until local gossip moves on and she is all but forgotten. But when her mother dies, she decides to return home, where, along with her baby girl, Allison, Constance carefully reinvents herself as a widow whose husband left her enough money to open a small dress shop. The town's old men can't keep their eyes off

Connie, "built like a brick shithouse." But the town is sympathetic. "It's a shame," says Peyton Place. "It's hard for a woman alone, especially trying to raise a child" (17). Still, the fears that haunted her mother are now her own. With every new visitor who comes "from away," with every glance at the forged birth certificate, with every misstep she imagines for her daughter, Constance expects the other shoe to drop. "In her worst nightmares she heard the voices of Peyton Place" (16).

Only the ability to cover up a daughter's "mistake" could save a family from ruin. In Betty's and Constance's fears of exposure and shame, we see the bitter limitations of female desire in postwar America, forever threatening "a form of punishment no man can begin to imagine."[13]

"Soon," Constance tells herself, "I will have to tell [Allison] how dangerous it is to be a girl" (51).

With so much at stake, the pressure on girls to give up their babies for adoption mounted throughout the decade. From the end of the Second World War until 1973, an estimated 1.5 million young women turned their infants over to strangers rather than risk the stigma of unwed motherhood for themselves and their families. One woman who decided to give up her child remembered "being really afraid of how [her mother] would act" if she learned that the teenaged daughter on whom she'd pinned her hopes was pregnant. "I was the one child of her four who just might make it through school, might make it out of our little town." In rural areas especially, postwar attitudes toward premarital sex represented a sharp departure from traditional ones. Before the war, whether in the North, South, or Midwest, unwed motherhood was a local affair, interpreted in the context of interwoven social relationships of long standing. Unwed mothers in small towns were valued as honest hard workers whose contributions to the family and community were far more important than their chastity.[14] Children, whether or not born out of wedlock, were also needed for their labor. Unwed motherhood was considered less a sign of immorality than of immaturity, and unwed mothers were deemed unfortunate but not necessarily bad.

New England was no exception. Our image of the iconic spinster and hidebound "prude," embodied by Bette Davis in her wartime film *Now, Voyager*, distorts the degree to which prenuptial sex remained an accepted part of rural Yankee life well into the middle of the twentieth century.

One Vermonter admitted that his New England neighbors took far more offense at his "wife smoking on the front porch" than at "the three local couples living together for years and having children all without the benefit of clergy."[15] Like the larger cultural reimagining of the region, Davis's chaste Charlotte Vale grafted sexual reticence onto the old-fashioned Yankee character, adding sexual repression and female purity to the supposed white Anglo-Saxon virtues and traditional American values.[16] Off screen, Davis augmented this image of the buttoned-up New Englander with personal anecdotes and advice. "Do not be afraid of the term prude," the New England native urged her fans. "Good sports get plenty of rings on the telephone, but prudes get them on the finger."[17] For rural working-class Yankee girls and women, however, the reality was far removed from popular mythology, often leaving those "from away" bewildered by the attitudes New Englanders actually took toward illicit sexuality.

One New York woman, who moved with her family to what they imagined would be a "strait-laced and chaste" New England village, was so startled by the prevalence of unwed motherhood and the town leaders' indifference to it that she felt compelled to send her story to the fledgling *Yankee* magazine. Published in the fall of 1936, the article by this incredulous newcomer portrayed her adopted hometown as riddled with sexual scandal. When she sought to enroll her children in the local school, the principal took her aside and warned her about the moral conditions she would find, explaining that only a few months before, "the president of the senior class and the head of the student council had been forced to leave the school, the one to take a job, the other to have a baby." Suspecting the principal of overreacting to one small fall from grace, she enrolled her son and daughter anyway. Soon after, a friend of her thirteen-year-old daughter, impregnated by a thirty-year-old man, was forced to marry him. Two years later the teenage bride had her second child. "During my first winter in New England," the woman wrote, "I had at various times five local girls, just past high school age, help me with my housework. Three had illegitimate babies. Two girls were of French, one of Swedish extraction—all had 'Yankee' names." This was not a New Yorker's New England. More troubling still, she wrote, was the fact that the townspeople "seemed to accept this condition without question." Local doctors offered free medical care to the "child mothers," while others provided them with nursing assistance and layettes. "As far as I could see nothing, absolutely NOTHING, was being done to remedy the situation," the author wailed. "Are these conditions common in New England?" she wondered fearfully.[18]

Although Metalious sets her scene in prewar New England, characters like Betty and Constance typify the transformations that occurred in the years following the war. If illegitimacy continued unabated, community responses changed radically. The professionalization of social services and extension of federal policies built new bridges to the nation's "island communities," dramatically undercutting regional traditions and local contexts. Interest and concern "moved away from the mother to the child."[19] Once deemed unfortunates in need of support, guidance, and education, rural white girls who became pregnant out of wedlock were rebranded in the language of the new experts as disturbed, maladjusted, deviant, abnormal, and, by the end of the decade, unfit mothers and undeserving citizens, abusers of taxpayers' money. In reaction to the civil rights movement, which made African American unwed mothers an especially convenient

"Quaint, perhaps, but I'll bet it's Peyton Place."

Figure 5. *Peyton Place* countered regionalist images of picturesque New England, drawing both humorous and serious attention to the "open secrets" behind this highly mythologized and romanticized region. Cartoon, *New York Review of Books*, February 3, 1957.

target, conservative lawmakers across the country introduced hundreds of bills criminalizing unmarried mothers with fines, jail time, and sterilization.[20] *Peyton Place* put them on sympathetic display.

From the letters sent to the author in the wake of its publication, we know that many readers were not unlike the women of *Peyton Place*. "I thought you had used a crystal ball and read my past," a woman wrote to "Mrs. Metalious" from El Cajon, California. "I'm Betty," they told her, or "I know just what Selena felt," or "I too am an outcast." Suspecting that Metalious was the "real" Allison, they wrote as if to one of their own, confiding their thoughts with the intimacy appropriate to a treasured friend. "No one else knows that I am writing you," or "Who would imagine I would tell you these things," they said. "Dear Grace," they presumed. They offered emotional support, assured her of their sincerity, wished her well, and pressed upon her the singularity of their act as they slowly felt their way into the conversation. "This may seem foolish for a 40 year old woman to do"; "How do I start this letter?"; "I want you to know I have never written to anyone before not even a movie star." They tested the waters—"You must be saying, another nut"—and they struggled to get going: "How to begin?" But begin they did: "Please don't think me crazy, but I just had to write you." More emphatically, "WHY AM I WRITING THIS TO YOU?" a Florida woman pondered. "*Why?*"

The history of the fan letter has yet to be written, but by World War II the practice of readers writing to authors was well established. Neither new nor unique to the twentieth century, it blossomed with modern celebrity culture and the popularity of fan clubs that sought to blur the distance between stars and fans while at the same time solidifying the elevated status of the celebrity. We can only speculate about the motives behind individual letter writers, but the genre of fan mail helped readers overcome their hesitations as they imagined themselves part of a larger collectivity of readers. "I had to write you," they wrote again and again, as they struggled to explain the feelings *Peyton Place* stirred in them. "This isn't the craziest thing I've ever done, however, at my age of 40 [it] may be foolish," wrote "Ginny," signing no last name. "Like most people I don't like to write letters," a man from New York began, "but . . . I have to write it." So "life like," a young boy from Georgia gushed. So "real to life," so "true," they affirmed, all so true, not earthy, as the critics claimed, but "down to earth," genuine, and authentic. "*I just had to write.*"

Certainly part of the imaginative labor of *Peyton Place* was to render the single girl and unconventional woman more visible and their visibility more sympathetic. Yet the women of *Peyton Place* did more than reveal the unspoken realities of women's sexual lives; they made them plausible, even possible, putting into print what once seemed to readers well beyond words. "Your story is so human, it gave me the courage to satisfy my urge to tell my story," wrote one reader. "Oh," another exclaimed, "there is so much to my story." Turning themselves into storytellers, letter writers worked through the emotional difficulties of their past, using the characters of *Peyton Place* as a narrative template to give order and meaning to what often seemed chaotic, random, and pointless. "I have been wanting to write to you since I saw and read Peyton Place," a "social outcast" from Maine wrote in a long letter to Metalious. "I did a lot of off color things," she confessed, which, in the wake of her reading, now seemed far less through any fault of her own. "Let me tell you about . . . ," she wrote, going on to tell of secret abortions, abusive husbands, sneering neighbors, two divorces, three out-of-wedlock pregnancies, and "the smart, threatening District attorney . . . that took advantage of me, with no friends and no one to turn to, and had me sign over my son by threatening to send me to jail if I could not pay my baby's board." Searching for the words to make something of themselves, readers found in fiction a way to contain, at least imaginatively, what seemed beyond their control. *Peyton Place* fostered as well a sense of collective relief: *"I am not alone."*

For some, the dust jacket said it all. "The extraordinary new novel that lifts the lid off a small New England town," it announced. In the mind's eye of the 1950s, Metalious's Peyton Place was geographically misplaced. Scenes of tarpaper shacks, incestuous fathers and drunken mothers, religious hypocrisy, clerical suicide, cats strangled by little boys, unwed mothers, sexually assertive girls, and Peeping Toms conjured the pellagra-ridden landscapes of the American South. "Everybody knew the South was degenerate," the well-known author Merle Miller wrote. "Grace Metallious's books insist—usually stridently—that Puritan New England has all the southern vices and a few others that not even William Faulkner had come across."[21] *Peyton Place*, one journalist noted, had brought *"Tobacco Road* up North" and given it a "Yankee accent."[22] Metalious, it seemed, needed to reset her compass.

Readers disagreed. Imaginatively recasting picturesque New England, *Peyton Place* pulled into the 1950s the starker vision of Edith Wharton's small towns, with their "dark, unsuspected life—the sexual violence, even incest—that went on behind the bleak walls of the farmhouses."[23] In Metalious's hands, New England becomes an abject place, a "silhouette of society on the unsteady edges of the self," its tarpaper shacks, queer folks, autonomous women, and inexact sexualities a haunting and disruptive presence in the national landscape.[24] "I too, am from the New England States," Vivian Freund wrote Grace Metalious from her home in Pennsylvania. "In the small village I was brought up in one 'respectable' married woman ran away (and had a baby) with one of the town's 'respectable' men!! And another 'nice' man hanged himself in his apple orchard. Still, another was a dope fiend, and a real church going girl had a child by her father!!! Etc. etc. etc. *BUT*," she continued, "I was a real sinner because I sneaked away and went into show business!!"

With her "dark complexion" and family secrets, Selena Cross troubles the confident myth of straitlaced New England and its ethnic sameness, her "slightly slanted" eyes and "gypsyish beauty" a transgressive specter as unsettling as the bleak interiors her family inhabits. Even the surname Cross, Sally Hirsh-Dickinson points out, "suggests ambiguity and hybridity, as well as a burden to be endured."[25] Along with Tom Makris, the new schoolteacher and "a goddamned Greek" (94), Selena infuses the region with the disorder and danger seen as inherent in the fluidity of border crossing and unregulated sexuality.

In popular culture, Selena represented as well a growing fascination with and controversy over girls who existed outside the confines of white middle-class respectability. In hit songs like "Patches," "Teen Angel," and "Town Without Pity," girls from "the wrong side of the tracks" were increasingly represented as victims of social circumstances and class prejudice, "good girls" wronged by society rather than by blood. Like Selena, they find romance on the other side of town with respectable middle-class boys who, unlike their disapproving parents, neighbors, and teachers, reject prejudice and class boundaries as old-fashioned and unjust. The narrative arc of these "wrong side of the tracks" stories, however, usually ends in suicide or separation, underscoring the difficulties, even the naïveté, of cross-class and, at times, interracial mingling, at least on a permanent basis. Metalious, by contrast, used the story of Selena as a potent vehicle for excoriating both the invented whiteness of New England and the indifference of town leaders and churchgoers to the problems of the rural working poor in general and to their daughters in particular. In an era of free education, the narrator of *Peyton Place* explains,

> the woodsmen of northern New England had little or no schooling. . . . "They're all right," the New Englander was apt to say, especially to a tourist from the city. "They pay their bills and taxes and they mind their own business. They don't do any harm." This attitude was visible, too, in the well-meaning social workers who turned away from the misery of the woodsman's family. If a child died of cold or malnutrition, it was considered unfortunate, but certainly nothing to stir up a hornet's nest about. The state was content to let things lie, for it never had been called upon to extend aid of a material nature to the residents of the shacks which sat, like running sores, on the body of northern New England. (29)

"You are quite right," a Mainer scribbled in her decorated letter just above a recipe for Indian pudding. "Facts are facts, and there is much more to be written, long buried facts in the countless graveyards of New England." Because it was frank rather than romantic, female-centered rather than sentimental, *Peyton Place* represented a radical leap in its conception of women characters, encouraging readers to recognize themselves or one of their neighbors in its pages. "What hurts in Peyton Place," one reader notes, "is that it hits home a little hard."[26]

New Englanders were not alone. Across the nation, readers felt the stab of recognition. The women of *Peyton Place* touched a national nerve, their true-to-life stories simultaneously well known and silenced, the subject of clandestine gossip and a will-to-not-know. Postmarked by rural postmistresses and big-city clerks, letters from every regional nook and cranny in America flowed into the Metaliouses' Gilmanton post office box. "Your story is my own," fans wrote again and again. "I live in Peyton Place." Even today, readers remember the shock of representation, the open secrets *Peyton Place* dared to name. "Metalious wrote about contemporary problems . . . that no one dared speak about in real life," one reader recalled. "I remember those days. I was about 13 when the book came out. . . . No one talked about incest and child abuse; no one even talked about premarital sex (you weren't supposed to have it) or nice, decent girls getting pregnant before marriage or having babies out of wedlock."[27] Another recalled how she used *Peyton Place* to categorize her neighbors: "I was alone and didn't quite fit in, so I simply gave my neighbors the names of characters in the book—that helped me understand them better and be nicer towards them. I was Allison, of course."[28]

Peyton Place invited readers to identify across sexual and gender difference, to engage with "narrative fantasy from a variety of subject positions and at various levels."[29] Allison, Norman, Selena, Betty, Constance: readers inserted themselves into one then into another, entwining selves, forging new ones, using difference to revise their understandings of identity, place, future, and past. "It made no difference," one elderly woman recalled, "they all drew me in. I imagined myself at once Norman and Allison."[30] One young gay man told me: "The only way I can explain my obsession with *Peyton Place* is that it was like a shadow world. You know, everything inside of me seemed less clear, blurry, and so I became Norman for a while, then Mike, then Allison and Selena. I think I kind of put masculinity and femininity together in ways that worked for me. But I could never really explain it."[31]

Social commentators seldom addressed the needs of readers who found reflections of themselves in *Peyton Place*. While liberal reformers sought to bring sex education into the schools, contraception and abortion remained fiercely opposed. Charges of child sexual abuse, rape, and incest: it was all lies and too much imagination. Unconventional sex was the stuff of locker room jokes. Girls were either "good" or "bad." Case closed. In his influential 1962 study *Growing Up Absurd: The Problems of Youth in the Organized Society*, Paul Goodman capped off a decade's dismissive attitudes toward young women like Connie, Allison, Betty, and Selena. "Our 'youth troubles,'" Goodman told readers, "are 'boys' troubles."[32] Like many postwar social commentators, Goodman equated "youth" with young men and boys. Girls, no matter their class, racial, or ethnic differences, were subsumed by the alchemy of female sameness and the certitude of gender expectations. Angry men, alienated Beats, ethnic bad boys, urban gang members, and unconventional beatniks symbolized for many the social underside of American materialism and prosperity, their troubled lives a source of highly visible concern, study, and drama.[33]

The story of American girls was sweet and simple. For good girls, marriage was a symbol of maturity, for bad girls a sign of reform, a return to respectability. Speaking for many, Goodman argued that the young girl is "not expected to make something of herself . . . for she will have children."[34] Increasingly understood as the single most important transition into adulthood, marriage took on a new inevitability in the fifties, with couples commonly marrying in their teenage years. "Except for the sick, the badly crippled, the deformed, the emotionally warped and the mentally defective," one expert noted, "almost everyone has an opportunity ('and, by implication, a duty') to marry."[35] By 1959, just under 50 percent of all brides married before they turned nineteen years old.[36] Children arrived not long after the honeymoon, with three offspring the new norm in popular songs and 3.2 in actuality. The year before *Peyton Place* was published, fewer than 10 percent of Americans believed that an unmarried person could be happy. "The family is the center of your living," an advice manual proclaimed. "If is isn't, you've gone astray."[37] To marry was to define oneself as "good"—a good person and a good citizen. "Should I get married? Should I be good?" Beat poet Gregory Corso asks while toying with the decade's most popular image of the "aproned young and lovely" wife "wanting my baby."[38]

Allison MacKenzie would have found him a crushing bore. "Don't you think it's just awful?" Allison's friend Kathy asks as they discuss Betty's pregnancy.

"Oh, I don't know" Allison responds. "I think it would be sort of exciting to have a child by one's lover."

Should Betty have married Rodney?

"No," Allison cries! "Marriage is for clods, and if you go and get married the way you plan, Kathy, that will be the end of your artistic career. Marriage is stultifying" (212).

In her wish to remain single yet sexually active, to delay marriage and pursue a career, Allison mapped out the terrain of the single girl who was yet to find a public voice. By the time Helen Gurley Brown offered advice to the sex-friendly single girl, *Peyton Place* had already assured an audience would be waiting.[39] Allison's mother, Constance, was equally prescient, her independence, career, and convoluted road to marriage foretelling second-wave shifts in the tidy progression of love, marriage, sex, and childbirth. The blond bombshell was nobody's fool.

Poised and "well built," the widowed Constance refuses to date, positions herself at a respectable distance from the town ("the only mother to have dinner instead of supper," Allison complains [18–19]). Yet despite her fair good looks, Constance avoids men. Indeed, after a scandalous youth, Connie becomes something of a New England prude when she returns home with her infant daughter. "Never having been highly sexed," she leads a sexless life. Economically autonomous, she retains a certain whiff of Victorian "single blessedness," wherein life without a man is both welcomed and preferred. "The truth of the matter," the narrator explains, "was that Constance enjoyed her life alone." Conforming to the social codes she knows so well, Mrs. MacKenzie keeps her worrisome past secret and her nose to the grindstone. "She stays in that shop of hers 'til six o'clock every night," townspeople approvingly observe (17). She is contained by honest work.

Still, Connie's undersexed life elicits both sympathy and suspicion. At a time when sexual fulfillment was growing into an accepted, even essential part of mature womanhood, Connie's contentment stood out. So odd was the woman without a husband that one study called such women "a separate species" who "inhabit a half-secret subculture."[40] In 1954 *Esquire* proclaimed the working wife "a menace."[41]

As new norms for female sexual response gathered momentum in the fifties, women who rejected marriage, and the sexual maturity it confirmed, lost the safe perch that "single blessedness" had once provided. In its place came dozens of expert explanations, scientific categories, and therapies constructed in relation to the new norm of mutual gratification and sexual satisfaction in the marriage bed. Was Constance a latent homosexual, one of *Peyton Place*'s "Lizzies"? Was she frigid? Or was she actually oversexed, her frigidity less a rejection of innate femininity than the result of repressed desire? Was Connie suffering from nymphomania?

How to read Constance MacKenzie?

Early in the novel, Connie explains her lack of sexual feelings as a product of her painful love affair with Allison's father. When she looks back, she decides that perhaps she never loved him and that he could not have loved her, for if he did, "his first thoughts should have been for her protection, coming ahead of his desire to lead her to bed" (119). His crime, she reasons, was not adultery but his failure to use contraception, a failure to offset the injuries that she alone would suffer. This was not love but sex, a foolish act that ruined her life and one she must now guard against. Marriage, she muses, is about companionship and friendship "based on

a community of tastes and interests, together with a similarity of background and viewpoint" (119), a brew of emotions called "love." Love and
marriage might go together in popular song, but sex, Connie reasons, has
nothing to do with it. Sex, she tells readers, is something altogether different. When one is young, sexual urges are a test of love, of a man's commitment, but later in life, sex is just a minor upset, "not unlike a touch of
indigestion," she tells herself (17).

Today's readers often compare Connie to Betty Draper of television's
Mad Men: cold, remote, and emotionally unavailable. In the early decades
of the twentieth century, she was a familiar type much deployed in literary
texts to connote the frigid woman. Typically blond, refined, upper class,
and Anglo-Saxon, the frigid woman represented a mélange of theories that
linked sexual coldness to "overcivilization" among delicate, upper-class,
urban, and urbane wives.[42] With the rise of the women's movement in
the early 1900s, sexual indifference and unresponsiveness quickly tran-
sited into the ranks of female pathology. What was once understood as an
aberration among men *and* women, a deficiency rather than a perversion,
became the inevitable result of women's "will to power," induced by a hidden desire to dominate and "triumph over men." As the century unfolded,
frigidity became solely a female malady, its causes located deep within the
woman herself, "an act of will," a choice, albeit an unconscious one, trig-
gered perhaps by an insult or "an indignity."[43]

While intense professional interest began to wane after World War II
(albeit with notable exceptions like the psychoanalyst Marie Bonaparte),
ideas about frigidity lingered in marriage manuals well into the 1960s
and 1970s. In the national imaginary, sexual coldness also continued to
take on a multitude of forms. In films, magazine stories, and paperback
novels, strong, domineering career women, suffocating mothers, and
Boston spinsters carried more than a suggestion of frigidity, often represented as repression in need of sexual awakening by a strong masculine
type. By the early fifties, neo-Freudian theories increased public interest
and uncertainty as professionals connected frigidity with nymphomania.
Simply put, women who were overly sexed might actually be suffering from an underlying lack of sexual desire. In the new formulation,
undersexed women were simply the other side of the nymphomaniac
coin, their desire just waiting to be released. "Not lascivious desires or hot
blood," experts argued, "but lack of sexual satisfaction most often bred

nymphomania."[44] How to unlock Connie's sexuality? How to restore her to sexual normalcy?

For most readers today, Connie's "sexual awakening" is not just difficult to understand; it makes no sense. It begins on a beach where Tom Makris takes Connie for a moonlight swim. Makris is the town's new school principal, "dark skinned, black haired," handsome in "an obviously sexual way." He stands in stark contrast to Connie, with her English features and the hard-shelled sexual repression she represents. Worse, in the eyes of Peyton Place's xenophobic establishment, Makris is "a goddamned Greek" (100, 94). But for Metalious, whose husband was Greek American, he represents the perfect figure of masculine virility to unleash Connie's sexual desires. They kiss, they partially disrobe, but when Connie refuses to have sex with him, Tom picks her up, drives her home, and forces himself on her.

"I'll have you arrested," she stammers. "I'll have you arrested and put in jail for breaking and entering and rape—"

> He stood on the floor beside the bed and slapped her a stunning blow across the mouth with the back of his hand.
>
> "Don't open your mouth again," he said quietly. "Just keep your mouth shut."
>
> He bent over her and ripped the still wet bathing suit from her body, and in the dark she heard the sound of his zipper opening as he took off his trunks.
>
> "Now," he said. "Now." (150)

It is a scene of violence and rape. Yet not one letter writer took note; not one objected. They liked Tom. Not one critic took aim at the scene or raised a voice against the violence directed at Connie. Metalious's publishers loved it. Indeed, they had asked her to write just such an episode to help explain Connie's engagement to Tom. Her editor, Leona Nevler, and publisher, Kitty Messner, wanted a hot, sexy scene on the beach between Tom and Connie. Metalious obliged, retreating to the publisher's office, where she hammered out the scene in half an hour. She thought it a good imitation of Mickey Spillane. It was. Whether the woman's problem was nymphomania or frigidity, "the love of a strong, forceful, masculine man" was a popular literary cure for many female problems.[45]

Rape, at least white-on-white rape, was seldom taken seriously in the years prior to second-wave feminism. Scenes of rough sex initiated by men were a staple of hard-boiled novels and magazine fiction. Many states demanded corroborating evidence of sexual assault, allowed the victim's sexual history into evidence at trial, and "required judges to invoke the seventeenth-century dictum, 'rape is the easiest charge to make and the most difficult to prove.'" In North Carolina, a victim first had to prove that she'd been a virgin before she could enter a claim of rape.[46] Among more than one hundred interviews I conducted, almost every reader remembered thinking of the scene at the time they read it as "steamy," "hot," "thrilling," a "big wow." Only later did they wonder at the prevalence of such scenes, their casual acceptance of them, and the depth of cultural tolerance for them. Even one college professor was surprised that he could still quote the scene's most famous line: "Your nipples are as hard as diamonds" (277).[47]

If the possibility of exciting married sex resolves Connie's conflicted relationships with men, her daughter finds resolution in the pursuit of a career and life as a sexually active single girl. Uncomfortable with the only options available to her, Allison is "peculiar and different," a dreamy girl at odds with the requirements of her gender. Like many readers, she imagines others to have the "attraction and poise" she lacks. The world around her is boring and uninteresting; only when reading or walking in the woods does she feel a "shred of happiness" (11). Yet Allison is not a conventional heroine, her discomfort and rebellion resolved by the arms of a strong man. Behind the façade of her femininity rest not only the vague rebellions of youth but also the masculine ambitions for independence and personal success. Sensitive, she avoids the sentimental, dismisses marriage, and is indifferent to motherhood. Rather than enter college, she leaves home to become a writer, moving to Greenwich Village, where she rooms with a bachelor girl daringly named Stevie, and eventually puts her hometown's talk into a best-selling novel.

In many ways Allison embodies the discontent, unrest, defiant pose, and outsider identity available to "Beat" boys and rebellious men in gray flannel suits. But she is also a new kind of female rebel, deeply in revolt against traditional femininity, capable of assuming "masculine" qualities that allow her to pursue sex without commitment and a career that will be her own. Before Helen Gurley Brown, *Cosmopolitan*, or Mary Tyler

Moore made sex and the single girl a popular cultural trope, Allison gave the single girl a powerful place in the cultural imaginary.

Teenagers wrote Metalious in gratitude and admiration for giving them Allison. Yet older readers were also drawn to the character, identifying less with her career ambitions than with her vague longings and loneliness. "I could write pages and pages to you," a Florida reader confided to "Grace"—"things I think, feel, do." Then a few lines down, she quotes from her favorite passage from *Peyton Place*—"But it was not the season that weighed heaviest on Allison. She did not know what it was. She seemed to be filled with a restlessness, a vague unrest, which nothing was able to ease"—adding, "I think a lot of women now feel this, not only myself, or you, at one time . . . that feeling of WHAT AM I HERE FOR? Perhaps some women feel only a vague restlessness they can't analyze . . . but it IS an unfruitful feeling, and just raising children to maturity doesn't seem the full answer. Perhaps too many modern conveniences have robbed a woman of her own creativeness in the home? Thus that creativeness has no full outlet?" Unlike Allison, the letter writer feels stuck in her small Florida town. "Where were my guts twenty years ago?" she wonders. For comfort she goes fishing and sends letters to Grace, to whom she had been writing since the summer of 1956. The letter was written in 1961, two years before Betty Friedan identified "the problem that had no name."

Allison is not the only woman in *Peyton Place* to represent inchoate yearnings and ambitions that would later be described as feminist. Among her circle of friends are the town's outsiders, an assortment of girls and boys who defy conventional roles. There's Selena Cross, of course, "her 13 year old eyes as old as time." She and Allison make a "peculiar pair" (6–7). If critics made a great hullabaloo out of the "outhouse" language Metalious used,[48] they failed to note her many uses of terms like "peculiar," "different," "odd," "queer," and "Lizzie." Metalious's biographer counted only three four-letter words in the entire text. Had she counted the vocabulary of social, sexual, class, and gender difference, she would have discovered a far more disruptive language, one that gave new meaning and motive force to outsider identities and the readers who would come to confirm and claim them. "If one reads her carefully," an astute critic noted in 1971, "an interesting pattern emerges, for Grace Metalious knew in her blood what it meant to be an outsider, hungering for respectability."[49]

The women of *Peyton Place* make their way without apology. They survive. At times they triumph, morally if not always materially. Selena has an abortion, gets over her boyfriend's rejection, and finds a good job at Connie's fashionable dress "shoppe." She "had never been one to let the opinions of Peyton Place bother her in any way," the narrator tells us. "Let 'em talk"—she didn't care. She knew that girls from the "backwoods" would "always be branded 'hotblooded,' so let 'em talk" (138–39). If Connie finds sexual satisfaction with Tom, she refuses to accept sex as a sign of love. "Speak to Tom," she tells Allison. "He's the one who taught me to call a spade a spade" (358). For Allison, the town's many voices turn into a career that makes her famous. And Betty, offstage, continues to haunt the town. In defiance of literary convention, she does not succumb to consumption, die in childbirth, or surrender her baby to a rich but barren couple. Rather it is boyfriend Rodney who pays the ultimate price. Unable to keep his eyes off his latest sexual conquest, who sits beside him in his convertible—"she was like something he had read about in what he termed 'dirty books' "—Rodney dies with her in a spectacular car crash as he reaches over to unbutton her blouse at fifty miles per hour (314).

Years later Metalious will write that she left Betty Anderson "pretty much up in the air." Her hope, in a projected third sequel, was "to focus more on Betty's happy life with her father-in-law and son, Rodney Harrington, Jr."[50] It is a book Grace will never write. Yet the women of *Peyton Place* do not disappear. They surface again and again, in novel form; in television's first, and most widely watched, primetime serialized drama; and in the 1960s, when they find social traction in the outsider identities and unconventional behaviors they made imaginable, real, and normal.

In the years immediately following publication of the novel, however, it is Grace Metalious who will become the most watched woman of *Peyton Place*, her life the most talked-about sequel she would ever produce.

8

Excitable Fictions

She put me on the wrong road early on, and I am better for it.

John Waters

In December 1956, just a few months after *Peyton Place* was published, WABD-TV in New York City invited Grace Metalious to appear on its new talk show *Night Beat*, a live production that was rapidly gaining critical attention. The brainchild of Ted Yates and Mike Wallace, whose irreverent and confrontational interviewing style quickly earned him the nickname "Mike Malice," *Night Beat* pioneered late-night programming, pulling in millions of viewers eager to watch the smoldering Wallace interrogate the rich and famous.[1] "What Yates persuaded me we should do on *Night Beat*," Wallace later recalled, "was to hurl a thunderbolt into that smug and placid world" of television news journalism and, by extension, the tepid topics it covered.[2] That night they hurled Grace Metalious.

The author arrived by limousine, her new boyfriend, New Hampshire deejay T. J. Martin, in tow.[3] Upset and uncomfortable, she fussed with her clothes, her girdle cutting into her prickling skin. "It's killing me," she told T. J. "Nerves," he replied. Was it possible to cancel? In the short ride from their plush room at the Plaza Hotel to the terrifying studios of channel 5, Grace's panic grew. She wanted the safety of her Gilmanton living room, the warm comfort of her fireplace. She wanted to pour herself a drink. T. J. held her tight. He was all smiles and warm assurances. Taking her arm, he pulled her gently out of the car. Resistant but unwilling to let him go, she entered the offices of the Dumont Broadcasting Company, where her host waited. Nervous and uneasy, Grace felt especially vulnerable under the *Night Beat* microscope, not only because of the show's hard-hitting reputation, but because it was being recorded live: an unedited hour of tight camera close-ups against a stark backdrop in a one-on-one exchange with Mr. Malice.

Grace takes her seat, and almost immediately klieg lights come up, illuminating her face. T. J. crouches underneath her chair, handing up glowing cigarettes. Wallace casually lights his own, slapping the smoke toward his guest like a police interrogator in a B movie. Already uncomfortable in the requisite panty girdle and skirt that replaced her comfortable dungarees and flannel shirt, Grace wilts under the leering gaze of her host.

"I thought your book was base and carnal," Wallace says with a sneer, his cigarette stabbing the bluish air.

"You did, huh?" Grace whispers.

"What gives you the right to pry and hold your neighbors up to ridicule?" he demands. Grace's eyes moisten.

Poised offstage in her embroidered dress, Schiffli pitchwoman Jackie Susann watched in fascination and horror as Wallace hammered away at America's most "sexsational" authoress. As Susann's biographer Barbara Seaman tells the story, Jackie prayed for divine intervention. "Don't let this woman cry in front of millions of people," she pleaded. "Get her through this show, God, and I won't smoke another cigarette tonight." Grace plays with her ponytail, twitches, pulls at her skirt; but she does not cry. Then suddenly she alters course, temporarily rattling Wallace by calling him by his hated birth name. "Myron," she taunts, "tell the audience how many times you've been married." Caught off guard, Wallace is speechless and angry. He refuses to talk about his three divorces, a taboo subject even on late-night television.[4]

It was a small victory in an otherwise unsettling experience. "Massacred" is how the author later described her television debut. For those who expected a cool confidence and sartorial flair from the woman who penned America's spiciest novel, Grace Metalious disappointed. "I expected her to be a seductress," *Night Beat* writer Burton Bernstein told her biographer. Al Ramrus, another writer for the show, had imagined the author of *Peyton Place* as "a very flamboyant, outspoken, colorful woman," but found instead an overweight wife and mother who "could just as easily have been sitting behind a drugstore counter."[5] Susann, with her "spiky false lashes, chain smoker's gravelly voice, and glittery dresses," was equally stunned by Metalious's plainness.[6] "How," the future author of *Valley of the Dolls* asked, "could this woman, chunky, depressed, and colorless," write a book that had become so popular "almost in spite of the author's publicity efforts?"[7]

How indeed?

It was a question that reverberated across a nation fascinated by television's display of instant fame and fortune: $64,000 television quiz prizes; game show winnings of sparkling white washing machines, refrigerators, sewing machines, even automobiles. Anyone, it seemed—country boys with guitars, runaway girls from backwoods homes, housewives with typewriters in their kitchens—could strike it rich.

It was the very qualities that disappointed *Night Beat* staffers that endeared Metalious to millions of other ordinary Americans. With her matronly suits, plump figure, and unadorned face, she exuded a disarming familiarity; this was a woman they could sit down and have a real chat with. "Dear Grace," they sympathetically wrote. If the press focused on her "paunchy," "plump," "stocky," and "bulky" body, viewers were drawn to her "startlingly candid" voice and quick tongue as she put into words what many only inarticulately felt. In her body and voice they found a woman refreshingly unbridled by the gendered constraints of her time. As Mike Wallace discovered, Metalious could give as good as she got. When Patricia Carbine of *Look* magazine (and later a founder of *Ms.* magazine) asked the author "whether sex ever seemed repulsive to her," the mother of three casually replied: "There are very few things which repel me—such as seeing the kids get a cut finger or pulling out their teeth. Far worse to me than any sex act is unattractive food, and I'm no gourmet."[8] Fame fell to earth.

Could celebrity be more prosaic? Or the famous less glamorous? In the rococo fifties,[9] Grace raised anti-glamour to new and respectable heights, eschewing the fashion-centered world that television personalities like Susann represented. Like her candid book, the body she presented to the world went unadorned. "I do have a lipstick that the Stork Club gave me," she confided to readers of *Look*, "but I never use it."[10] Unlike many post-war consumers who welcomed the flood of stylish goods that began soon after the end of wartime rationing, Metalious viewed the beauty industry with discomfort and frustration. New products like eye, cheek, and lip coloring, ready-to-mix hair color, curling perms and chemical straighteners that invited millions of women to make up new identities, fulfill fantasies, and try on new selves seemed to Grace ubiquitous and irritating reminders of a body she could not transform. Cosmetics intimidated and even depressed her; nylons made her itch; wearing dresses and high heels oppressed her. "I hate clothes," she confessed. "I'd go naked if I could."[11] On another TV talk show, she almost did. In the midst of a live interview with screenwriter and novelist Ben Hecht, Metalious began to fidget with her clothes as her mandatory girdle suddenly snapped with a loud *whang*.

Figure 6. The idealized sculpted body of the "New Look" by fashion designer Christian Dior, January 1952. Photographer: Paul Radkai for *Harper's Bazaar*.

"Clutching her stomach oddly," the stricken guest "waddle[d] off towards the ladies room."[12]

Smart, frank, unassuming, even poignantly awkward at times, Grace Metalious made her entrance onto the public stage at a portentous moment in postwar America. At the peak of Cold War anxiety over gender and sexual normalcy, female fame was exerting a new influence. In a decade of highly standardized gender performances, which circulated more and more widely with the expanding reach of television, Grace Metalious established new representational grounds on which gender differences, sexual expressiveness, and sartorial rebellions could be conceptually played out. Rarely had the speaking female subject been less mediated and more publicly available.

"There was nothing like her," a ninety-year-old woman from Ohio recalled in 2004. "When I saw her for the first time, I just stared. I just knew right then and there something in my life had changed. You could see it, you know—you could see something out there was happening. So I ran out and bought *Peyton Place* and my husband thought I had gone mad."

"Not a bad thing to be," she added with a smile, "in 1957." [13]

Hardly unique to modern times, celebrity culture nevertheless gained considerable power after the war as it inserted into public life a discursive focus for matters normally outside the bounds of polite discussion. Under the gaze of fame, the celebrity became the embodiment of individuality and its unique potential. But as a cultural space of debate and discussion, the celebrity also produced new publics: fans or critics who became themselves proxies for change.[14]

Grace Metalious called excitable publics into being. The very terms of her fame established the sharp divisions along which readers and viewers organized themselves into fans, critics, and commentators. She named an argument as her book fame circulated in tandem with a most unorthodox personal life. Like a sudden storm, Metalious seemed all at once to be everywhere, explosive, turbulent, and then gone, her presence felt only in the upended social landscape she left behind. But between 1956 and 1964 she dragged into polite conversation the inconvenient truths silenced by gender, sexual, and class "normality." Like *Peyton Place*, Grace Metalious served as a potent signifier, the "wrong road" suddenly full of danger and possibility. Her life became a series of well-publicized stories. Readers used them to make sense of their own lives, shape new social identities, rebel against social constraints, negotiate conventional meanings, and perhaps change them, too. Still, like any other commodity, her celebrity was used as well to sell magazines and books, to hustle up new customers, to pitch films and a television series, and to cheat her out of a small fortune. Grace's fame was always at work.

In the beginning, however, success seemed a long way off. Anticipating the skeptical Jacqueline Susann, publicists at Messner and Dell had serious doubts about *Peyton Place* and its unusual author. Both firms predicted modest sales for the novel, and during the long year of editorial revisions Grace turned into a difficult author, insecure, needy, and emotionally unstable. She refused to work with Leona Nevler, whose comments and changes she found overwhelming and insulting. Kitty Messner, who genuinely admired Grace's talent, took over the editing, providing what would become a lifetime of support and encouragement. Kitty also hired outside talent, a publicist named Alan "Bud" Brandt, who together with a Messner editor, Howard Goodkind, took charge of publicity.

Both thought the book "very dirty" and "very naughty," a most unlikely piece of work for a New England housewife.[15] How to pitch it? With little money to invest in advertising, they crafted a split image of Grace Metalious, promoting their new author in *Publishers Weekly* as both an ordinary housewife and a representative of a postwar generation of "emancipated" modern woman writers. The portrait that spread over two pages of the magazine and covered the book's dust jacket—the young novelist in blue jeans, a man's soft flannel shirt, and sneakers, crouched over her typewriter—marked the beginning of a campaign that visually emphasized the author of *Peyton Place* as a perfectly average wife and mother, her old-fashioned typewriter symbolically located in the kitchen, her hair in a simple ponytail, her face without a touch of makeup. Captioned "Pandora in Blue Jeans," the photograph accentuated Grace's youth and unpretentious demeanor while confirming her identity as the daring housewife writer who shockingly "lifted the lid off a small New England town."

"Publishing circles," the gossip columnist Dorothy Kilgallen announced a few weeks later, "are gabbing about a forthcoming novel titled *Peyton Place*—a shocker about life in a small New England town. The author, mother of three, is the wife of a school principal in New Hampshire."[16] Now the public could gab too.

Figure 7. Taken by Larry Smith of the *Laconia Evening Citizen*, the photograph that became known as "Pandora in Blue Jeans" was shot in Laurie Wilkins's kitchen, where Grace often came to hide when reporters camped outside her cottage. In her blue jeans, sneakers, and flannel shirt, Metalious offered women a sartorial counterpart to the antiestablishment Beats.

Exactly how Grace Metalious imagined herself in relation to the "lady novelists" she so admired is difficult to know, but that her enfranchisement as a writer found traction in the incongruity between her position as a New England housewife and her notoriety as the author of the "shocking" *Peyton Place* was clear from the beginning.[17] "Meet a New England housewife who . . . ," *Look* magazine invited its national readership. "Grace Metalious, Housewife-Authoress," women's editors of the Associated Press news service called her in 1957 as they voted her woman of the year in the field of literature for her "sensational story of life in a New England village," casually adding, "Mrs. Metalious is the mother of three children."[18] Conjoining popular images of a sleepy, "puritanical" New England with the decade's sanitized visions of female domesticity, these news flashes stirred intrigue and interest, curiosity and controversy, simultaneously putting the author in and outside her gendered place.

In small-town New England, where advance copies of *Peyton Place* stirred up early interest and local furor, conversations swirled over the tale Metalious told and what it said about the woman who wrote it. In Gilmanton, rumor and gossip about the book and the schoolteacher's unconventional wife had been spreading for years. "They say there's something [in it] about everyone," a retired telephone employee told a local reporter. "I'm not worried myself," he hastened to add, "but everyone sure is talking about the book."[19] In the August heat, talk singed village ears. "If the shoe fits . . . ," Grace coolly retorted. Local authorities fumed. Grace fumed back. "Everyone who lives in town," she told an influx of reporters (Boston newspapers printed a map to Gilmanton), "knows what's going on—there are no secrets—but they don't want outsiders to know."[20] That week members of the Gilmanton school board scheduled meetings to discuss contract negotiations with their grammar school's principal-teacher.

Small towns in New England, especially those located in the northern recesses of the region, continued to fascinate a postwar nation schooled in folksy images of covered bridges, rural simplicity, flinty independence, quaint blue laws, and hardy Yankee stock. Here, after all, was where Robert Frost versified about boyhood birches and good fences (the irony and darkness of his poetry swept under the rug of a higher provincialism), where Norman Rockwell celebrated the American Thanksgiving, and where the Farm Security Administration instructed its photographers to "pour maple syrup" over their portraits of the region.[21] It was here too, in 1953, that Scott and Helen Nearing celebrated "the Good Life"—self-sufficiency, vegetarianism, and sustainability—in their classic manifesto against modernization, wage dependency, standardization, and urbanization. Here, in other words, was the iconic north country, which both before and after the war functioned as a salve for a nation's battered psyche, conjuring up a place where Place still mattered.[22]

Gilmanton was shaped by this cultural labor and legacy. Long a destination for rusticators and summer people, the town drew its share of more recent neo-Yankees, urbanites who moved north after the war in search of an "imagined New England."[23] They came to town meeting, served as selectmen, and sat on the school committee. In the mind's eye of town fathers, Gilmanton was their own *Our Town*, a Grover's Corners where Anglo identity was emptied of any ethnic residue, carefully naturalized over time as a native brand, the "Yankee" shaped in opposition to the hyphenated Others who occupied the conceptually darkened edges of New England.

Peyton Place seemed to threaten all of this, ominously rekindling discourses of social and cultural decline: the doleful, isolated New England of abandoned farms and closed mills, of feeblemindedness and rural degeneracy, what Edith Wharton described in her popular memoir as the "still grim places" where "insanity, incest, and slow mental and moral starvation were hidden away behind the paintless wooden house-fronts."[24] No less nor more "real" than the regionalist imaginings, Wharton's New England nevertheless called attention to the very problems neo-Yankees wanted to leave behind, politicians sought to ignore, and Grace Metalious exposed.

To be sure, regionalists were a diverse and complicated lot, but whether selling stories, magazines, paintings, or books, they served the emotional needs of Americans seeking to escape the kinds of troubles modernization spawned. State leaders, businessmen, and entrepreneurs had long recognized the opportunities artists offered, and the neo-Yankees arrived just as advertising was making new inroads into the tourist market of auto vacationers, reframing the remote "grim places" as secluded camps, lakeside getaways, and scenic roadside sights. In 1936 Maine officially became "Vacationland." Twenty years later, preservationists, neocolonialists, and politicians all helped make New England America's unofficial homeland, not just a symbol of traditional values in the face of a communist threat but *the* place where American democracy began, to be preserved now in living-history settings like Old Sturbridge Village, Plimoth Plantation, and Strawbery Banke.[25]

When, in the summer of 1957, filmmakers showed up in Gilmanton to scout the village as a possible location for shooting the movie version of *Peyton Place*, neo-Yankees led the charge to kick them out. Like the citizens of Woodstock, Vermont, the filmmakers' earlier choice, residents were horrified by the prospect of identifying Gilmanton with the scandalous *Peyton Place*. They were even more furious, however, when 20th Century–Fox rejected their town as "too ugly." Gilmanton, the location scouts explained, "was simply not New England enough."[26] What the regionalists began, Hollywood continued: the imaginary heart of New England drifted Down East, where *Peyton Place* morphed into picturesque Camden, Maine.

Loyal to her adopted home, Grace was equally offended by the remarks of the film crew, refusing to speak directly to them ever again. Still, as much as she loved the place ("They can tar and feather me," she said, "but I won't leave Gilmanton"),[27] her portrait of New England was forged in the fires of her difference. "I have to chuckle to myself when people refer to me as a rock-bound New Englander," she wrote in a rare autobiographical article. "If there was ever a New Hampshire household that was un-Yankee, it was ours."[28] A "Canuck" to her Yankee neighbors (French was her first language), by her marriage to a Greek American, Grace further accentuated her alienation from and resentment of Anglo hypocrisy and pretention. Like Wharton, Metalious purposefully set her New England in sharp opposition to the one seen through the "rose-colored spectacles" of her predecessors.[29] "New England towns are small and they are often pretty," she acknowledged in her first interview, "but they are not just pictures on a Christmas card. To a tourist these towns look as peaceful as a postcard picture, but if you go beneath that picture, it's like turning over a rock with your foot—all kinds of strange things crawl out."[30] The comment flew over the wires of the Associated Press in a revival of regionalist rivalries that surprised many pundits who had long declared regionalism dead in an age of postwar consensus.

If memories of the depression were fading, images of poverty—tarpaper shacks, migrant mothers, dust bowls, and toothless farmers—continued to circulate in the postwar visual economy as things specifically southern. Little Rock, Emmett Till, and snarling police dogs expanded the already troubling portrait of regional backwardness and intolerance. The North conceptually expanded in direct opposition: liberal, tolerant, modern, healthy, and suburban, its countryside picturesque and bountiful, not depleted and desolate. *Peyton Place* overturned these regional stereotypes. Not surprisingly, southern and western reviewers applauded the novel's "great realism," while readers praised the author's courage and honesty. "Not only do I like your style of writing," a Washington, D.C., bureaucrat wrote Metalious, "but am proud that some one would write about the North. It is usually the South the writers try to lowrate!"

It was too much for Gilmanton; the entire Metalious family was shunned. People crossed the road to avoid Grace. Her children were off limits to school friends. But she refused to leave. She intended to stay put. "I live here because I couldn't stand to live anywhere else," she explained to those who suggested she move. "George just shuts the door and I can be perfectly safe."

"You just have to watch out for bears," husband George deadpanned.[31]

It's worth speculating whether or not *Peyton Place* might have claimed so much early publicity if the novel had been set in some other region or if the author had herself been "from away." Having already suffered under the economic and social pressures of being a New England schoolteacher's wife, Metalious understood the cultural capital available to her when Hal Boyle came to town. "I feel pretty sure of one thing," she "cheerfully" told the Pulitzer Prize–winning journalist. "[*Peyton Place*] will probably cost my husband his job."[32]

Whatever the truth of the matter (some thought it more an expression of New England xenophobia, a question of "ethnic compatibility"), the three-member school board terminated George's contract a few days before Boyle's article went to press. The publicity department at Messner was thrilled as Grace massaged the juicy story: "To a majority of people who live here it's a dirty book. Word got around that it's a shocking book. People suddenly decided that George is not the type to teach their sweet innocent children."[33]

A short month before its official publication, *Peyton Place* became a hot story about a scandalous New England town and the housewife who exposed its depravity. "TEACHER FIRED FOR WIFE'S BOOK," announced the *Boston Traveler* with a bold three-inch headline. "TEACHER'S WIFE DEFIES TOWN OVER HER NEW BOOK," declared another. "FUROR OVER WIFE'S NOVEL GETS PRINCIPAL SACKED," still another shouted. "SHOCKER WRITTEN BY VILLAGE WIFE," the headline of a piece by Sterling North declared, while others joined in lamenting that a wife and mother "should publish a book in language approximating a bellicose longshoreman."[34]

On the wings of a New England wife's apostasy, *Peyton Place* took off.

The speed of sales, the staggering numbers, and news of a film contract pushed Grace farther onto the public stage. The split image of the author as New England housewife and "racy" novelist gained the publishers advantageous publicity while simultaneously extending the literary reach of *Peyton Place*. As an emancipated authoress, "Grace Metalious" represented a figure Kitty Messner and Helen Meyer at Dell wagered would have wide appeal among disparate audiences, including highly educated readers who might otherwise reject paperback books. Yet the seeming ordinariness of "Grace" as an average small-town wife and mother would strike a chord, they believed, among more general readers as well, authorizing what might otherwise be seen as trashy and inappropriate reading material. By collapsing the borders between author and novel, publishers blurred the boundaries that separated writings publics, crossing generations and genres. Enormously successful as a marketing strategy, the tactic also meant that novel and author were easily conflated as subjects of critique and debate—the cultural labor of *Peyton Place* increasingly tethered to the gender performance of its author.

Can good wives write "bad" books?

Beginning in late 1957 and continuing until well after her death, the story of the "New England housewife who wrote a best-seller" tumbled out in the national press: her sudden separation from husband George; her adulterous love affair with disc jockey T. J. Martin; the bitter divorce from George in 1958, then a highly publicized marriage to T. J. three days later. Two years after that, T. J. the deejay was gone, and Grace triumphantly remarried the father of her three children the next day. Selling her story to the syndicated Sunday supplement the *American Weekly*, Grace explained to 50 million readers not simply why she had left Martin but "Why I Returned to My Husband."[35]

"Grace," Mike Wallace later admitted, "was a hell of a woman."[36]

Because female celebrity encapsulated the tensions of the era, fame was a propulsive force in postwar negotiations over gender and the borders of sexual and social propriety. Crystallizing in the 1920s with the advent of mass entertainment and the Hollywood star system, celebrity accrued new power in the fifties as visual culture increasingly penetrated the everyday through expanded pictorial coverage in photographic magazines, newspaper supplements, movies, and the dramatic growth of television. When World War II ended, only a small fraction of American households (0.02 percent) possessed a television set, but by 1955 a majority did. Five years later, only 10 percent of American homes lacked a magic box, in front of which the rest of their countrymen spent an average of five hours a day.[37]

Complementing the visual economy created by mass-market magazines and newspaper supplements, television, with its real-time capability and embodied voice, expanded the expressive possibilities available to viewers. It also promised a more unguarded and seemingly authentic glimpse of the celebrity than was possible on radio or the silver screen. Audiences could more easily identify with and recognize televised personalities as similar to themselves.[38] Television hostesses, or "femcees," like Arlene Francis, Betty Furness, Bess Myerson, and Joyce Donaldson, already offered an evolving contrast to the Hollywood film star, whose celebrity seemed remote and exotic to the average viewer. Though they often acted as co-hosts with male personalities on daytime television shows, their primary function was to sell the sponsors' products to female viewers, who made up the vast majority of audiences. By melding beauty and fashion with more accessible traits of "likability, magnetism, and amiability," the femcee gained access to ordinary consumers while modeling a female style that promoted casual sartorial fare along with up-to-date beauty and labor-saving products.[39]

More important, as one scholar has argued, by putting women onstage in a radically new and widespread public sphere, television "validated femininity's power to be seen and heard."[40] Whether women appeared as TV hostesses, female contestants, or interviewees, their voices gained an unprecedented place on the public stage. Unlike glamorous stars of stage and film with their scripted talk, they constituted a "speaking subject" that emphasized the importance of women's unrehearsed words and the power of female utterance. Yet as the femcees quickly discovered, television, like print culture, had the ability to control the meaning of their words tightly through context and camera angle, emphasizing woman's role as "feminine spectacle, eroticized or brimming over with emotion."[41] Like the contestants on their shows, the femcees typically spoke through the mediation of the male host and cameramen.

Live talk shows like *Night Beat* sought similar control, but it was precisely those out-of-control moments when celebrity guests did the unexpected and said the unspeakable that made them popular among viewers. The lack of restraint was also what banished them to the demimonde of late-night programing, where a presumably older and more sophisticated audience would tune in. Where else could one hear the taboo word "divorce" spoken on television or see a female guest talk back to her male host? Over the next few years after her first interview on *Night Beat*, Grace

Figure 8. Like many "femcees" of daytime television, Arlene Francis offered millions of viewers in the fifties an appealing alternative to the glamour of the "New Look" fashion plate and the Hollywood starlet. Along with Bess Myerson, Betty Furness, Mary Costa, and Barbara Britton, Francis embodied charm and likability, suggesting newer forms of female expression and opening up different possibilities for self-presentation.

Metalious appeared on dozens of TV talk shows and radio programs, offering Americans and Canadians a model of womanhood both unconventional and uncontained.

Audiences found Metalious's sudden success variously puzzling, dazzling, and hopeful, her journey from ordinary struggling housewife to literary celebrity a tale that seemed to confirm postwar consumerist narratives and the fantasies they enacted. Like Susann, viewers scratched their heads over the seeming plainness of the new jackpot celebrity being trumpeted as part of a new class of "millionaire writers." Her story also confirmed the narrative content and therapeutic messages of the daytime television shows the femcees co-hosted—popular programs like *It Could Be You* (1956–1961), *The Big Payoff* (1951–1959), *Who Do You Trust?* (1957–1963), and *Strike It Rich*, where the winning confessions of struggling housewives merited rewarding, either through sudden wealth or, as on *Queen for a Day* (1956–1964), with an array of dazzling consumer products.[42] In newspapers, magazines, Sunday supplements, and expanded television coverage, the story of Grace Metalious blended into familiar rags-to-riches tales: a once impoverished New Hampshire housewife who now lived the American Dream. In this sense her celebrity participated in the optimistic hopes of postwar capitalism, holding aloft the promises of consumerism and confirming among even the nation's worst-off workers their membership in an upwardly mobile middle-class society.

Indeed, many hoped to emulate Grace's literary path to fame and fortune. "I'm certain Peyton Place was a gold mine," a typical fan wrote. "How do you go about getting material published?" a financially strapped sixty-four-year-old widow asked. "Do you have to use a type writter [*sic*] or do some accept long hand?" From Massachusetts a "would-be author" wanted to know if she needed an agent. Fame was not her motive; as she explained, "I just enjoy writing and I want to earn some money, to put it bluntly." Suddenly authorship seemed within the average person's reach. "When I read about you it reminds me that it is possible for a Nobody to get up and go forth!" a Detroit wife and mother wrote. "I said to my husband, 'If Grace can write, why can't I?'" There were begging letters, too, in which downtrodden strangers asked for money, but mostly what they wanted was advice: "How do you get published?" Even those few who wrote to rail against *Peyton Place* congratulated Metalious on her success—for "pulling a fast one" on the American public, as one correspondent put it. "The filth nauseated me—I do admit, however, that if I had the talent to write and the opportunity to make so much money, I'd probably would have written as you did." Still, no one was more inspired by Grace Metalious than *Night Beat* pitchwoman Jacqueline Susann, who saw in Grace's ordinariness the road that would finally take her burning ambition (and Hollywood contacts) into the lucrative Valley of the Dolls.

As a representational model of female fame, however, Grace's story also complicated celebrity fictions by bringing into view both the persistent hardships of the rural poor (whose once ubiquitous faces all but disappeared in the official portraits of postwar prosperity) and the complexities of female desire, aspiration, and longing. For Metalious, poverty and hypocrisy, not sex and violence, were the engines that drove *Peyton*

Figure 9. On television talk shows, as well as in mass-market magazines and newspapers, the turbulent life of Grace Metalious unfolded in a visual narrative that simultaneously emphasized her "jackpot" success, ordinary domestic life, and scandalous behavior. Here, standing at the right, Grace is with her son Mike and daughter Marsha at a favorite getaway, the Plaza Hotel in New York City. *Look*, March 18, 1958. Courtesy Library of Congress, Duplication Services.

Place skyward, and she used her fame to bring attention to the failures of the American Dream. Her husband, after all, was a college graduate, a teacher and school principal, and yet she struggled to put food on the table, keep the car running, and clothe her three children. "In her new role as a celebrity," Patricia Carbine wrote in a six-page spread for *Look* magazine, "the stocky housewife finds herself being asked the same question again and again: 'How did you come to write the book?' Her answer," Carbine tells readers, "is typical of her disarming and often startling candor. Grace always starts her reply with: 'Well, I thought about it a good long time . . .' And her ending is always, '. . . and, frankly, I needed the money.'"[43]

Published in March 1958, the *Look* article blended easily into popular narratives of overnight success with titles like "How a Bestseller Happens," "How to Write a Bestseller," and "You Too Can Write a Bestseller." But in a follow-up to the *Look* profile, Grace wrote a piece that painted a portrait of rural middle-class poverty which poked gaping holes in the promises of the Consumer Republic.

Published as a three-part series for the *American Weekly*, a Sunday newspaper supplement owned by the Hearst empire, "All about Me and Peyton

Figure 10. Grace Metalious as happy housewife, playing here with her dog at her beloved Cape Cod–style house in Gilmanton. *Look*, March 18, 1958. Courtesy Library of Congress, Duplication Services.

Figure 11. Grace Metalious as "ordinary" American wife and mother, seen with a ponytail, a Coke, and a copy of *Peyton Place*. *Look*, March 18, 1958. Courtesy Library of Congress, Duplication Services.

Place" reached an estimated 50 million readers. It constituted what Grace called "my getting a turn," an opportunity to tell the "unvarnished truth" and correct the "café society" reputation her fame had created. The opening sentences set the tone. "It makes me so mad," she began, "when I hear, or read about, people who try to tell you what a chore it is to be rich and famous. While it is true that being wealthy and well-known will not solve all your problems, having money will keep you less hungry while you are suffering through them and, being well-known, will cause a great many more people to care about your troubles than if you were a poor nobody."[44]

Unlike the remote Hollywood celebrity or the consumerist femcee, Grace spoke in the no-holds-barred language of the struggling housewife, a "nobody" intimately familiar with the consequences of poverty, the missteps of young love, and the bitter pitfalls of female sexuality:

> Some of you who read this will know what it is like to try to care for a family of five, including three children, without water. When you have no water you do not wash your face in the morning because, as soon as the kids get up, they are going to want a drink and besides you want to make coffee and you haven't taken the empty milk cans down to the spring which is two miles away. You thank God that your children will eat cold cereal in the morning, but when you go to the refrigerator you discover that there is only a quart of milk left.
>
> But wait. In the kitchen cupboard there is one envelope of powered milk which you have cleverly kept for just such an emergency. Oh, really? What the hell are you going to mix it with, smarty? Spit?

"So you fix lettuce and tomato sandwiches for your children," she continued, "and you divide the half quart of milk three ways and you hope you can convince them that this is fun because it is like a picnic at eight o'clock in the morning. Self-pity? Right. But poverty and hardship cause more self-pity in people than cancer does. . . . I allowed myself $20 a week for food because no matter how I figured and fumed, I simply could not feed us for less."[45]

In all of her writing, Metalious made the unsatisfied longings of women a major theme. In *Peyton Place*, Selena loves to go to Connie's store, the Thrifty Corner Apparel Shoppe, where she gazes at "the dresses which hung, shimmering gorgeously, from padded white hangers" (35). When new clothes came in, Selena "looked as if in a trance . . . her fingers aching to touch the lovely fabrics" (39). Rodney Harrington, Metalious informs readers, had "three thousand dollars' worth of convertible coupé" (135). Metalious knew what it meant to go without, to imagine, like Selena, the MacKenzie living room "with its big chairs and its wrought-iron magazine rack" (40). In the sequel *Return to Peyton Place*, Allison succeeds as a writer, but her fame does not soften her longings for middle-class comfort and confidence: "Walking through the lobby of the Plaza, Allison looked at the expensively groomed, beautifully dressed women who sat chatting or strolling about. They were at their ease, in their element; places like this were a customary part of their daily lives. For them there was nothing dreamlike or exotic about stopping at the Plaza for cocktails. Will it ever be like that for me? Allison wondered."[46] Readers wondered along with her.

Her life story echoed the emotions *Peyton Place* stirred and touched in its readers. It validated their sense of having missed something, of being "gypped," shut out from the refined worlds they saw so vividly described in *Life, The American Home, Ladies' Home Journal*, or *Coronet*. "I must say you've been a great inspiration to me," a typical reader told Grace, "not because I've read any of your books . . . but because I am a nobody like you were." Another fan expressed similarly: "I too am a nobody, and after reading your story felt inspired to write my own and put it on the market. . . . This will solve all my problems." If Grace could speak of such things, then so could they. "I am a 'nobody,'" another fan, a Belfast, Maine, woman echoed, "'an outcast' too who had an abortion, married three times and let me tell you my life would make a book." Seeing Grace's story as their own, they used Grace's tale as a narrative template to structure their own experiences, even, in a way, to make them up.[47] "I too am poor and no fault of my own," a letter writer explained to someone who she could see had been there. "It used to be fun being a Nobody," a midwesterner acknowledged, "but I guess I am tired of the role."

There was something in her awkwardness, her voice, her modesty, and her chaotic life as a working wife and mother that made her familiar to those she had never met. Readers became protective. "It is a shame," a housewife from nearby Maine wrote, "that some interviewers cannot bring out the real person that you are and allow you to be sincerely your real self, for your reticence can be felt even over the air waves—and it is only natural for you to be on the defensive." Or "I had the oddest sensation of kinship with you," another confessed. "I feel I had the pleasure of seeing," a fan wrote after reading Grace's story, "the inner most recesses of the soul of a real person."

It's not unusual for fans to project their own thoughts and feelings onto a celebrity, who becomes an empty screen for their own fantasies and desires. It was the detailed, candid, and serial-like unfolding of Grace's story, however, that made her seem to many readers emblematic of deeper social problems. She wrote of her emotional "ups and downs," her despair, her struggles with a body she could not escape. They followed her story over the years, seeing in her turbulent life a pattern of dissatisfaction and loneliness they knew as women who felt different from their peers. "Women like us have few good women friends," a longtime fan wrote. "I think . . . because the docility of most women bores us to tears, and to them we are simply nuts or eccentric, so there is no mutual meeting ground." As unconventional women, letter writers found in Grace a kindred spirit and wrote in hopes of finding, if not a friend, then a pen pal. "I'm still looking around for a woman similar to me to be friendly with . . . one I could exchange thoughts with." Husbands were all right, the writer confessed, but they were "quiet," good perhaps, she said, for "holding me within some bounds. But what about my thoughts that he can't share? Where is the outlet for this?" In the golden age of solitary domesticity, fan mail was all some women had.

Reflecting the discourses of familiarity and "sympathetic identification" shaped by the television "personality," Grace represented for many the quotidian concerns and interests of common folk, her longings as well as her missteps welcomed as a way to navigate and narrate their own. "My life is so like yours," a woman from far-off El Cajon, California, wrote after reading Grace's story in the *American Weekly*. "Oh, Mom, she sounds just like you!" the daughter of another fan exclaimed as she read Grace's reply to her mother's first letter. Thanking Grace for responding to her "crazy, mixed up letter," the middle-aged wife and mother concluded, "Maybe that's why I had written to you because I felt a closeness—that you are a down-to-earth person and not a snob." In a world where being "nobody" was the norm, Grace gave readers a sense that their stories were still unfolding, still unfinished, and full of possibility.[48]

Her candor was stunning. In interviews and articles Grace spoke of her unhappy childhood, stormy divorce, excessive drinking, and, to the chagrin of her lawyer and publisher, the adulterous affair with T. J. Martin. "He made me feel beautiful," she said. "I who had been the ugly duckling in the family, was suddenly beautiful, desirable, intelligent, and adorable."[49] Shortly before she divorced George and married T. J., Grace and the family took an extensive road trip out West, eventually ending up in Hollywood, where the author was to act as a consultant on the film. There they met with Jerry Wald, a sharp-eyed up-and-coming producer who was busy turning Grace's novel into a major motion picture for 20th Century–Fox. Known in his later years as the "Wald Machine" for his influential grip on the industry, Wald pioneered the idea of using "tie-ins" that bound authors and their hardback firms to paperback publishers and Hollywood studios. Grace got an office, a fabulous suite in the Beverly Hilton, and invitations to meet studio stars. But it soon became clear to everyone, including Grace, that she was to have no part in crafting the film. John Michael Hayes, who was writing the film adaptation of *Peyton Place*, met her only once—not at the studio, but at lunch in the exclusive Hollywood restaurant Romanoff's. Just one question, he asked when introduced to the author. "Was *Peyton Place* your autobiography?" Grace threw her Bloody Mary in his startled face.[50]

Hollywood, she later wrote, was a "wasteland," a "junk heap," the treatment of women "dreadful," with actresses sorted and branded like "cattle." What Wald wanted was simply the publicity generated by Grace's presence, although he thought the Bloody Mary was a bit much. "The whole trouble with Hollywood and me," she later reflected, "was that we did not know each other's language."[51] Readers sympathized. Friends worried that Grace misunderstood as well the language of fame.

Kitty Messner and Grace's lawyer, Bernard Snierson, feared that traveling openly with T. J. could ruin her career. Nobody, absolutely nobody—not even Lana Turner, who played Connie in the film version of *Peyton Place*—could expect to admit adultery publicly without suffering serious consequences. (Turner kept a tight lid on her own extramarital affair, at least until her daughter stabbed Turner's lover to death.) For one article Metalious provided photographs of George, her husband, and then on the next page of her lover: T. J. with the kids, T. J. and Grace having dinner by candlelight, T. J. and Grace in New York City. Draped around Grace's frank story, the photographs highlighted for readers the twists and turns a woman's life could take until she found true happiness. Images of her smiling children playfully tossing sand at her handsome boyfriend promoted the benefits for the entire family. "I did not like being Mrs. Schoolteacher," Grace boldly confided to readers. "I did not like belonging to Friendly Clubs and Bridge Clubs. I did not like being regarded as a freak because I spent time in front of a typewriter instead of a sink. And George did not like my not liking the things I was supposed to like."[52]

"She may outrage you," the writer Merle Miller later quipped, "but she never bores you."[53]

To be sure, a fair number of readers were outraged by the revelations Grace provided, including a man from Indiana who scrawled, "I knew that anyone who would write 'Peyton Place' must be a drunken old bag and your story in 'The American Weekly' proves that I was right." But the series generated a new wave of supportive letters from readers who used Grace's story to legitimize and reimagine their own. "When I read your story in the *American Weekly*," a "plain old housewife" wrote, like so many others, "I thought you had used a crystal ball and read my past." Letter writers typically confessed, "I devoured every word written on your personal life," before defending Grace's divorce and then plotting their own. Many thanked her for giving them as well "the courage to attempt . . . to tell my own story" of an illicit affair, divorce, abortion, abuse, miscarriage, or alcoholism. They applauded her courage: "Wonder where *my* 'guts' were when I was younger by 20 years." Divorced women and men wrote of their own difficulties trying to get a divorce; some wrote to ask her how to get one. "Where do I go?" a man from Alabama inquired. Others spoke of a daring post-marriage freedom: "Oh, what a villain one is when the fetters of dependency are loosened!" a recently divorced woman confided.

Others wrote in confidence about their own struggles with alcohol, marriage, hard times, and homosexuality, a topic Grace hinted at with *Peyton Place*'s Norman Page, and featured in *The Tight White Collar*, her third novel. Word of the book's subject matter spread, and readers wrote to ask where they could find it. "No one seems to be carrying it," a would-be reader lamented. "Will you send me a copy if I send you the price?" Kitty Messner complained of the "creaky system of bookstore merchandising," especially in New England communities where "distribution is impossible."[54] Fans were not deterred. "I understand also that you are presently working on number 4 concerning homosexuality or something in that realm," a twenty-five-year-old postal worker wrote from New Jersey. "As soon as it goes to press you can rest assured that I will purchase a copy!" White collars were loosening.

When she married T. J., fans politely switched salutations. "You know Miss Martin," a Canadian man wrote in response to Grace's reply to his first letter, "I think that if more people got down and wrote what they thought or were thinking. We and all the rest of the people could try and understand them better. . . . It seem's like you know how to say thing's to people and have them understand everyword." Missteps and poverty were transformed from matters of shame and victimization to subjects of discussion and evaluation. "You are quite right," a Maine woman gratefully wrote, "that poverty breeds bitterness." Writers unburdened themselves of all sorts of concerns. "Dear Grace," one confided, "I'm buried in self-pity today so I thought I'd write to someone who would understand. . . . Your story [of divorce] jacked me up."

What sounded shocking and offensive to some seemed "real" and "human" when Grace wrote about it. If *Peyton Place* was risky for a woman to write, her articles were even more daring, prompting readers to lend encouragement, gratitude, and a word or two of kindness. "Like a prospector you took leave of one vein of ore and sought another. You are so brave. Keep on writing honey—it is inspiring to people," urged a grateful fan. "I read [*Peyton Place*] and recognized it for what it really was—a triumph over good and evil, and you, for what you are, a good woman," a reader from New York City enthused as he defended her from the charges of critics.

Metalious's voice in the *American Weekly* series brought largely unspoken subjects like divorce, female alcoholism, and adultery out into the public domain. As Betty Friedan moved through the New York suburbs to collect her interviews, readers from small towns, rural states, working-class neighborhoods, and big cities across the country spontaneously sent their opinions to Grace. Compelled and buoyed by her story, they named the problems women faced but no one would talk about: unhappy marriages, the difficulty getting a divorce, low wages and poor jobs, the stigma of widowhood, single motherhood, and the sheer lack of public discussion. "I find myself in a similar circumstance and I had to find a way to thank you," a not untypical letter writer told her. Using Grace's story of divorce as inspiration to file for her own, she concluded, "So with heart felt thanks, I believe I can find my way." From Texas a woman wrote in relief that she was not alone. "My life was so very much like yours," she said. "Nothing has turned out and I find myself turning to drink as you say you did." Now threatened with going to jail for "a theft I did not commit," the letter writer found "courage in your willingness to write of these things." Grace and the characters of *Peyton Place* overlapped and flowed into one. "I am Connie"; "I am you"; "a nobody for sure," but "like you, a woman with a story." And Grace wrote them back, the "somebody" they could talk to.

If fame and celebrity culture have most often been explored and held accountable for their hard work in the service of capitalist hegemony, particularly as a "consumption ideal," Grace's fame operated in ways that connected those on the other side of American prosperity to a new story about themselves and the world in which they lived.[55] If the extreme lifestyles of mainstream stars—their enormous houses, manicured lawns, fast cars, planes, horses, and healthy tanned bodies can be thought of as "an extrapolation of a consumer subjectivity," Grace's celebrity aligned fans with an ethos of social critique and the narrative possibilities her candor and unconventionality opened up to public view.[56]

For historians, then, this is where celebrity culture turns useful: not because it necessarily reveals anything true about the famous, but because it insists on the excitable fictions of transgressive behavior in the form of out-of-control publicity. Like all commodities, fame sold a certain belief in individual endeavor and the potential of the Consumerist Republic. It also sold books, and if given the chance, Ivory soap and Rice Krispies. But in the combustible behaviors enacted by and through postwar systems of celebrity, especially live television interviews, audiences were not simply opened up to the narrative possibilities of difference; they were in many ways made up by them. When it came to Grace Metalious, readers seemed compelled to take sides. They honed arguments, pulled others into the battle—"Have you read this?" "Did you hear about that?" "Everyone, Grace, is talking about your . . ."—and ultimately readers sorted themselves into loose bands of critics, fans, emulators, interpreters, and authorities of all sorts. New publics emerged along the wrong-way roads she mapped.

Scandal, in other words, is the very essence of celebrity, exposing for public consumption the private departures and offstage escapes from social norms that the hue and cry surrounding it are supposed to regulate and enforce.[57] Readers took note. Grace's fans took more: hope, courage, confirmation, validation. They also took autographs, photos, even wall-paper from her home—anything to establish a link, a connection, and a pathway that could lead them, perhaps, toward alternatives not yet fully imagined, not yet quite worked out. All fame carries with it a certain dis-cursive power, a cascading of effects that are difficult to pinpoint and hard to track. Yet in readers' letters to Grace Metalious we see female fame in motion, its grip holding fast to the imagination of fans, its vision of differ-ence penetrating the visual economy of the everyday. And certainly among the many tales that permeate the here and now, it is the scandalous that must be counted as the easiest to grasp and, in the end, the most unsettling.

Writing, Grace always said, was a way for her to escape—to leave real-ity behind in "oceans of words." Increasingly, however, it became an eco-nomic necessity. Grace loved the grand gesture. At times she would call up her friend Laurie late at night and suggest a trip to the Plaza. Together they piled kids, food, beer, and down sleeping bags into Grace's wagon and drove all night to New York City. When they arrived at the Plaza, often with goose feathers stuck in their hair, the entourage was greeted with a polite dismissal until Grace triumphantly introduced herself. In addition, life with T. J. was not cheap. If George represented the unfulfilled ambi-tions of a "beer budget," T. J. stood for the champagne possibilities of fame. "There comes a time when you look at someone and you begin to think of all the things you've never had, and of the person you've never been. You think of all the places you haven't seen, the fun you haven't had, the laughs you haven't laughed, the warmth and joy of love which somehow has been just out of your reach."[58] George was the schoolteacher: humorless, stern, responsible. T. J. was fun. Royalties flowed in and whooshed out.

In April 1958, a little more than a year following the unpleasantness at Romanoff's, Jerry Wald telephoned Grace at her Cape Cod house in Gilmanton. Convinced that lightening could strike twice, he asked her for a ten-page script that could be turned into a sequel by his team. Grace hung up. He called again. She had forgiven Hollywood but was already hard at work on *The Tight White Collar*. She would think about it. He called again and put $25,000 on the table. "Ten pages," he said, "that's all." Her agent, Jacques Chambrun, called from New York urging her to accept. Then he came up to New Hampshire to push the deal.[59] Fans wrote, hoping the rumors were true: "I hope that you are contemplating writing more about Allison, Joey, Selena, Constance, Mike, etc. . . . I'm sure the American public shares my same feeling." Continue, they pleaded, "no matter what they say!"

Shortly after publication of *Peyton Place* in 1956, 20th Century–Fox had taken legal control of the brand. For $125,000, Wald purchased not only movie and television rights but rights to the name "Peyton Place" as well. No one in the fall of 1956, after all, had any idea that the book would sell as it did. For Metalious, there would be no residual rights, ever. "Peyton Place" became a brand name, a commodity completely uncoupled from its author. It could return or not, in films, book sequels, or television episodes, written by Metalious or not. With ten pages from Metalious, Wald's team could finish the rest and still claim the cultural capital of the increasingly popular author of *Peyton Place*.

Grace stormed around the house. She hung up the phone. She said to everyone, "No, no, no, no, no." Her hope was to prove that she was a serious writer. *Peyton Place* was a starting point, not the end. "No, I don't think it's a good book," she meekly confessed. "God, how I hope the next one is better!"[60] Bills piled up. Distant and not so distant relatives wrote her asking for handouts. Strangers begged for loans. Carpenters overcharged her. And she was always generous with her money, and careless, too. When fights with T. J. grew combustible and he left home, she would charter a plane to fetch him back. The Plaza Hotel kept a suite ready, while the Gilmanton house turned into a bottomless pit of repairs and additions. Arms in the air, Grace slammed the door to her study, hunkered down at her typewriter, and reluctantly returned to the New England town so many of her characters longed to escape.

It took Grace thirty days to write *Return to Peyton Place*. What began as a ten- and then a twenty-page "original screenplay" huffed and puffed its way into a ninety-eight-page "novelization," which Dell agreed to publish if Wald came through with a movie version. Wald had cleverly reversed the "tie-in" process, so *Return* became the first published book that originated as a movie treatment, a practice Wald perfected and which turned him into one of Hollywood's most successful and powerful producers. It made Grace Metalious angry and sick. *Return*, she told reporters, was just "so much sludge. "It was written for the gentlemen of Hollywood who will do anything to make a quick buck. I wish that I had never let it happen."[61]

She hoped that readers would understand the book for what it was: a "Hollywood treatment. It was never intended as anything else," she insisted. Readers loved it. "Congratulations on your book, Return to Peyton Place," a "bookworm" from Charlotte, North Carolina, wrote. "I liked it better than Peyton Place. By next year this time I hope there will be a new Peyton Place book out." The literary sequel took hold. Three weeks after hitting the bookshelves, *Return to Peyton Place* sold almost 3 million paperback copies, which, according to Dell Publications, "made it the fastest selling paperback since Peyton Place."[62] Fans were insatiable. "Please," implored a reader from Brookline, Massachusetts, "give us another book soon!"

But *Return* gave Grace the literary shakes. "It was a foul, rotten trick. They made a hell of a lot of money on Peyton Place and they wanted to ride the gravy train. . . . I've been played a sucker all around."[63] Critics blasted the sequel. "Whatever the inspiration that sent a flat-wheeled caboose clattering after Author Metalious' steam-powered first novel, *Peyton Place*," *Time* magazine declared, "the sequel bears all the marks of a book whacked together on a long weekend."[64] The popular critic Elizabeth Bayard, a great admirer of *Peyton Place*, was irked by *Return*. "It takes more than spying on the eating, drinking, and love-making habits of Mr. Mrs. And Miss America to make a memorable novel," she scolded.[65] Publicity increasingly irritated Grace, then bruised her, rekindling a deep sense of inadequacy—not pretty enough, never able to fit in, unloved and ultimately unlovable. Tom Makris, a long-ago friend of George's, sued her for supposedly using his name in *Peyton Place* and again in *Return*. Her mother filed suit over a car accident. Soon she would discover that her agent and friend Jacques Chambrun had been cheating her for years.[66] "The bottle is empty," Grace told a friend, "and I can see myself at the bottom."[67]

Fights with T. J. escalated. She finished *The Tight White Collar*, but it was uneven, rushed, "some of the best writing" she'd done, yet "badly organized," Kitty Messner wrote. Jerry Wald pressed for a third *Peyton Place*. "She shouldn't do it," Kitty told Wald. She wrote Grace to say the same: "I would be happier if you would stick to your 'creative' writing, the sooner to prove that 'Peyton Place' wasn't a flash in the pan." Besides, the publisher pointed out, "a 'big' book by you would pay off better than a minor one."[68]

Life grew chaotic. To readers she tried to explain her emotional swings, her "ups and downs" with men, agents, publishers, and reporters. She clung to her children, the fireplace, and a bottle of rye. "I don't think you are an 'in between' sort of person, either Grace," a "kindred spirit" wrote. "You are either very low down, or very high . . . very discouraged or very enthused . . . very 'all out' in all ways." A diagnosis of bipolar disorder, we might speculate today. Publicity of all kinds rekindled her sense of inadequacy. When reporters hounded her, she hid in her friend Laurie's farmhouse kitchen. "She was a very scared girl," Gilmanton neighbor Ken Crain remembered. "After the book came out, nobody let her be, and she was even more scared."[69]

Yet through it all Grace remained loyal, generous, and big-hearted. When Kitty Messner offered the inexperienced author the firm's lawyer to negotiate the film rights to *Peyton Place*, Grace instead engaged the services of a local New Hampshire attorney who, years before, had helped her solve a minor legal problem. She was loyal as well to all the stores in the area that had been good to her when she was broke. Even with reporters "who played it straight," Grace opened up, offering them rides in her beach wagon, inviting them into her home, and at times treating them to dinner at her favorite tavern in Laconia. "I hate the sight of red meat," she told one startled journalist. Instead she ordered snails to go with her rye highball. "We had a swell time," two reporters wrote their boss, "and look forward to a return."[70]

In the final installment of the *American Weekly*, Grace's story seemed to come full circle. Finally, she and T. J. Martin marry. It is the spring of 1958, some twenty months after the publication of *Peyton Place* and a year before *Return* hits the bookstores. "My life has assumed a pattern now," Grace optimistically tells readers. "It is time to go back to work, to return to normalcy, to be happy with my husband and my children. The only thing that is over is the storm. At last I have found my way safely home."[71]

Readers were left to ponder what on earth Grace Metalious meant exactly by a "return to normalcy." Certainly nothing in her past offered them the faintest clue as to what that fashionable term might mean to the controversial author of *Peyton Place*. But Grace would not disappoint them. Her turbulent life once again on display, on October 6, 1960, Mrs. T. J. Martin divorced her husband. Three days later she remarried the father of her children. The judge in the divorce case was furious. Divorce could not be predicated on a pending marriage, he said, and he accused Metalious of misleading the court. "We may be in the soup," her lawyer warned her.

"I heartily suggest that you do not discuss the situation any further with the newspapers."[72]

It was not to be. Ever in need of money, Grace sold the story of why she had returned to her husband to the *American Weekly*. "I love you," George had told her. "Yes, I know," Grace responded. "And all of a sudden I was cooking meals again, joking with my children and thinking that it was a pretty good-looking old world after all." She was pleased by the reviews for *The Tight White Collar* and planned another lengthy book about a Franco-American family. "Now I'm ready," she told George, "to come home."[73]

Yet, like many of her readers, Grace found the ideals of home and domestic life forever elusive and unsatisfying. She left George again, this time forever, in 1963. The motel they owned together, one of the many distractions Kitty Messner had feared, went bankrupt. The only constant in her life was the pressure to make money, to bail out others, and to keep herself afloat. "I could write another book," she wrote her new agent in despair and desperation. "But as of December 12th, 1963, I feel that a contract and all the worry that involves would be impossible for me. Is there a magazine market which could be met from Gilmanton, is there a newspaper market for Gilmanton gossip?"[74] This time, Kitty could not write back. She was dying of breast cancer, another taboo subject Grace "outed" in her last novel, written in homage to her friend. Laurie Wilkins was also lost to Grace, swallowed by grief over her young son's death.

Throughout another winter of horrors, Grace retreated to her beloved Cape Cod cottage, embracing the fireplace "as if it was the rock of Gibraltar." At least "here I was safe," she wrote. "I drank. I wept."[75] Here was a place of writing—a place where Grace's difference and outsider identity found expression in oceans of words. And perhaps, like Allison's secret nookery, Road's End, this too was where Grace "saw the starry tree of Eternity, put forth the blossom Time . . . and remembered Mathew Swain and the many, many friends who were part of Peyton Place. I lose my sense of proportion too easily, [Allison] admitted to herself. I let everything get too big, too important and world shaking. Only here do I realize the littleness of the things that can touch me" (371). At the end of *Return*, Allison tells a friend: "I'm glad you came. You've helped me a lot . . . by reminding me that the world isn't full of monsters waiting to cut me down. And by showing me that work will exorcise all the ghosts that haunt me."[76] For

Allison, Grace always imagined a happy ending, the kind of happily-ever-after finale she dreamed a literary life could ultimately provide for herself. To the delight of her fans, Grace Metalious wrote two more novels after *Peyton Place* and its sequel, but in the end, words failed her. They were never enough; the demons always returned.

On February 25, 1964, Grace Metalious died suddenly in Boston of "chronic liver disease," a polite euphemism for cirrhosis which she would have found hypocritical and sneaky. She returned to Gilmanton for the last time in the spring, where she was buried on the sloping margins of Smith Hill, her grave a sparkling white against the dark New Hampshire woods. She was thirty-nine years old.

Epilogue

MEMENTO MORI

Perhaps it is pure coincidence that in the Autumn of 1964, when Peyton
Place first went on the air, the American people, and I among them, voted
for Lyndon Johnson to keep us out of war. And in 1965, when President
Johnson decided to bomb North Vietnam, perhaps it was pure coincidence
that the number-one show on television was Peyton Place. But if anyone
really wants to know how we stumbled so deeply into the quicksands of
Vietnam, at a time when the whole country was watching the thrice-weekly
efforts of Rodney Harrington (Ryan O'Neal) to regain the affections of
Allison MacKenzie (Mia Farrow), perhaps we should take a retrospective
look at the half-forgotten phenomenon of Peyton Place.

OTTO FRIEDRICH, "FAREWELL TO PEYTON PLACE"

Books suffer many deaths. When the writer Otto Friedrich published
his poignant "Farewell to Peyton Place" in 1971, Grace Metalious and
her literary phenomenon were already "half-forgotten."[1] Amidst the
exploding demands for women's liberation and sexual freedom, *Peyton
Place* seemed trivial and irrelevant, its participation in the unbuttoning
of America unnoted and unnoticed. What had once embroiled a nation
became, by century's end, the symbol of lightweight literature and frivolous hanky-panky, the tawdry yardstick against which a nation measured
sexual intrigue and scandal. In the fall of 1998, when President Bill Clinton
was accused of covering up a sexual affair with a White House intern,
the U.S. representative from South Carolina, Lindsey Graham, rose on

the House floor to denounce the House Judiciary Committee's hearings regarding the impeachment of the president. Irritated and dismissive, Graham shouted at his colleagues, "Is this Watergate or *Peyton Place?*" No one needed an explanation. *Peyton Place* had migrated to the historical margins of the political, reduced to common shorthand for idle philandering, its edginess dulled by the mystic chords of memory.

Bold, iconoclastic, and highly female, *Peyton Place* was swept away over time by a wave of nostalgia for a more virile 1950s: the petulant Jack Kerouac, bad-boy Beats, hard-boiled detectives, and brooding cowboys who gave the "popular" a new gravitas. *Peyton Place?* "I don't know," an undergraduate mused when asked some years ago what the name meant. "It's kind of like *Valley of the Dolls*, right? Sex, drugs, and rock 'n' roll?" Or, as another guessed more recently, "Some kind of chick lit?" Right?

Death, here is thy sting.

In recent years, however, the retrospective Otto Friedrich began in 1971 has been gaining momentum. In the decade that followed the novel's 1999 reissue, *Peyton Place* received new scholarly and popular attention, including a proposed feature film on the life of Grace Metalious. The Internet has also added to its revival with virtual museums and fan clubs, clips from the film and television series, and homages to cult figures like Diane Varsi (Allison MacKenzie in the film version), Lana Turner (Constance MacKenzie), and Grace Metalious. Still, no matter how many new fans *Peyton Place* attracts, it continues to suffer from what *New Yorker* television critic Emily Nussbaum described as a "classic misunderstanding," the "assumption that anything stylized (or formulaic, or pleasurable, or funny, or feminine, or explicit about sex rather than about violence, or made collaboratively) must be inferior." Writing in defense of the iconoclastic television series *Sex and the City*, Nussbaum noted how quickly, in just fifteen years since its 1998 debut, the show had "shrunk and faded, like some tragic dry-clean-only dress tossed into a decade-long hot cycle."[2] Elbowed off the Mount Olympus of television history, even by viewers who once raved about the show, *Sex and the City* has become a cultural cliché—at best a guilty pleasure remembered, at worst an embarrassment even to women.

Like the fall of *Sex and the City*, the downgrading of *Peyton Place*, classically misunderstood, was unnervingly swift. Its devolution was structured by the processes through which cultural taste takes shape and finds meaning. We are all trained in the hierarchies of good taste. We all know what we should read, what we should admire, and what we ought to think, especially about television shows like *Sex and the City* and books like *Peyton Place*. "If I'm a lousy writer," Grace Metalious told her finger-wagging critics, "a hell of lot of people have got lousy taste."[3] Exactly so.

For so many of my generation, literary taste in the 1950s and 1960s was a nerve-racking business, its acquisition a serious marker of class and gender identity. Among the aspiring middle classes, there were only two ways to traverse the borders of the mediocre middlebrow. One was to follow the road marked "Literature" and take up serious books that cultural authorities deemed both universal and timeless. The other, far riskier path was to embrace the reading habits of what Margaret Widdemer called the "tabloid addict class," whose proclivities for cheap paperback novels—mysteries, romances, science fiction, westerns, and the more salacious texts alternately referred to as "sexy," "racy," and "sleazy"—defined for the middle classes the demimonde of the socially deviant and the culturally impoverished.[4] Here, our teachers and parents agreed, was the literary landscape of the low: inexpensive books with hard-hitting stories and fast-paced writing, their jackets promising the "inside" story, "true" romance, or "frank, uninhibited" tales of violent emotions.

In the northern New Jersey community where I grew up, excursions out of the middlebrow were allowed only if we took the high road. Socially aspiring parents would nod proudly as we toted around our prep school Lit, books whose very absence from the best-seller list virtually confirmed their distinction and our high purpose. Did we even notice the lack of female authors? Even the rare African American "great" (and I think it was in fact a singular event back then) was male. Only gradually did it dawn upon us that many of these admirers of quality literature were themselves either in some confusion over the exact boundaries of the middlebrow or else travelers on a secret literary road we had yet to discover. My friends and I found hidden under beds, pushed to the back of bookshelves, and in private drawers the artifacts of our parents' silent rebellions and guilty pleasures. *Forever Amber, Naked Came the Stranger, Kings Row, Mandingo, A Room in Paris*—and *Peyton Place*. Where I grew up, only the intellectually confident and socially secure could risk reading *Peyton Place* in public. My mother kept her copy safely tucked away.

I was eight years old when *Peyton Place* was published. When I entered high school, we spoke of *Peyton Place* with great confidence and meaning, but none of us had actually read the book. The film missed us entirely. But I was intrigued when my parents bought a small television set for their bedroom in order to watch the thrice-weekly series. By then, however, a serious defanging of *Peyton Place* was under way.

Fans of the novel were the first to notice. "I so disliked the movie," they wrote Metalious. "It's not at all true like your book."⁵ A woman who'd read *Peyton Place* and *Return to Peyton Place* several times over wondered why the author seemed "satisfied with what Hollywood did to the story. To me it was not enough like the book." A few astute reviewers took up their cause, noting not just radical changes to the plot but a softening of tone. "There is no sense of massive corruption here," the *New York Times'* critic lamented. "The shocking impact of despicable qualities concealed by superficial respectability" had vanished.⁶ A warm syrup oozed over Hollywood's version of *Peyton Place*, melting the cold truthfulness that ran through the novel like a vein of ice. The film was nominated for nine Academy Awards.

The choice of Camden, Maine, as the location for the film was emblematic of the screenplay's elevation to "good taste." Screenwriter John Michael Hayes, *Cue* magazine noted, made "a clean story out of the literary mess he had to begin with." What to fans of the novel had been a welcome airing of "long buried facts in the countless graveyards of New England" emerged rebottled and corked by the film.⁷ The tarpaper shacks of the north woods receded amidst the tree-lined streets and handsome white houses of coastal Camden. The Crosses' messy yard seemed a gross anomaly on the outskirts of town. Selena became Yankier and Yankier, her "dark, gypsy" features morphing into the blond, blue-eyed figure of the starlet Hope Lange. While the rape she suffers is graphic and violent, the town does not turn its back on the attractive girl, nor does Selena's boyfriend, Ted, desert her. Unlike Metalious's Ted, who fears that the publicity over Selena will ruin his future career and so walks away from her grief, his television counterpart, played by David Nelson, responds to the situation with the benefit of all the noble moral lessons *Ozzie and Harriet* imparted week after week. Finding solace and acceptance in his love, Selena becomes a romantic victim rather than the courageous and strong-willed girl who defied the town and succeeded on her own merits. The women of *Peyton Place* fall into line.

Allison's quest for independence and selfhood does not entirely disappear, but the film views her longings as nothing more than the normal angst of modern youth, something Allison will presumably overcome when she grows up. The restless, career-oriented, and material yearnings that forged female ambitions in the novel exit the stage. As Allison narrates her tale, she sounds wistful, unsure, and dreamy. The real storytellers are now the men of *Peyton Place*: Tom Makris, Doc Swain, Leslie Harrington, even "little Norman Page," transformed by Hollywood from an "odd," "queer" boy into a shy but capable wartime hero, played with warm charm by Russ Tamblyn. Even the iron bars of *Peyton Place*'s class structure weaken and give way. The girl from the shacks dates middle-class Ted and no one blinks an eye. The great divide between Rodney Harington, son of the mill owner, and Betty Anderson, daughter of a mill worker, finds resolution in a chastened Leslie Harrington, who reaches out to Betty during a memorial for soldiers killed in action, including his self-centered son Rodney, now a movie-made war hero.

"Andy Hardy could have lived here," the *Times'* critic snorted.[8]

It was the television series, however, that most radically transformed *Peyton Place* in popular memory, aggressively relocating it within a narrative more in tune with the prevailing conservative politics of domesticity, social consensus, sexual conformity, and male privilege. Adrian Samish, director of programing for ABC, regarded the novel as both immoral and sensational. On the show, "we always do the right thing," he told a reporter in 1964. "Our villains get punished. When people do what they shouldn't do, we draw the moral conclusions and either they suffer the consequences or are changed. We would never favor violence. Violence is taboo."[9] Sixty million viewers, one in three Americans—the largest in television's history—tuned in.[10]

The director of the television show, Paul Monash, "hated" the novel, calling it "a negativistic attack on the town, written by someone who knew the town well and hated it." Selena, along with all "the novel's unsavory aspects," is cut out of the show and child sexual abuse moved back into the shadows. Doc Swain, in any case, is hardly fit to perform an abortion, since the producers recast him as the placid new editor of the *Peyton Place Clarion*, turning him from town conscience to town apologist. Metalious's Norman Page, overly involved with his mother and subject to unconventional sexual urges, finds himself the second son of the widower Rod Harrington Sr., himself transformed into a powerful but likeable industrialist. "Ours is a love affair with the town," said Monash. "Our people are not hostile to their environment. The general feeling we have of the town is of people evolving towards the light."[11] And if that light felt a bit soapy, it may be because the show's "creative consultant," Irna Phillips, was also a well-established writer of daytime television melodramas like *The Guiding Light* (premiered 1952), *As the World Turns* (1956), and *Days of Our Lives* (1956).[12]

In the guiding hands of Monash and Phillips, *Peyton Place* got a moral facelift. Drunks sobered up (or at least became middle class); abortion, incest, and child sexual abuse disappeared, the very idea pushed beyond the realm of the imaginable. There were no winter binges in locked cellars filled with barrels of hard cider. Gossipy old men, eccentric old maids, impoverished woodsmen, sexually aggressive girls, economically independent women, ambitious females, odd boys, and cranky Yankees took flight from the manicured landscapes of television's *Peyton Place*. Immigrants and their children lived elsewhere; blacks seemed not to exist anywhere at all.[13] The ache of poverty, a pattern that runs through the novel, disappears, as does the Thrifty Corner Apparel Shoppe. The TV Constance MacKenzie runs a respectable bookstore, the kind where novels like *Peyton Place* would never be sold.

While the brilliant actress Dorothy Malone managed to convey the heat of Connie's sexual desire, performers Ryan O'Neal (Rodney) and Mia Farrow (Allison) offered little more than the insipid charm and optimism of tepid youth. "Though an episode ends in a cliff-hanger," the show's producer noted, "you can await the sequel without anxiety. For unlike the world we live in, villains will always be punished, justice will always be done, character will be improved by adversity. You are safe among friends."[14]

And no place seemed safer in the turbulent sixties than Ye Olde New England. What Metalious tore down, corporate executives built up. Studio carpenters nailed together a plywood fantasy set complete with a town square, a ship chandler's, a bookstore, and, in a weird stab at colonial "authenticity," a pillory smack in the center of the tidy square. Following Hollywood's lead, Monash moved Peyton Place seaward, abandoning the dark forests and impoverished hills of interior New England for the postcard picturesque coast, heavily coded as quaint and old-timey. A lifeboat stood at the ready, hung ignobly (and oddly unusable) over the chandler's front door. A wooden schooner, complete with an antique loading chute, stood ready to move its imaginary cargo of cod out of Peyton Place's waterless harbor. The Elm, Chestnut, and Maple streets that Metalious had walked as a child in Manchester, New Hampshire, and readers knew as the center of *Peyton Place*'s intrigue, were replaced with Faith, Hope, and Charity, words Metalious neither used nor held in high esteem.

The *Times* was right: Andy Hardy *could* have lived here. "It has," a reviewer noted in 1965, "no discernable Negroes, no obvious Jews, no bigotry, no religious or political division."[15] A perfect place, in other words, for the future television sleuth and mystery writer Jessica Fletcher to call home. In the 1980s and 1990s the former set of *Peyton Place* would become known to millions of viewers as Cabot Cove, the quintessential New England village reimagined by the writers of *Murder, She Wrote* as the "real" Maine. According to the Maine Turnpike information center, the question most frequently asked by tourists in the summer of 1993 was "Where is Cabot Cove?" If the murder rate seemed a bit excessive, the town itself was clothed in respectability, offering viewers a beautiful paean to a mythical lost past and a nostalgic authenticity. In this town, Allison MacKenzie, Selena Cross, Norman Page, Tom Makris, and Doc Swain would have been arrested.

Eviscerated of its harsh social commentary and female voice, *Peyton Place* turned from shocking to sleazy, as issues of sexual difference and female desire were reduced to the generically provocative and "sexy." The phrase "Peyton Place" was increasingly adopted by mass-market publishers to signal the sensationalism and sexual thrills that awaited readers. The colorful covers of one bodice-ripper after another now promised "the torrid tale of a town more wicked than Peyton Place." The repackaging was a sharp departure from the original black dust jacket that had no images on it at all. Even the paperback version was muted. The title, in bright yellow letters, was the flashiest part, positioned above a small Edward Hopper–like image of a lonely train station, its soft after-hours light inviting readers to imagine themselves travelers drifting into the secret lives of *Peyton Place*. It is mysterious, wistful, and evocative.

Advertisements for the 1957 film and translations of the book deployed more sensational images. Colorful, even gaudy posters, ads, and record albums featured a blue-eyed, blond-haired Lana Turner, her head thrust upward in erotic ecstasy, the top of her red dress pulled down slightly as a dark-haired man holds her firmly and presses his mouth into her pale-skinned bare shoulder. While Allison and Selena disappear from the

Figure 12. The original paperback cover of *Peyton Place* with its almost Hopper-like image, conjuring a sleepy place with a hint of wistful nostalgia and mystery. Courtesy Dell Publishing.

Figure 13. 20th Century–Fox spiced up the film version of *Peyton Place* with posters of a panting Lana Turner and a shoulder-nibbling Lee Philips.

Figure 14. Cover design for the Italian edition of the novel, *I Peccati di Peyton Place* (The Sins of Peyton Place), translated by Adriana Pellegrini. Milan: Longanesi, 1961.

visual economy of *Peyton Place*, a lusty Constance and lustful Tom move to the imaginative center.

This is the *Peyton Place* of "classical misunderstandings," low in hierarchies of taste, subject to profit-driven revisions and purposeful misreadings. It was the imagined *Peyton Place* that second-wave feminists and conservative politicians shared. And it was the only *Peyton Place* many of my generation knew. The letters Grace Metalious kept, however, were from those who had read her novel and recognized the many ways in which it had shaken their world. From them the author discovered the depth of emotion her story aroused, the hopes her characters put into play, and the pain and longing that echoed her own. Hovering over them is a landscape the original *Peyton Place* validated: the terrain of female desire, ambition, economic autonomy, and difference, a woman-centered place of dreams denied and hope rekindled. Did their reading ignite a cultural revolution? They don't say. Did *Peyton Place* inspire readers to push back or act up? On this, too, the letters are silent.

What they do tell us is that *Peyton Place* mattered not only to individual readers but also to the imagined communities and writing publics the novel called forth and set to work. When Helen Gurley Brown wrote *Sex and the Single Girl*, an audience was already waiting. When Betty Friedan published *The Feminine Mystique*, readers of *Peyton Place* had no trouble recognizing themselves. They had imagined it all before in the harsh truths, restless desires, and radical vision that defined the women of *Peyton Place*. Yet the politics of *Peyton Place* are easily orphaned by the classificatory terms available to scholars. In the tidy categories that pigeonhole the literary, it is difficult to capture the kinds of class, gender, and outsider emotions that structure *Peyton Place*. Among the many things I have tried to show in these pages is that the political meanings of the novel were never simple, its readers seldom silent. Political agency is easily denied when it comes to things female, sexual, and popular.

We lose authors, too. By 1970 Grace Metalious had fallen off the authorial wall of fame. "Grace Metalious," Friedrich admitted, "never conformed to our image of the lady novelist." Like Humpty Dumpty, we might argue, the author of *Peyton Place* did not fall; she was pushed. "The middle class book reviewers on the middle class newspapers could have forgiven her such literary sins if she had just gone to college and become a lady," said Friedrich, "one of those elegant creatures who write so tirelessly about the sensitive and misunderstood. But Grace Metalious never got beyond high school, and she was fat and homely, and she wore blue jeans and sneakers without socks, and she swore, and drank too much (blended whiskey, one suspects, rather than vodka martinis), and she was basically vulgar."[16]

In 1955 Kitty Messner asked her new author to write a short autobiography for the publisher's file. Metalious complied: "I was born. I married. I reproduced." Short and terse. We can imagine from later events that the new author may just have needed to run to the bathroom to adjust the girdle she felt compelled to wear in her new role. Or perhaps she simply hated bureaucracy. But her statement speaks as well to another classic misunderstanding: the assumption that in the discursive formulations that continually construct and reconstruct the category "woman," this is essentially all that matters. That Grace Metalious resisted those constraints even as she sought to perform them is part of her legacy to modern feminism. That writers as diverse as Jacqueline Susann, Harold Robbins, Barbara Delinski, Carolyn Chute, John Waters, and Stephen King now point to *Peyton Place* as informing and inspiring their own work is a legacy she never would have imagined. That historians, literary critics, filmmakers, writers, and feminists are beginning to think of *Peyton Place* as historically important and politically meaningful would deeply surprise her.

It is my hope in writing this book that no one will ever again be surprised to find *Peyton Place* the subject of historical inquiry or fail to imagine the importance of its cultural labor in the making of modern America.

NOTES

Introduction: Small Talk

1. The term "invisible everyday" is from Paul Leuilliot, preface to Guy Thuillier, *Pour une histoire du quotidien au XIXe siècle en Nivernais* (The Hague: Mouton, 1977), xii, quoted in Michel de Certeau, Luce Giard, and Pierre Mayol, *The Practice of Everyday Life*, vol. 2, trans. Timothy J. Tomasik (Minneapolis: University of Minnesota Press, 1998), 171.

2. On fantasy and critique, see Joan Wallach Scott, *The Fantasy of Feminist History* (Durham: Duke University Press, 2011), 23–44.

3. Robert Monroe, interview with the author, April 1, 2004; Barbara Wolfson, "Who's Taking Care of the Babysitter?" *Women: A Journal of Liberation* 6, no. 2 (1979): 18.

4. It took only eighteen months for *Peyton Place* to surpass the twenty-five-year record of *Gone With the Wind* as the nation's best-selling novel. Ten years after publication, *Peyton Place* remained the top-selling fiction title in America, with *God's Little Acre* and *Gone With the Wind* ranked third and fourth, respectively. It was not until 1975, when marketing practices and movie rights dramatically altered the literary landscape, that *The Godfather* would edge out *Peyton Place*'s 10,070,000 copies with a blockbuster 11,750,000 copies. As late as 1988, *Peyton Place* was ranked third in overall sales. See Alice Payne Hackett, *70 Years of Best Sellers, 1895–1965* (New York: R. R. Bowker, 1967), 12, 40, 201; Alice Payne Hackett and James Henry Burke, *80 Years of Best Sellers, 1895–1975* (New York: R. R. Bowker, 1977), 10, 33; Marilyn Slade, *New Hampshire Profiles*, May 1988, 55–93 (Metalious folder, Gale Memorial Library, Laconia, N.H.). On sales statistics, see also Maurice Zolotow, "How a Best-Seller Happens," *Cosmopolitan*, August 1957, 37.

5. Charles Slovenski, "Staying in with the Dog," http://www.amazon.com/exec/obidos/tg/detail/-/1555534007/ref=cm_rev_all_1/102–8026639-, Amazon Reviews, posted November 23, 2001 (accessed June 25, 2002).

6. For a detailed discussion of the impact of Stowe's novel on the nation, see David S. Reynolds, *Mightier Than the Sword: Uncle Tom's Cabin and the Battle for America* (New York: W. W. Norton, 2011), x.

7. Grace Metalious, *Peyton Place* (1956; repr., Boston: Northeastern University Press, 1999), 11; subsequent quotations are from this edition and are cited by page in the text.

8. Betty Friedan, *The Feminine Mystique* (New York: W. W. Norton, 2001), 261.

9. Patricia Craig, *Asking for Trouble: The Story of an Escapade with Disproportionate Consequences* (Belfast: Blackstaff Press, 2007), viii.

10. Unless otherwise noted, all letters to Grace Metalious from fans and readers were sent between the publication of *Peyton Place* in 1956 and her death in 1964 and can be found in the Metalious Family Collection (private collection in possession of the family) and the Grace Metalious folder, Paul Reynolds Collection, Butler Library, Columbia University, New York.

11. Quoted in "New Biography of Peyton Place," *Laconia (NH) Evening Citizen*, July 4, 1981.

12. Melissa Fay Greene, *Praying for Sheetrock: A Work of Nonfiction* (Cambridge: Da Capo Press, 2006), xi.

13. Regina Kunzel, "Pulp Fictions and Problem Girls: Reading and Rewriting Single Pregnancy in the United States," *American Historical Review* 100, no. 5 (December 1995): 1465–87.

14. Otto Friedrich, "Farewell to Peyton Place," *Esquire*, December 1971, 163.

15. Denise Riley, *The Words of Selves: Identification, Solidarity, Irony* (Stanford: Stanford University Press, 2000), 3.

16. Gunnar Myrdal, *An American Dilemma: The Negro Problem and Modern Democracy* (New York: Harper & Row, 1962), 179.

17. Rickie Solinger, "Extreme Danger: Women Abortionists and Their Clients before *Roe v. Wade*," in *Not June Cleaver: Women and Gender in Postwar America, 1945–1960*, ed. Joanne Meyerowitz (Philadelphia: Temple University Press, 1994), 335; Elizabeth Pleck, *Domestic Tyranny: The Making of American Social Policy against Family Violence from Colonial Times to the Present* (Urbana: University of Illinois Press, 2004), 155.

18. The scholarly turn toward popular fiction and the habits of general, working-class, and mass readers is enormous and growing. I list here a few works that have been especially important to me in mapping different kinds of readers and thinking about the cultural labor that reading performs: Lisa Walker, "Afterword," in Valerie Taylor, *The Girls of 3-B* (New York: Feminist Press, 2003), 91; Michael Denning, *Mechanic Accents: Dime Novels and Working-Class Culture in America* (London: Verso, 1987); Carolyn Stewart Dyer and Nancy Tillman Romalov, eds., *Rediscovering Nancy Drew* (Iowa City: University of Iowa Press, 1995); Janice Radway, *A Feeling for Books: The Book-of-the-Month Club, Literary Taste, and Middle-Class Desire* (Chapel Hill: University of North Carolina Press, 1997); Richard Brodhead, *Cultures of Writing: Scenes of Reading and Writing in Nineteenth-Century America* (Chicago: University of Chicago Press, 1993); Elizabeth Long, *Book Clubs: Women and the Uses of Reading in Everyday Life* (Chicago: University of Chicago Press, 2003).

19. Benedict Anderson, *Imagined Communities: Reflections on the Origin and Spread of Nationalism* (London: Verso, 1991), 44.

20. Natalie Zemon Davis, "Printing and the People," in *Society and Culture in Early Modern France* (Stanford: Stanford University Press, 1975), 214.

21. Terry Eagleton, *Literary Theory: An Introduction*, 2nd ed. (Oxford: Blackwell, 1997).

22. Quoted in M. M. Manring, *Slave in a Box: The Strange Career of Aunt Jemima* (Charlottesville: University Press of Virginia: 1998), 58.

23. On the problem of truth in history, see Jacquelyn Dowd Hall, "Partial Truths," *Signs* 14, no. 4 (Summer 1989): 902–11.

24. John Burrow, *A History of Histories: Epics, Chronicles, Romances, and Inquiries from Herodotus and Thucydides to the Twentieth Century* (New York: Random House, 2009), 317.

25. Here I draw on the works of Patricia Meyer Spacks, who makes this case for gossip alone, and Jane Kamensky, who expands gossip to include talk in its many forms and its deep historical links to social life and the politics of gender. Patricia Meyer Spacks, *Gossip* (New York: Knopf, 1985), 263; Jane Kamensky, *Governing the Tongue: The Politics of Speech in Early New England* (New York: Oxford University Press, 1997).

26. Allesandro Portelli, *The Death of Luigi Trastulli* (Albany: State University of New York Press, 1990).

27. Ibid., 279.

28. Quoted in Frank Kermode, "Lives of Dr. Johnson," *New York Review of Books* 53, no. 11, June 22, 2006, 28–29. See also Gwin J. Kolb and Robert Demaria Jr., *Johnson on the English Language: The Yale Edition of the Works of Samuel Johnson*, vol. 18 (New Haven: Yale University Press, 2006).

29. Judith Butler, *Excitable Speech: A Politics of the Performative* (New York: Routledge, 1997), 91; G. B. Madison quoted in Harlene Anderson, *Conversation, Language, and Possibilities: A Postmodern Approach to Therapy* (New York: Basic Books, 1997), 112; I use Anderson's notion here of "a narrating self" (108–9).

30. Michel de Certeau, *The Practice of Everyday Life*, trans. Steven Rendall (Berkeley: University of California Press, 1984), xxi.

31. Denise Riley, *Impersonal Passion: Language as Affect* (Durham: Duke University Press, 2005), 1, 4.

32. Butler, *Excitable Speech*, 91.

33. Portelli, *The Death of Luigi Trastulli*, ix–xii.

34. The term is from John Demos, *Entertaining Satan: Witchcraft and Culture in Early New England* (New York: Oxford University Press, 1985), 209. I thank Michele Morgan for pointing it out.

35. James D. Hart, ed., *The Oxford Companion to American Literature* (New York: Oxford University Press, 1995); Susan Ware and Stacy Braukman, eds., *Notable American Women: A Biographical Dictionary*, vol. 5, *Completing the Twentieth Century* (Cambridge: Belknap Press of Harvard University Press, 2004); Greil Marcus and Werner Sollors, eds., *A New Literary History of America* (Cambridge, Massachusetts: Belknap Press of Harvard University Press, 2009); Armand B. Chartier, "The Franco-American Literature of New England: A Brief Overview," in *Ethnic Literature since 1776: The Many Voices of America*, vol. 1, ed. Wolodymyr T. Zyla and Wendell M. Aycock (Lubbock: Texas Tech Press, 1978), 193–216; Robert B. Perreault, "In the Eyes of Her Father: A Portrait of Grace Metalious," *Historical New Hampshire* (Fall 1980): 318–27; Richard Sorrell, "A Novelist and Her Ethnicity: Grace Metalious as a Franco-American," *Historical New Hampshire* (Fall 1980): 284–317; Madonne Miner, *Insatiable Appetites: Twentieth-Century American Women's Bestsellers* (Westport, Conn.: Greenwood, 1984). In the 1990s *Peyton Place* began to attract more scholarly interest but primarily as an example of "trashy" best-sellers. See especially Jack Stillinger, *Multiple Authorship and the Myth of Solitary Genius* (New York: Oxford University Press, 1991), 139–50; Ruth Pirsig Wood, *Lolita in Peyton Place: Highbrow, Middlebrow, and Lowbrow Novels of the 1950s* (New York: Garland, 1995). Since the republication of the novel by Northeastern University Press in 1999, a number of studies have emerged that focus on the 1957 film or the television series. See Moya Luckett, "A Moral Crisis in Prime Time: *Peyton Place* and the Rise of the Single Girl," in *Television, History, and American Culture: Feminist Critical Essays*, ed. Mary Beth Haralovich and Lauren Rabinovitz (Durham: Duke University Press, 1999), 75–97;

Jane Hendler, *Best-Sellers and Their Adaptations in Postwar America* (New York: Peter Lang, 200), 185–225. The only scholarly biography at this writing is Emily Toth, *Inside Peyton Place: The Life of Grace Metalious* (1981; repr. Jackson: University Press of Mississippi, 2000). In more recent years, however, *Peyton Place* has gained new scholarly attention in the excellent studies by Anna G. Creadick, *Perfectly Normal: The Pursuit of Normality in Postwar America* (Amherst: University of Massachusetts Press, 2010), 118–41; Evan Brier, *A Novel Marketplace: Mass Culture, the Book Trade, and Postwar American Fiction* (Philadelphia: University of Pennsylvania Press, 2010), 102–26; and Sally Hirsh-Dickinson, *Dirty Whites and Dark Secrets: Sex and Race in Peyton Place* (Durham: University of New Hampshire Press, 2011).

36. Brodhead, *Cultures of Writing*, 10.

37. Carla Kaplan, *The Erotics of Talk: Women's Writing and Feminist Paradigms* (New York: Oxford University Press, 1996), 4.

38. Nancy Hewitt, ed., *No Permanent Waves: Recasting Histories of U.S. Feminism* (New Brunswick, N.J.: Rutgers University Press, 2010), 8.

39. "Ordinary affects," the anthropologist Kathleen Stewart explains, "are the varied, surging capacities to affect and to be effected that give everyday life the quality of a continual motion of relations, scenes, contingencies, and emergencies." See Kathleen Stewart, *Ordinary Affects* (Durham: Duke University Press, 2007), 2.

40. Iris Young, *Justice and the Politics of Difference* (Princeton: Princeton University Press, 1990), 6.

41. Stewart, *Ordinary Affects*, 4.

42. Roland Barthes, "The Third Meaning: Research Notes on Some Eisenstein Stills," in *The Responsibility of Forms: Critical Essays on Music, Art, and Representation*, trans. Richard Howard (Berkeley: University of California Press, 1985), 318; Stewart, *Ordinary Affects*, 3.

43. Mary Ellen Brown, *Soap Opera and Women's Talk: The Pleasures of Resistance* (New York: Sage Publications, 1994), 79.

44. Brodhead, *Cultures of Writing*, 10.

1. The Novel Truth

1. Writers of letters to Metalious between 1956 and 1964 have been given pseudonyms to protect their privacy.

2. Julia Child to Avis DeVoto, October 2, 1957, in *As Always, Julia: The Letters of Julia Child and Avis DeVoto*, ed. Joan Reardon (Boston: Houghton Mifflin Harcourt, 2010), 300.

3. Quoted in Elisabeth B. Nichols, "Blunted Hearts: Female Readers and Printed Authority in the Early Republic," in *Reading Acts: U.S. Readers' Interactions with Literature, 1880–1950*, ed. Barbara Ryan and Amy M. Thomas (Knoxville: University of Tennessee Press, 2002), 1.

4. Ibid., 1–2.

5. Cora Kaplan, *Sea Changes: Culture and Feminism* (London: Verso, 1986), 121–24.

6. Quoted in Jill Lepore, "Just the Facts, Ma'am," *The New Yorker*, March 24, 2009, 82.

7. Henry Dwight Sedgwick, "The Mob Spirit in Literature," *Atlantic Monthly*, July 1905, 9.

8. Ibid., 15.

9. Nan Enstad, *Ladies of Labor, Girls of Adventure: Working Women, Popular Culture, and Labor Politics at the Turn of the Twentieth Century* (New York: Columbia University Press, 1999), 49.

10. Quoted ibid.

11. Cora Kaplan, quoted in Barbara Taylor, *Mary Wollstonecraft and the Feminist Imagination* (Cambridge: Cambridge University Press, 2003), 72.

12. Betty Friedan, *The Feminine Mystique* (New York: W. W. Norton, 2001), 261.

13. Nichols, "Blunted Hearts," 1.

14. Enstad, *Ladies of Labor*, 206.

15. When fiction sales dipped in 1943, the American Library Association noted that "the devotees of light reading are now canning, doing Red Cross work, working in factories and taking care of their own housework." Quoted in John Tebbel, *A History of Book Publishing in the United States*, 4 vols. (New York: R. R. Bowker, 1972–1981), 4:47.

16. Lepore, "Just the Facts," 82.

17. This is not to deny the many ways in which female teachers, librarians, and other sharp-eyed women recorded both local, national, and international events. The history of women as fiercely engaged amateur historians is clear and unfolding, especially in the years that followed the Civil War. Yet for the vast majority of literate women, the history of their worlds came into view most sharply in and through the pages of fiction. See Bonnie G. Smith, *The Gender of History: Men, Women, and Historical Practice* (Cambridge: Harvard University Press, 1998); Julie Des Jardins, *Women and the Historical Enterprise in America: Gender, Race, and the Politics of Memory, 1880–1945* (Chapel Hill: University of North Carolina Press, 2003); Ellen Gruber Garvey, *Writing with Scissors: American Scrapbooks from the Civil War to the Harlem Renaissance* (New York: Oxford University Press, 2012).

18. Truman Capote, *Breakfast at Tiffany's* (New York: Random House, 1958), 69.

19. Michel de Certeau, *The Practice of Everyday Life*, trans. Steven Rendall (Berkeley: University of California Press, 1984), 173.

20. Kaplan, *Sea Changes*, 117.

21. Eric Homberger, obituary, "*Forever Amber*," *Guardian America*, June 4, 2003.

22. For a brief discussion of the term "dirty" in relation to *Peyton Place*, see Richard Dyer, *Heavenly Bodies: Film Stars and Society* (New York: St. Martin's Press, 1986), 156.

23. The trend toward better venues was helped as well by new censorship laws that began to shift responsibility for "pornography" away from shop owners and toward publishers. See Tebbel, *History of Publishing*, vol. 4, esp. 77–98.

24. Jack Denton Scott, "Big Money Writing," *Cosmopolitan*, August 1959, 35.

25. Kaplan, *Sea Changes*, esp. 139.

26. Rose Feld, review of *Peyton Place*, *New York Herald Tribune*, September 23, 1956.

27. Emily Toth, *Inside Peyton Place: The Life of Grace Metalious* (1981; repr. Jackson: University Press of Mississippi, 2000), 137.

28. John Michael Hayes, quoted in Gwen Filosa, "Metalious's Peyton Place Was Controversial," *Concord (N.H.) Monitor*, March, 27, 1999.

29. On the uncanny, see the classic essay by Sigmund Freud, "The Uncanny," in *The Standard Edition of the Complete Psychological Works of Sigmund Freud*, vol. 17, ed. James Strachey (London: Hogarth Press, 1955), 234–35; and E. Foust, "Monstrous Image: Theory of Fantasy Antagonists," *Genre* no. 13 (Winter 1980): 440–53.

30. Prof. June Carter, letter to the author, undated. Unless otherwise noted, anonymous comments in this discussion are from audience members who attended the following public presentations: "Women and Popular Culture" conference, University of Maine, spring 1999; Camden Public Library, Camden, Me., August, 2000; Oyster Pond Historical Society, Orient, N.Y., March 2003; Gale Memorial Library, Laconia, N.H., March, 2003; "Fifty Years of Grace," Manchester Historic Association, Manchester, N.H., April 10, 2006; Bethel Historical Society, Bethel, Me., August, 2010.

31. "Metropolitan Diary," *New York Times*, January 14, 2008.

32. Patricia Craig, *Asking for Trouble: The Story of an Escapade with Disproportionate Consequences* (Belfast: Blackstaff Press, 2007), 141–42.

33. Letter to the author, March 15, 2010.

34. Alberto Manguel, *A History of Reading* (New York: Penguin Books, 1996), 12.

35. Laura Lippman, "The Women of 'Peyton Place,'" *Baltimore Sun*, June 14, 1999.

36. Susan Stewart, *On Longing: Narratives of the Miniature, the Gigantic, the Souvenir, the Collection* (Durham: Duke University Press, 1993), 136.

37. Lippman, "The Women of 'Peyton Place.'"

38. Elaine Sciolino, "Hell at the Library: Eros in Secret," *International Herald Tribune*, January 2008.

39. *Hell at the Library, Eros in Secret*, exhibition catalog, Bibliothèque nationale, Paris.

40. Robert Monroe, interview with the author, April 1, 2004, Portland, Me.

41. William H. Whyte Jr., *The Organization Man* (New York: Simon and Schuster, 1956), 252–56.

42. See especially Judith E. Smith, *Visions of Belonging: Family Stories, Popular Culture, and Postwar Democracy, 1940–1960* (New York: Columbia University Press, 2004).

43. Ibid., 90.

44. Elaine Tyler May, *Homeward Bound: American Families in the Cold War Era* (New York: Basic Books), 1988.

45. Stephanie Coontz, *The Way We Never Were: American Families and the Nostalgia Trap* (New York: Basic Books, 2000), 186, 39, 253; Whyte Jr., *The Organization Man*, 253.

46. On the changing meanings of "normal" after World War II, see Mary Louise Adams, *The Trouble with Normal: Postwar Youth and the Making of Heterosexuality* (Toronto: University of Toronto Press, 1997), 83–84; Anna G. Creadick, *Perfectly Normal: The Pursuit of Normality in Postwar America* (Amherst: University of Massachusetts Press, 2010), esp. 1–14. As Adams points out, what was seen as an innate quality before the war was increasingly used to describe "something for which to strive" in the years that followed (84).

47. Smith, *Visions of Belonging*, 6–7.

2. The Sheep Pen Murder

1. Laurie Wilkins, interview with author, October 10–13, 1998; "Gilmanton Girl Confesses Shooting Father Last Christmas," *Laconia Evening Citizen*, September 6, 1947.

2. See Natalie Davis, *Fiction in the Archives: Pardon Tales and Their Tellers in Sixteenth-Century France* (Stanford: Stanford University Press, 1987).

3. "Girl Admits Slaying Father, Hiding Body," *Boston Daily Globe*, September 6, 1947.

4. Quoted in Jane Scriven Cumming with Barbara Donahue, *Gilmanton Summers: Memories of a New Hampshire Village in the Early 1900s* (Gilmanton, N.H.: published by the author, 1993), 2.

5. Edith Wharton, quoted in R. W. B. Lewis, *Edith Wharton: A Biography* (New York: Harper & Row, 1975), 137.

6. Quoted in Raymond Smith, "Barbara Hunted Chief Night She Killed Dad," *Laconia Evening Citizen*, September 12, 1947.

7. Interview with John Chandler, attorney at law, Meredith, N.H., June 18, 2003.

8. Ebba M. Janson, "Barbara, Quiet Black-clad Girl of 20, Tells Where She Dragged Dad's Body," *Laconia Evening Citizen*, September 6, 1947.

9. Ibid.

10. Louisa May Alcott, "A Whisper in the Dark," reprinted in Karen Jacobsen McLennan, *Nature's Ban: Women's Incest Literature* (Boston: Northeastern University Press, 1996), 159–96.

11. Linda Gordon, "Incest and Resistance: Patterns of Father-Daughter Incest, 1880–1930," *Social Problems* 33. no 4. (April 1986): 253; see also Judith Herman, *Father-Daughter Incest* (Cambridge: Harvard University Press, 1981); "Family Secrets: Child Sexual Abuse," special issue, *Feminist Review* 28 (Spring 1988); Louise Armstrong, *Rocking the Cradle of Sexual Politics: What Happened When Women Said Incest* (Reading, Mass.: Addison-Wesley, 1994).

12. Stephanie Coontz, *The Way We Never Were: American Families and the Nostalgia Trap* (New York: Basic Books, 2000), 35.

13. Quoted in Douglas Martin, obituary, "Maritta Wolff," *New York Times*, July 14, 2002.

14. Linda Gordon, "The Politics of Child Sexual Abuse: Notes from American History," *Feminist Review*, no. 28 (January 1988): 56.

15. See Jeffrey Moussaieff Masson, *Final Analysis: The Making and Unmaking of a Psychoanalyst* (New York: HarperPerennial, 1990), 174, 175–77. I thank Nancy MacKay for this source.

16. Gordon, "The Politics of Child Sexual Abuse," 57.

17. "Gilmanton Girl Confesses," "Barbara, Quiet, Black-clad Girl," *Laconia Evening Citizen*, September 6, 1947.

18. "Report of the Interim Commission of the State of New Hampshire to Study the Cause and Prevention of Serious Sex Crimes," Concord, N.H., 1949, 8–9, New Hampshire State Archives, Concord.

19. Ibid., 12.

20. Gordon, "The Politics of Child Sexual Abuse," 61.

21. The practice of providing offenders bus tickets out of town was a well-known, if unacknowledged, practice throughout rural New England that began in the depression era and continued in some small towns well into the 1970s.

22. "Report of the Interim Commission," 14.

23. Quoted in Bill Donahue, "Bad Dirt," *Salon* Books, April 15, 1999, salon.com/1999/04/15/peyton (accessed April 20, 1999).

24. William J. Lewis, "Girl Admits Slaying Father, Hiding Body," *Boston Globe*, September 6, 1947; "Door to Roberts Kitchen Taken to State Police Office," *Laconia Evening Citizen*, September 8, 1947.

25. "Barbara Hunted Chief," *Laconia Evening Citizen*, September 12, 1947.

26. "Girl Admits Slaying," *Boston Globe*, September 6, 1947.

27. On the functions of the grotesque in southern literature, see Patricia Yaeger, *Dirt and Desire: Reconstructing Southern Women's Writing, 1930–1990* (Chicago: University of Chicago Press, 2000).

28. Laurie Wilkins, interview with the author, September, 2001.

29. "Barbara Taken to State Prison," *Laconia Evening Citizen*, December 3, 1947.

30. See Holly McCammon, *United States Women's Jury Movement and Strategic Adaption: A More Just Verdict* (New York: Cambridge University Press, 2012), 48–49.

31. "Barbara Taken," *Laconia Evening Citizen*, December 3, 1947.

32. Otto Friedrich, "Farewell to *Peyton Place*," *Esquire*, December 1971, 163.

33. Anonymous reader quoted in Ardis Cameron, "Open Secrets: Rereading Peyton Place," introduction to Grace Metalious, *Peyton Place* (Boston: Northeastern University Press, 1999), xvi.

3. Scenes of Writing

1. Laurie Wilkins, interview with the author, September 12, 1998, and December 3, 2002; John Wilkins, interview with the author, August 1999; Wendy Wilkins, interview with the author, December 3, 2002; Joanne Wilkins, interview with the author, December 3, 2002.

2. "The one steady pull more" is from the poem "A Servant to Servants," by Robert Frost, *North of Boston* (New York: Henry Holt and Company, 1914).

3. For population rates, see Robert Eisenmerger, *The Dynamics of Growth in New England's Economy, 1870–1964* (Middletown, Conn.: Wesleyan University Press, 1967), 61–65; Hal Barron, *Those Who Stayed Behind: Rural Society in Nineteenth-Century New England* (Cambridge: Cambridge University Press, 1984); Irvin Sobel, "Labor Market Behavior in Small Towns," *Industrial Labor Relations Review* 9 (October 1955): 54–76.

4. J. K. Galbraith, "Abandoned Farms, Unabandoned Hopes," *New York Times Magazine*, September 13, 1953, 25.

5. On Frost's fowl and life in New Hampshire, see Jay Parini, *Robert Frost: A Life* (New York: Henry Holt and Company, 1999), 72.

6. On Old Home Week and the "invention" of New England, see Dona Brown, *Inventing New England: Regional Tourism in the Nineteenth Century* (Washington, D.C.: Smithsonian Institution Press, 1995), 135–50.

7. Jane Scriven Cumming with Barbara Donahue, *Gilmanton Summers: Memories of a New Hampshire Village in the Early 1900s* (Gilmanton, N.H.: published by the author, 1993), 2.

8. "Mountain View Hotel," undated brochure. See also Brown, *Inventing New England*, 145.

9. Galbraith, "Abandoned Farms," 26.

10. New Hampshire State Planning and Development Commission quoted in Elizabeth Forbes Morison and Elting E. Morison, *New Hampshire: A Bicentennial History* (New York: W. W. Norton, 1976), 188.

11. Laurie Wilkins MacFadyen, quoted in Laura Lippman, "The Women of Peyton Place," *Baltimore Sun*, June 14, 1999.

12. Quoted in Emily Toth, *Inside Peyton Place: The Life of Grace Metalious* (1981; repr. Jackson: University Press of Mississippi, 2000), 81.

13. Tamara K. Hareven and Randolph Langenbach, *Amoskeag: Life and Work in an American Factory City* (New York: Pantheon Books, 1978), 10–11.

14. Grace Metalious, "All about Me and Peyton Place," *American Weekly*, May 18, 1958, 8, 11. This was a three-part series published in *American Weekly* on May 18, June 1, and June 8, 1958. On the importance of the library, see George Metalious and June O'Shea, *The Girl from Peyton Place* (New York: Dell Publishing, 1965), 25–26.

15. Metalious and O'Shea, *The Girl from Peyton Place*, 38.

16. Laurie Wilkins, "Publishers Spotlight Gilmanton, *Laconia Evening Citizen*, July 17, 1956; James Dobson, "Pandora in Blue Jeans," *Yankee*, September 1990, 94.

17. Grace Metalious, "Why I Returned to My Husband," *American Weekly*, January 29, 1961, 4; Grace Metalious, "Me and Peyton Place," *American Weekly*, June 1, 1958, 11.

18. Laurie Wilkins, "Publishers Spotlight," *Laconia Evening Citizen*, July 17, 1956.

19. John Rees, interview with the author, October 2, 2002.

20. Quoted in Toth, *Inside Peyton Place*, 79.

21. Ibid., 107.

22. Quoted in Gwen Filosa, "Metalious's Book Was Controversial, Popular," *Concord Monitor*, March 27, 1999.

23. Ibid.

24. Laurie Wilkins, interview with the author, October 6, 1998.

25. Quoted in Patricia Carbine, "Peyton Place," *Look*, March 18, 1958, 108.

26. Estelle B. Freedman, "'Uncontrolled Desires': The Response to the Sexual Psychopath, 1920–1960," *Journal of American History* 74, no. 1 (June 1987): 90, 106.

27. Metalious and O'Shea, *The Girl from Peyton Place*, 51; Grace Metalious interviewed by Joyce Donaldson, *The Joyce Donaldson Show*, Canadian Broadcasting Company, ca. 1957, Metalious Family Collection.

28. Quoted in Lippman, "The Women of Peyton Place," *Baltimore Sun*, June 14, 1999.

29. Toth, *Inside Peyton Place*, 78; Metalious and O'Shea, *The Girl From Peyton Place*, 82–83; Dobson, "Pandora," 94.

30. Laurel Thatcher Ulrich, *A Midwife's Tale: The Life of Martha Ballard, Based on Her Diary, 1785–1812* (New York: Alfred A. Knopf, 1990), 219. The idea of a house as "an adversary" I owe to Ulrich.

31. John Rees, "Grace Metalious' Battle with the World," *Cosmopolitan*, September 1964, 56; Evic Jarvin, quoted in Merle Miller, "The Tragedy of Grace Metalious and Peyton Place," *Ladies Home Journal*, June, 1965: 112.

32. Metalious and O'Shea, *The Girl from Peyton Place*, 83.

33. Metalious, "Me and Peyton Place," *American Weekly*, June 1, 1958, 10.

34. Metalious, "Me and Peyton Place," *American Weekly*, May 18, 1958, 11; Maurice Zolotow, "How a Best-seller Happens," *Cosmopolitan*, August 1957, 39.

35. On advertising in books, see Megan Benton, " 'Too Many Books': Book Ownership and Cultural Identity in the 1920s," *American Quarterly* 49, no. 2 (1997): 280.

36. Quoted in Metalious and O'Shea, *The Girl from Peyton Place*, 26.

37. Michel de Certeau, *The Practice of Everyday Life*, trans. Steven Rendall (Berkeley: University of California Press, 1984), xxi.

38. Metalious, "Me and Peyton Place," *American Weekly*, May 18, 1958, 13–14.

39. On the culture of longing and the politics of envy in working-class life, see Carolyn Kay Steedman, *Landscape for a Good Woman* (New Brunswick, N.J.: Rutgers University Press, 1987), 15.

40. Metalious and O'Shea, *The Girl from Peyton Place*, 23.

41. Preface to the *Complete Poems of Robert Frost* (New York: Henry Holt and Company, 1949).

42. Metalious and O'Shea, *The Girl from Peyton Place*, 22–23.

43. Metalious, "All about Me and Peyton Place," 11.

44. Rees, "Grace Metalious' Battle," 56.

4. The Other Side of Writing

1. Richard Brodhead, *Cultures of Letters: Scenes of Reading and Writing in Nineteenth-Century America* (Chicago: University of Chicago Press, 1993), 110.

2. Grace Metalious, "All about Me and Peyton Place," *American Weekly*, May 18, 1958, 12.

3. Grace Metalious, *Return to Peyton Place* (Hanover, N.H.: University Press of New England, 2007), 61.

4. Maurice Zolotow, "How a Best-Seller Happens," *Cosmopolitan*, August 1957, 40. The dictum is from Mary Heaton Vorse in a letter to Sinclair Lewis, quoted in Metalious, "All about Me and Peyton Place," 12.

5. R. Jackson Wilson, *Figures of Speech* (New York: Knopf, 1989), 12.

6. Linda Brodkey, *Academic Writing as Social Practice* (Philadelphia: Temple University Press, 1987), 54–81.

7. See P. David Marshall, *Celebrity and Power: Fame in Contemporary Culture* (Minneapolis: University of Minnesota Press, 1997); Loren Glass, *Authors Inc.: Literary Celebrity in the Modern United States, 1990–1980* (New York: New York University Press, 2004). Elizabeth Long sees the writer-writes-alone image as part of a longer narrative tradition with modernism advancing "just one version." Elizabeth Long, *Book Clubs: Women and the Uses of Reading in Everyday Life* (Chicago: University of Chicago Press, 2003), 1. On the gendered image of the "independent writer and reader," see Janice Radway, *A Feeling for Books: The Book-of-the-Month Club, Literary Taste, and Middle-Class Desire* (Chapel Hill: University of North Carolina Press, 1997), 189–90.

8. Metalious, *Return to Peyton Place*, 72.

9. The phrase is from Brodkey, *Academic Writing*, 55.

10. Brodhead, *Cultures of Letters*, 5, 11.

11. Laurie Wilkins, interview with the author, December 3, 2002.

12. Marshall, *Celebrity and Power*, 15. Housed within the celebrity, Marshall argues, is "the exceptional with the ordinary, the ideal with the fundamentally everyday (22–23).

13. Robert Byrne, *Writing Rackets* (New York: Lyle Stuart, 1969), 16; Margaret Wallace, "Young Women Novelists Steal the Headlines," *Independent Woman*, April 1952, 107–8; Jack Denton Scott, "Big Money Writing," *Cosmopolitan*, August 1959, 35–41.

14. "Eight Ways to Become an Authoress," *Saturday Review*, October 8, 1955, 20–21; Verona Backus, "Sell Your Family," *Writer*, February 1946, 52–52.

15. *Time*, September 10, 1956, 124; Marynia F. Farnham, "The Pen and the Distaff," *Saturday Review of Literature*, February 22, 1947; Inez Holden, "Some Women Writers," *The Nineteenth Century and After* 1460 (August 1949): 130–37; Wallace, "Young Women Novelists Steal the Headlines," 99–100; Abbe Dimnet, "A Letter to an American Woman Who Says 'She Would Like to Write,'" *Vogue*, November 1, 1954, 101–3; Susan Kuehn Boyd, "Authoress in an Apron," *Writer* 72 (October 1959): 15–17; Gerald Walker, "Typewriters in the Kitchen," *Cosmopolitan* 149 (August 1960): 36–41.

16. The term "Consumers' Republic" is from Lizabeth Cohen, *A Consumers' Republic: The Politics of Mass Consumption in Postwar America* (New York: Vintage, 2003).

17. T. F. James, "The Millionaire Class of Young Writers," *Look*, March 18, 1958, 40.

18. Nancy Walker, "Humor and Gender Roles: The 'Funny' Feminism of the Post–World War II Suburbs," *American Quarterly* 1 (Spring 1985): 113; Eva Moskowitz, "'It's Good to Blow Your Top Off': Women's Magazines and a Discourse of Discontent, 1945–1965," *Journal of Women's History* 18 (Spring 1985): 98–113.

19. Mary Kelley, *Private Woman, Public Stage: Literary Domesticity in Nineteenth-Century America* (Oxford: Oxford University Press, 1984), 135. Kelley argues against the term "sentimentalists" traditionally used to designate these popular women writers, preferring instead "literary domestics" to call attention to their historical importance not only as writers but as economically autonomous women often acting as the family breadwinner. See esp. ibid., 139.

20. The quote is from George Orwell, *Keep the Aspidistra Flying* (New York: Harcourt, 1956), 204. Sales of Miss Laura Jean Libby brought in $15 million and also, like most of these novelists, caustic complaints from critics. Quentin Reynolds, *The Fiction Factory: From Pulp Row to Quality Street* (New York: Random House, 1955), 158–59. For an excellent history of this early revolution, see Kenneth C. Davis, *Two-Bit Culture: The Paperbacking of America* (Boston: Houghton Mifflin, 1984), 1–83. One of the earliest chroniclers remains one of the best: Mary Noel, *Villains Galore: The Heyday of the Popular Story Weekly* (New York: Macmillan, 1954). See also John Tebbel, *A History of Book Publishing in the United States*, 4 vols. (New York: R. R. Bowker, 1972–1981), 2:170–74; Lehman-Haupt Hellmut with Lawrence C. Worth and Rollo G. Silver, *The Book in America: The History of the Making and Selling of Books in the United States* (New York: Bowker, 1952); Radway, *A Feeling for Books*, esp. chap. 4; Michael Denning, *Mechanic Accents: Dime Novels and Working-Class Culture in America* (London: Verso Press, 1987).

21. Tebbel, *A History of Book Publishing*, 2:504.

22. Ibid., 25.

23. See especially Radway, *A Feeling for Books*, 132–35. Raymond Williams notes that the meaning of "Literature," which came into use in English in the fourteenth century to convey the "sense of polite learning through reading," became more closely linked to the practice of writing as conveying "literary merit," "literary reputation," and skill with words during the eighteenth century as the profession of authorship became more self-consciously developed with the rise of the bookselling marketplace. Raymond Williams, *Keywords: A Vocabulary of Culture and Society* (New York: Oxford University Press, 1976), 184–85.

24. Davis, *Two-Bit Culture*, 35.

25. On literary celebrity, see especially Glass, *Authors Inc.;* and John Cawelti, "The Writer as Celebrity: Some Aspects of American Literature as Popular Culture," *Studies in American Fiction* 5, no. 1 (Spring 1977): 161–74.

26. Glass, *Authors Inc.*, 18.

27. Radway, *A Feeling for Books*, 129–31.

28. Anonymous letter from a bookseller quoted in Tebbel, *A History of Book Publishing*, 2:504.

29. Ibid., 506.

30. Julian Hawthorne, "Inspiration 'Ex Machina,'" *Appleton's Booklovers Magazine* 17, no. 6 (June 1906): 814.

31. Kelley, *Private Woman*, 20.

32. Noel, *Villains Galore*, 5–7.

33. Michael Denning, *The Cultural Front: The Laboring of American Culture in the Twentieth Century* (New York: Verso, 1997), 178.

34. Henry Holt, "The Commercialization of Literature," *Atlantic Monthly*, November 1905, 578.

35. On the role of series books and children's reading, see Nancy Tillman Romalov, "Children's Series Books and the Rhetoric of Guidance: A Historical Overview," in *Rediscovering Nancy Drew*, ed. Carolyn Stewart Dyer and Nancy Tillman Romalov (Iowa City: University of Iowa Press, 1995), 113–20.

36. Quoted ibid., 117.

37. Tebbel, *A History of Book Publishing*, 3:510. See also Davis, *Two-Bit Culture;* Freeman Lewis, *A Brief History of Pocket Books* (New York: Pocket Books, 1967); John Tebbel, *Paperback Books: A Pocket History* (New York: Pocket Books, 1964). Harper editor Maxwell Aley estimated that by the close of the 1920s, 25 million Americans, or about a quarter of the 90 million literate public, were in the habit of buying books. With increased advertising and distribution, best-selling novels were reaching annual sales of 800,000, while nonfiction could top a million. Maxwell Aley, "How Large Is Our Book-Reading Public?" *Publishers Weekly*, June 6, 1931, 2691. Notoriously unreliable, sales numbers were nevertheless carefully compiled by Alice Payne Hackett, whose surveys of books were published in each issue of *Publishers Weekly* and collected in *70 Years of Best Sellers: 1895–1965*, ed. Alice Payne Hackett (New York: R. R. Bowker, 1967).

38. Deidre Johnson, "From Paragraphs to Pages: The Writing and Development of the Stratemeyer Syndicate Series," in Dyer and Romalov, *Rediscovering Nancy Drew*, 29–32. See also, Tebbel, *A History of Publishing*, 3:482.

39. Lorrayne Carroll, *Rhetorical Drag: Gender Impersonation, Captivity, and the Writing of History* (Kent, Ohio: Kent State University Press, 2007).

40. Tebbel, *A History of Book Publishing*, 3:481.

41. Ibid., 492.

42. Quoted ibid., 481.

43. Advertisement, *The Writer*, September 1953, 205.

44. Quoted in Byrne, *Writing Rackets*, 16–17.

45. Advertisement, *The Writer*, November 1953, 362.

46. Denning, *The Cultural Front*, 226–27.

47. See Allen Maple, "Off the Cuff," *Writer's Magazine*, November 2, 1953, 361.

48. On correspondence schools, see especially Byrne, *Writing Rackets;* and Jessica Mitford, "Let Us Now Appraise Famous Writers," *Atlantic Monthly*, February 1970, 45–54.

49. Edwin Seaver, "The Age of the Jackpot," *Saturday Review of Literature*, February 15, 1947, 29.

50. Henry Seidel Canby, "Clear the Shelves," *Saturday Review of Literature*, December 6, 1930, 411.

51. Tebbel, *A History of Book Publishing*, 2:143.

52. Ibid., 581.

53. Henry Holt, "The Commercialization of Literature," *Atlantic Monthly*, November 1905, 581–82.

54. Radway, *A Feeling for Books*, 189.

55. James Thurber, "The American Literary Scene," *The New Yorker*, July 30, 1949, 21–22.

56. Ted LeBerthon, "Writers Who Once Were Men," *Catholic World* 162 (December 1945): 219–22.

57. Benjamin Appel quoted in Denning, *The Cultural Front*, 227.

58. Brodhead, *Cultures of Letters*, 107–41.

59. Ibid., 119.

60. Denning, *The Cultural Front*, 229.

61. Moran, *Star Authors*, 16.

62. Cawelti, "The Writer as Celebrity," 166.

63. Quoted in Michael Kammen, *American Culture, American Tastes: Social Change and the 20th Century* (New York: Knopf, 1999), 57.

64. Leo Lowenthal, *Literature, Popular Culture, and Society* (Englewood Cliffs, N.J.: Prentice-Hall, 1961); Marshall, *Celebrity and Power*, 10.

65. See especially André Schiffrin, *The Business of Books: How International Conglomerates Took Over Publishing and Changed the Way We Read* (London: Verso, 2000).

66. Jane Howard, "Whiskey and Ink," *Life*, July 21, 1967, 67; "An American Story," *Time*, December 13, 1954, 42–43; see also James Steel Smith, "Life Looks at Literature," in Peter Davison, Rolf Meyersohn and Edward Shils, eds., *Literary Taste, Culture, and Mass Communication*, vol. 12 (Cambridge: Chadwyck-Healey, 1978), 52, 147–49.

67. Joshua Gamson, *Claims to Fame: Celebrity in Contemporary America* (Berkeley: University of California Press, 1994), 132.

68. Grace Metalious, interview with Joyce Donaldson, Canadian Broadcasting Company, 1957.

69. Richard Dyer, *Heavenly Bodies: Film Stars and Society* (New York: St. Martin's Press, 1986), 156.

70. Marshall, *Celebrity and Power*, 91.

71. Metalious, "All about Me and Peyton Place," 11.

72. Metalious, *Peyton Place*, 35, 92, 212, 213.

73. Metalious, *Return to Peyton Place*, 70, 102.

74. Otto Friedrich, "Farewell to *Peyton Place*," *Esquire*, December 1971, 162, 164.

75. Michel de Certeau, *The Practice of Everyday Life*, trans. Steven Rendall (Berkeley: University of California Press, 1984), xv, xxi.

76. Anderson wrote this in regard to Gertrude Stein in "Four American Impressions," *The New Republic*, October 11, 1922, 171–73.

77. Zolotow, "How a Best-Seller Happens," 36.

78. Metalious, "All about Me and Peyton Place," 12.

5. The Gendered Eye

1. Maurice Zolotow, "How a Best-Seller Happens," *Cosmopolitan*, August 1957, 36–37.

2. Grace Metalious, "All about Me and Peyton Place," *American Weekly*, May 18, 1958, 11.

3. Anne Bernays and Justin Kaplan, *Back Then: Two Literary Lives in 1950s New York* (New York: Perennial, 2002), 100.

4. Quoted in Emily Toth, *Inside Peyton Place: The Life of Grace Metalious* (1981; repr. Jackson: University Press of Mississippi, 2000), 86.

5. Edith Wharton, *The Age of Innocence* (New York: Simon & Schuster, 1996), 64.

6. Bernays and Kaplan, *Back Then*, 5.

7. John Tebbel, *A History of Book Publishing in the United States*, 4 vols. (New York: R. R. Bowker, 1972–1981), 2:390–91.

8. Michael Korda, *Another Life: A Memoir of Other People* (New York: Dell Publishing, 2000), 48–49.

9. James Silberman, interview with the author, July 23, 2002.

10. Korda, *Another Life*, 44.

11. "Reminiscences of Helen Meyer: An Oral History," 1979, 7, Columbia University Oral History Collection, Butler Library, New York.

12. Korda, *Another Life*, 47.

13. Tebbel, *A History of Book Publishing*, 3:583.

14. Edith M. Stern, "A Man Who Was Unafraid," *Saturday Review*, June 28, 1941, 27.

15. Jay Satterfield quoted in Evan Brier, "The Accidental Blockbuster: *Peyton Place* in Literary and Institutional Context," *Women's Studies Quarterly* 33, nos. 3 and 4 (Fall–Winter 2005): 57.

16. Susan K. Ahern, "Julian Messner," in *Dictionary of Literary Biography*, vol. 46 (Detroit: Gale, 1986), 235.

17. Ibid., 59; Brier, "The Accidental Blockbuster," 58; Tebbel, *A History of Book Publishing*, 3:334–35.

18. Brier, "The Accidental Blockbuster," 56.

19. Ibid. 58–59.

20. Ibid. 61. Who actually came up with the title *Peyton Place* is much disputed. Emily Toth tells us that it was the brainchild of Aaron Sussman (*Inside Peyton Place*, 96), although she cites no sources. Leona Nevler, the editor who discovered the novel, thought that the title had been in the wings from the beginning, although she also remembered "The Tree and the Blossom" as the original title of the manuscript she read (interview with the author, September 18, 2002). George Metalious claims that he and Grace came up with the title one night during a snowstorm (interview with the author, April 9, 1999). Grace Metalious was always silent on the point.

21. Harcourt, Brace & Howe led the way in the 1920s, when Ellen Eayres, house stenographer and bookkeeper, traveled throughout the Midwest speaking to women's book clubs and school libraries about the new firm. Sales soared, and Eayres became something of a legend. Harcourt became the first firm to put women on an equal basis with men, granting equal vacation rights and equal access to upper-level positions. Tebbel, *A History of Book Publishing*, 3:133, 19, 273–78. More typically, women earned considerably less than men in most other firms and were only rarely given top positions, as confirmed in surveys by *Publishers Weekly*; see especially Stella Dong, "Publishing's Revolving Door," *Publishers Weekly*, December 19, 1980, 20; Margaret Harding, "The Professional Services of Women in Book Publishing," *Pi Lambda Theta Journal*, May 1943; Tebbel, *A History of Book Publishing*, 4:728; Kenneth C. Davis, *Two-Bit Culture: The Paperbacking of America* (Boston: Houghton Mifflin, 1984), 361–62.

22. All quotations are from Rona Jaffe, *The Best of Everything* (New York: Simon & Schuster, 1958), 28–29.

23. Marjorie Shuler, Ruth Adams Knight, and Muriel Fuller, *The Lady Editor: Careers for Women in Publishing* (New York: E. P. Dutton & Co., 1941), 178.

24. Tebbel, *A History of Book Publishing*, 4:387.

25. Ibid. 75.

26. Toth, *Inside Peyton Place*, 102.

27. In the years that followed the Second World War, competition for the paperback market escalated as many close to the trade witnessed the new popularity of paper-bound books in Europe. Businesses founded by moguls like magazine publisher George Delacorte Jr., who launched Dell Publishing in 1942, were joined by Bantam Books, Basic Books, New American Library, and eventually Doubleday's Anchor and Knopf's Vintage in the early 1950s to bring quality paperbacks to academic, literary, and other more "highbrow" audiences who avoided drugstore and train station venues. For a good overview of these events, see Tebbel, *A History of Book Publishing*, 4:74, 350; and Davis, *Two-Bit Culture*, 83, 146.

28. Davis, *Two-Bit Culture*, 145.

29. Shuler, Knight, and Fuller, *The Lady Editor*, 179, 182, 184. On salaries in publishing, see also Tebbel, *A History of Book Publishing*, 4:728.

30. Shuler, Knight, and Fuller, *Lady Editor*, 179.

31. Helen M. Strauss, *A Talent for Luck: An Autobiography* (New York: Random House, 1979), 52.

32. Quoted in John F. Baker, *Literary Agents: A Writer's Introduction* (New York: Macmillan, 1999), 31–32.

33. Korda, *Another Life*, 84.

34. Strauss, *A Talent for Luck*, 69.

35. Ted Morgan, *Maugham: A Biography* (New York: Simon & Schuster, 1980), 462.

36. Ibid.

37. Jeffrey Meyers, *Somerset Maugham: A Life* (New York: Alfred A. Knopf, 2004), 247.

38. Metalious, "All about Me and Peyton Place," 2.

39. Zolotow, "How a Best-Seller Happens," 36.

40. James Silberman, interview with the author, July 23, 2002.

41. Leona Nevler, interview with the author, September 18, 2002.

6. Sex Talk

1. T. F. James, "The Millionaire Class of Young Writers," *Cosmopolitan*, August 1958, 40.

2. Quoted in Kenneth C. Davis, *Two-Bit Culture: The Paperbacking of America* (Boston: Houghton Mifflin, 1984), 179.

3. From Grace Metalious to Bob and Dora Athearn, November 6, 1956, quoted in Emily Toth, *Inside Peyton Place: The Life of Grace Metalious* (1981; repr. Jackson: University Press of Mississippi, 2000), 151.

4. The calling card resides in the Metalious Family Collection (private collection in possession of the family).

5. See Ardis Cameron, "Open Secrets: Rereading Peyton Place," introduction to Grace Metalious, *Peyton Place* (Boston: Northeastern University Press, 1999), xxvii.

6. *Nashua Telegraph*, Vertical File, Gale Memorial Library, Laconia, N.H.; Michael Callahan, interview with the author, November 2005.

7. Daniel Radosh, "The Culture Wars: Why Know?" *The New Yorker*, December 6, 2004, 46.

8. William Loeb, "The Filth They Live By," *Manchester Union Leader*, January 1957, Metalious Folder, Gale Memorial Library.

9. Jesse Helms to Robert Coe, American Broadcasting Company, May 6, 1964. In his request to cancel *Peyton Place*, Helms quoted a "Christian mother" who objected to the moral content of the novel. In response, Coe suggested that this "type of viewer" might tune in elsewhere, unless such viewers had "so little self-discipline, or discipline within their homes." Station manager Helms was furious and shot back, "We members of the 'fringe' element have been put in our place." Helms to Coe, March 3, 1965. My thanks to Bryan Thrift of Tougaloo College for copies of these letters. For more on Helms and early television, see Bryan Thrift, *Conservative Bias: How Jesse Helms Pioneered the Rise of the Right-Wing Media and Realigned the Republican Party* (Gainesville: University of Florida Press, 2014).

10. Dan Lacy in *Publishers Weekly*, October 15, 1956, 170, 1879.

11. Ibid., 170, 1878.

12. Leslie Hansom, *Laconia Evening Citizen*, Vertical File, Gale Memorial Library.

13. Quoted in *Publishers Weekly*, October 15, 1956, 1859.

14. Elaine Tyler May, *Homeward Bound: American Families in the Cold War Era* (New York: Basic Books: 1999), 95–97, 81–82.

15. Carlos Baker, "Small Town Peep Show," *New York Times Book Review*, September 23, 1956, 4.s

16. Edmund Fuller, "New Hampshire: Activities for Strong Stomachs," *Chicago Sunday Tribune Magazine of Books*, September 23, 1956.

17. Julia Child to Avis DeVoto, October 2, 1957, in *As Always, Julia: The Letters of Julia Child and Avis DeVoto*, ed. Joan Reardon (Boston: Houghton Mifflin Harcourt, 2010), 300.

18. Phyllis Hogan, review of *Peyton Place, Times Literary Supplement*, September 20, 1956.

19. Baker, "Small Town Peep Show," 4.

20. I thank Annelise Orleck for this information.

21. *Catholic World*, September 1956, 152.

22. Fanny Butcher, "A Selection of Outstanding Books That Were Published in 1956," *Publishers Weekly*, January 21, 1957, 34–37. For a more through exploration of these concerns and their relationship to *Peyton Place*, see Evan Brier "The Accidental Blockbuster: *Peyton Place* in Literary and Institutional Context," *Women's Studies Quarterly* 33, nos. 3 and 4 (Fall–Winter 2005): 51.

23. John D'Emilio and Estelle B. Freedman, *Intimate Matters: A History of Sexuality in America* (Chicago: University of Chicago Press, 1997), 277, 285

24. Quoted in Carol Groneman, *Nymphomania: A History* (New York: W. W. Norton, 2000), 88.

25. Quoted in Patricia Carbine, "Peyton Place," *Look*, March 18, 1958, 108.

26. Alfred Kinsey, Wardell B. Pomeroy, and Clyde E. Martin, *Sexual Behavior in the Human Male* (Philadelphia: W. B. Saunders, 1948), 10.

27. Judith E. Smith, *Visions of Belonging: Family Stories, Popular Culture, and Postwar Democracy* (New York: Columbia University Press, 2004), 4.

28. Aleksander Hemon, "The Aquarium," *The New Yorker*, June 13, 2011, 56.

29. Kinsey, Pomeroy, and Martin, *Sexual Behavior in the Human Male*, 10–11.

30. Michel Foucault, *The History of Sexuality: An Introduction*, vol. 1, trans. Robert Hurley (New York: Vintage Books, 1990), 36.

31. Ibid., 27.

32. Smith, *Visions of Belonging*. See also Anna G. Creadick, *Perfectly Average: The Pursuit of Normality in Postwar America* (Amherst: University of Massachusetts Press, 2010), 23.

33. Regina G. Kunzel, "White Neurosis, Black Pathology: Constructing Out-of-Wedlock Pregnancy in the Wartime and Postwar United States," in *Not June Cleaver: Woman and Gender in Postwar America, 1945–1960*, ed. Joanne Meyerowitz (Philadelphia: Temple University Press, 1994), 304–31; Mary Louise Adams, *The Trouble with Normal: Postwar Youth and the Making of Heterosexuality* (Toronto: University of Toronto Press, 1997); Donna Penn, "The Meaning of Lesbianism in Post-War America," *Gender & History* 3, no. 2 (Summer 1991): 190–203.

34. Mira Komarovsky, *Blue-Collar Marriage* (New York: Random House, 1964), 13–14, 261; Betty Friedan, *The Feminine Mystique* (New York: W. W. Norton, 2001), 258.

35. Quoted in Creadick, *Perfectly Average*, 9–11.

36. Ibid., 29; Wendy Kozol, *Life's America: Family and Nation in Postwar Photojournalism* (Philadelphia: Temple University Press, 1994).

37. Creadick, *Perfectly Average*, 11.

38. "Normal Isn't as Normal Does," *America*, September 8, 1956, 520–21.

39. W. Norman Pittenger, *The Christian View of Sexual Behavior: A Reaction to the Kinsey Report* (Greenwich, Conn.: Seabury Press, 1954), 16–17.

40. David Riesman with Nathan Glazer and Reuel Denney, *The Lonely Crowd: A Study of the Changing American Character* (New Haven: Yale University Press, 1969); Creadick, *Perfectly Average*, 9.

41. Estelle B. Freedman, "'Uncontrolled Desires': The Response to the Sexual Psychopath, 1920–1960," *Journal of American History* 74, no. 1 (June 1987): 83–106; Donna Penn, "The Sexualized Woman: The Lesbian, the Prostitute, and the Containment of Female Sexuality in Postwar America," in Meyerowitz, *Not June Cleaver*, 358–81.

42. John Tebbel, *A History of Book Publishing in the United States*, 4 vols. (New York: R. R. Bowker, 1972–1981), 4:574.

43. As Anna Creadick makes clear, the term "normality" was the precise keyword used in the *Reader's Guide* throughout this time period. Creadick, *Perfectly Average*, 2–4.

44. Groneman, *Nymphomania*, 88–89.

45. Michel Foucault, *The History of Sexuality: An Introduction*, vol. 1, (New York: Vintage Books, 1990), 22.

46. George Chauncey, Jr., "The Postwar Crime Panic," paper presented at the Organization of American Historians, April 1986.

47. Stephanie Coontz, *The Way We Never Were: American Families and the Nostalgia Trap* (New York: Basic Books, 2000), 186; May, *Homeward Bound*, 82.

48. Sterling North, "Shocker Written by Village Wife," *New York World Telegram*, September 29, 1956.

49. J.O., "Not for Kiddies," Vertical File, Metalious Folder, Gale Memorial Library.

50. May, *Homeward Bound*, 83.

51. Penn, "The Sexualized Woman," 359.

52. Ibid.; Freedman, "Uncontrolled Desires," 83.

53. Freedman, "Uncontrolled Desires," 83.

54. By 1955 the American Psychiatric Association listed no fewer than 106 mental disorders, up from the twenty-two it had identified in the wake of World War I. That year the *Diagnostic and Statistical Manual of Mental Disorders* expanded as well, needing 130 pages to contain the growing list of psychic, sexual, emotional, and social disorders threatening Americans. An anxious audience was in the making. Even Sloan Wilson's "man in the gray flannel suit" took up the cause of mental health, leaving his career in publishing in order to join the crusade to educate Americans about the increasing importance of and expanding risks to the nation's mental health.

55. Hazel Carby, "Policing the Black Woman's Body in an Urban Context," *Critical Inquiry* 18, no. 4 (Summer 1992): 739.

56. Kunzel, "White Neurosis," 304–31, esp. 308, 314–21.

57. Tricia Rose, *Longing to Tell: Black Women Talk about Sexuality and Intimacy* (New York: Farrar, Straus and Giroux, 2003), 395, 361, 5, 96, 98.

58. Smith, *Visions of Belonging*.

59. Barbara Ehrenreich, Elizabeth Hess, and Gloria Jacobs, *Re-Making Love: The Feminization of Sex* (Garden City, N.Y.: Anchor Books, 1986), 68.

60. Brett Harvey, *The Fifties: A Women's Oral History* (New York: HarperCollins, 1993), 32, 89.

61. Alice McDermott, *That Night* (New York: Harper & Row, 1987), 108.

62. Annie Dillard, *An American Childhood* (New York: Harper & Row, 1987), 194.

63. Benita Eisler, *Private Lives: Men and Women of the Fifties* (New York: Franklin Watts, 1986), 133.

64. John Preston, *Winter's Light: Reflections of a Yankee Queer* (Hanover: University Press of New England, 1995), 155.

65. Foucault, *History of Sexuality*, 84.

66. Barbara Dyer, "Peyton Place in Camden," speech given at the 2007 Maine Literary Festival, November 6, 2007.

67. Eisler, *Private Lives*, 33. See also D'Emilio and Freedman, *Intimate Matters*, 280–88.

68. John Howard, *Men Like That: A Southern Queer History* (Chicago: University of Chicago Press, 1999), 30–31.

69. Preston, *Winter's Light*, 21, 130.

70. Eisler, *Private Lives*, 133.

71. Foucault, *History of Sexuality*, vol. 1, 11.

7. The Women of Peyton Place

1. Kenneth C. Davis, *Two-Bit Culture: The Paperbacking of America* (Boston: Houghton Mifflin, 1984), 258–59.

2. Carol Groneman, *Nymphomania: A History* (New York: W. W. Norton, 2000), 90.

3. Alfred Kinsey et al., *Sexual Behavior in the Human Female* (Philadelphia: W. B. Saunders, 1953), 356.

4. James H. Jones, *Alfred C. Kinsey: A Public/Private Life* (New York: W. W. Norton, 1997), 688–89.

5. Alan Petigny, "Illegitimacy, Postwar Psychology, and the Reperiodization of the Sexual Revolution," *Journal of Social History* 38(1) (Fall 2004): 64; Alexandra M. Lord, *Condom Nation: The U.S. Government's Sex Education Campaign from World War I to the Internet* (Baltimore: Johns Hopkins University Press, 2010), 93–114.

6. In 1939 investigators for the U.S. Children's Bureau found that "Maine had one of the highest illegitimacy rates in the country." Mazie Hough, *Rural Unwed Mothers: An American Experience, 1870–1950* (London: Pickering & Chatto, 2010), 151.

7. Petigny, "Illegitimacy," 72.

8. Allen Churchill and Pierre Rube, "Nymphos Have No Fun," *Esquire*, August 1954, 21, 104–6; Groneman, *Nymphomania*, 82.

9. Groneman, *Nymphomania*, 37–42.

10. June Carter, interview with the author, July 2002.

11. Hough, *Rural Unwed Mothers*, 9.

12. Ann Fessler, *The Girls Who Went Away* (New York: Penguin, 2006), 102.

13. Caitlin Flanagan, "Sex and the Teenage Girl," *New York Times*, January 13, 2008.

14. Hough, Rural Unwed Mothers, 9, 21.

15. "Nice Clean Little Town," *Yankee Magazine*, September 1936, n.p.

16. For works especially concerned with the imagined New England, see Dona Brown, *Inventing New England: Regional Tourism in the Nineteenth Century* (Washington, D.C.: Smithsonian Institution Press, 1996); Edward Ayers et al., *All Over the Map: Rethinking American Regions* (Baltimore: Johns Hopkins University Press, 1995); Joseph A. Conforti, *Imagining New England: Regional Identity from the Pilgrims to the Mid-Twentieth Century* (Chapel Hill: University of North Carolina Press, 2001).

17. Bette Davis, "Is a Girl's Past Ever Her Own?" *Photoplay*, October 1941, 74.

18. "Nice Clean Little Town." I thank Joe Conforti for providing me with this article.

19. Hough, *Rural Unwed Mothers*, 1.

20. Rebecca M. Kluchin, *Fit to Be Tied: Sterilization and Reproductive Rights in America, 1950–1980* (New Brunswick, N.J.: Rutgers University Press, 2009), 77–79.

21. Merle Miller, "The Tragedy of Grace Metalious and *Peyton Place*," *Ladies' Home Journal*, June 1965, 111.

22. Hal Boyle, "Grace Unfolds to Hal Boyle Hazard of Husband Losing Job," syndicated column, *Laconia Evening Citizen*, August 29, 1956.

23. R. W. B. Lewis, *Edith Wharton: A Biography* (New York: Fromm International Publishing, 1993), 140.

24. William H. Truettner and Thomas Denenberg, "The Discreet Charm of the Colonial," in *Picturing Old New England: Image and Memory*, ed. William H. Truettner and Roger B. Stein (New Haven: Yale University Press, 1999), 79–110. While I was writing this book, several new works were published on *Peyton Place*, including a full-length literary analysis that astutely brings into focus gender and racial transgression. See Sally Hirsh-Dickinson, *Dirty Whites and Dark Secrets: Sex and Race in Peyton Place* (Durham: University of New Hampshire Press, 2011), 58.

25. Hirsh-Dickenson, *Dirty Whites*, 58–59.

26. Helen Brown, letter to the editor, *Laconia Evening Citizen*, September 1956, Metalious File, Gale Memorial Library, Laconia, N.H.

27. Anonymous post to Amazon.com from nerverwithoutespresso, Revere, Mass., January 6, 2004.

28. Sherri Hughes, interview with the author, May 20, 2004.

29. Cora Kaplan, *Sea Changes: Culture and Feminism* (London: Verso, 1986), 120.

30. Anonymous informant, interview with the author, June 25, 2004.

31. Robert Monroe, interview with the author, April 4, 2004.

32. Paul Goodman, *Growing Up Absurd: The Problems of Youth in the Organized Society* (New York: Vintage Books, 1960), 11.

33. Wini Breines, *Young, White, and Miserable: Growing Up Female in the Fifties* (Chicago: University of Chicago Press, 1992).

34. Goodman, *Growing Up Absurd*, 13.

35. Paul Landis, quoted in Stephanie Coontz, *The Way We Never Were: American Families and the Nostalgia Trap* (New York: Basic Books, 2000), 26.

36. Brett Harvey, *The Fifties: A Women's Oral History* (New York: HarperCollins, 1993), 70.

37. Quoted in Stephanie Coontz, *The Way We Never* Were, 24.

38. Gregory Corso, "Marriage," *The Happy Birthday of Death* (New York: New Directions, 1960).

39. See Jennifer Scanlon, *Bad Girls Go Everywhere: The Life of Helen Gurley Brown* (New York: Oxford University Press, 2009).

40. Morton M. Hunt, *The World of the Formerly Married* (New York: McGraw-Hill, 1966), vii, xi.

41. Coontz, *The Way We Never Were*, 24–25, 32.

42. Ibid., 105, 201; Groneman, *Nymphomania*, 88.

43. Peter Cryle and Alison Moore, *Frigidity: An Intellectual History* (London: Palgrave Macmillan, 2012), 161, 219, 221, 219.

44. Groneman, *Nymphomania*, 42, 83.

45. Ibid., 165–69.

46. John D'Emilio and Estelle B. Freedman, *Intimate Matters: A History of Sexuality in America* (Chicago: University of Chicago Press, 1997), 314.

47. Walter Licht, interview with the author, July 2002.

48. Sterling North, "Shocker Written by a Village Wife," *New York World Telegram*, September 29, 1956.

49. Otto Friedrich, "Farewell to Peyton Place," *Esquire*, December 1971, 307.

50. Grace Metalious to Oliver Swan, undated, Metalious File, Paul Reynolds Collection, Rare Book and Manuscript Library, Columbia University.

8. Excitable Fictions

1. Mike Wallace with Gary Paul Gates, *Between You and Me: A Memoir* (New York: Hyperion, 2005), 1–4; Mike Wallace with Gary Paul Gates, *Close Encounters* (New York: William Morrow and Company, 1984), 22, 40.

2. Wallace, *Close Encounters*, 23.

3. The account that follows is drawn from Emily Toth, *Inside Peyton Place: The Life of Grace Metalious* (1981; repr. Jackson: University Press of Mississippi, 2000), 163–65.

4. Barbara Seaman, *Lovely Me: The Life of Jacqueline Susann* (New York: William Morrow and Company, 1987), 239–42.

5. Quoted in Toth, *Inside Peyton Place*, 162–63.

6. The description is from Michael Korda, "Wasn't She Great?" *New Yorker*, August 14, 1995, 66.

7. Seaman, *Lovely Me*, 240.

8. Patricia Carbine, "Peyton Place," *Look*, March 18, 1958, 108.

9. The term is from Kathy Peiss, *Hope in a Jar: The Making of America's Beauty Culture* (New York: Henry Holt and Company, 1998), 245.

10. Ibid., 114.

11. Quoted in Carbine, "Peyton Place," 110.

12. Seaman, *Lovely Me*, 241.

13. Anonymous informant, interview with the author, May 19, 2004.

14. See David P. Marshall, *Celebrity and Power: Fame in Contemporary Culture* (Minneapolis: University of Minnesota Press, 1997), 47, 72, 244.

15. For a complete description, see Toth, *Inside Peyton Place*, 118; Howard Goodkind, interview with the author, September 2002.

16. Dorothy Kilgallen, syndicated column, August 7, 1956, quoted in Toth, *Inside Peyton Place*, 120.

17. See Evan Brier, "The Accidental Blockbuster: *Peyton Place* in Literary and Institutional Context," *Women's Studies Quarterly* 33, no. 34 (Fall–Winter 2005): 53–54.

18. Dorothy Roe, "Queen Elizabeth Woman of the Year," *San Francisco Call-Bulletin*, December 26, 1957. Thanks to David Richards, associate director of the Margaret Chase Smith Library in Skowhegan, Maine, for sending me this article.

19. Robert L. Zanes, "Gilmanton Folks Answer Grace's Freeze Out Charge," *Laconia Evening Citizen*, August 30, 1956.

20. Hal Boyle, "Grace Unfolds to Hal Boyle Hazard of Husband Losing Job," *Laconia Evening Citizen*, August 29, 1956.

21. The directive advises New England–bound photographers to highlight "autumn pumpkins, raking leaves, roadside stands . . . you know, pour maple syrup on it . . . mix well with white clouds and put it on a skyblue platter." Roy Stryker quoted in F. Jack Hurley, *Portrait of a Decade: Roy Stryker and the Development of Photography in the 1930s* (Baton Rouge: Louisiana State University Press, 1974), 148. Thanks to Donna Cassidy at the University of Southern Maine for this reference.

22. See Kathleen Stewart, *A Space on the Side of the Road: Cultural Poetics in an "Other" America* (Princeton: Princeton University Press, 1996).

23. Joseph A. Conforti, *Imagining New England: Regional Identity from the Pilgrims to the Mid-Twentieth Century* (Chapel Hill: University of North Carolina Press, 2001), 260–309.

24. Edith Wharton, *A Backward Glance* (New York: Scribner's, 1964), 293.

25. Conforti, *Imagining New England*, 310.

26. Laurie Wilkins, interview with the author, September 2001. For a slightly different version, see Toth, *Inside Peyton Place*, 174.

27. Quoted in Harold Banks, "'Peyton Place's Author Finds Utopia," *Pictorial Living*, October 21, 1962, 18.

28. Grace Metalious, "All about Me and Peyton Place," *American Weekly*, May 18, 1958, 11–12. This was a three-part series published in *American Weekly* on May 18, June 1, and June 8, 1958.

29. Wharton, *A Backward Glance*, 293.

30. Quoted in Banks, "'Peyton Place's Author," 18.

31. Quoted in Olivia Skinner, "Pandora of Small-Town New England Writes the 'Truth as I See It,'" *St. Louis Post Dispatch*, April 21, 1961.

32. Hal Boyle, "Grace Unfolds."

33. Ibid.

34. Sterling North, "Shocker Written by Village Wife," *New York World Telegraph*, September 29, 1956; J. O., "Not for Kiddies," *Laconia Evening Citizen*, September 29, 1956. Metalious Folder, Gale Memorial Library, Laconia, N.H.

35. Carbine, "Peyton Place" 108–18; Metalious, "All about Me and Peyton Place"; "Why I Returned to My Husband," *American Weekly*, January 29, 1961, 4–6; Skinner, "Pandora of Small-Town New England"; Banks, "Peyton Place's Author Finds Utopia," 18–19; Harvey

Ewing, "Author Says Vineyard Won't Be Novel Locale," *Laconia Evening Citizen*, October 27, 1960.

36. Quoted in Emily Toth, *Inside Peyton Place*, 164.

37. Lynn Spigel, *Make Room for TV: Television and the Family Ideal in Postwar America* (Chicago: University of Chicago Press, 1992), 1–2.

38. Susan Murray, "Our Man Godfrey: Arthur Godfrey and the Selling of Stardom in Early Television," *Television and New Media* 2, no. 3 (August 2001): 196.

39. Faye Hammill, *Women, Celebrity, and Literary Culture between the Wars* (Austin: University of Texas Press, 2007), 1–2; Catherine Gourley, *Gidgets and Women Warriors: Perceptions of Women in the 1950s and 1960s* (Minneapolis: Twenty-First Century Books, 2008), 44; Marsha Cassidy, *What Women Watched: Daytime Television in the 1950s* (Austin: University of Texas Press, 2005), 21–22. See also Mary Ellen Brown, "Motley Moments: Soap Operas, Carnival, Gossip, and the Power of the Utterance," in *Television and Women's Culture: The Politics of the Popular*, ed. Mary Ellen Brown (London: Sage Publications, 1990), 183–98.

40. Mary Ann Doane, *The Desire to Desire: The Women's Film of the 1940s* (Bloomington: Indiana University Press, 1987), 184.

41. Cassidy, *What Women Watched*, 206.

42. Ibid., 23–24.

43. Carbine, "Peyton Place," 108.

44. Metalious, "All about Me and Peyton Place," 11.

45. Ibid., 10.

46. Grace Metalious, *Return to Peyton Place* (Hanover, N.H.: University Press of New England, 2007), 60.

47. For a brilliant discussion of the uses of pulp fiction in the lives of unmarried mothers, see Regina Kunzel, "Pulp Fictions and Problem Girls: Reading and Rewriting Single Pregnancy in the Postwar United States," *American Historical Review* 100, no. 5 (1995): 1465–87.

48. Stuart Ewen, *All Consuming Images: The Politics of Style in Contemporary Culture* (New York: Basic Books, 1988), 92–96; Joe Moran, *Star Authors and Literary Celebrity in America* (London: Pluto Press, 2000).

49. Grace Metalious, "Why I Returned to My Husband," *American Weekly*, January 29, 1961, 4.

50. Toth, *Inside Peyton Place*, 173.

51. Otto Friedrich, "Farewell to Peyton Place," *Esquire*, December 1971, 310.

52. Metalious, "All about Me and Peyton Place," June 1, 1958, 10.

53. Merle Miller, "The Tragedy of Grace Metalious and *Peyton Place*," *Ladies' Home Journal*, June 1965, 111.

54. Kathryn G. Messner to George Metalious, February 23, 1961, Paul Reynolds File, Butler Library, Columbia University, Rare Book and Manuscript Library, New York.

55. Richard Dyer, *Heavenly Bodies: Film Stars and Society* (New York: St. Martin's Press, 1986); P. David Marshall, *Celebrity and Power: Fame in Contemporary Culture* (Minneapolis: University of Minnesota Press, 1997); Joe Moran, *Star Authors: Literary Celebrity in America* (London: Pluto Press, 2000); Jonathan Gray, Cornell Sandvoss, and C. Lee Harrington, *Fandom: Identities and Communities in a Mediated World* (New York: New York University Press, 2007).

56. Moran, *Star Authors*, 100–101.

57. Ibid., 101–02.

58. Metalious, "Me and Peyton Place," June 8, 1958, 20, 22.

59. Susan Stamberg, interview with the author, March 2004.

60. Carbine, "Peyton Place," 108.

61. Quoted in John Rees, "Grace Metalious' Battle with the World," *Cosmopolitan*, September 1964, 54.

62. Friedrich, "Farewell," 310.

63. Quoted ibid., 310.

64. "Son of Peyton Place," *Time*, November 30, 1959.

65. Elizabeth Bayard, quoted in Friedrich, "Farewell," 310.

66. While visiting her French publisher in Paris, Grace discovered that there was "a problem with Chambrun," as her French editor put it. It turned out that Chambrun had failed to notify Metalious of her many translated editions and had had all royalty payments sent directly to him, never passing them on to her. No paper contracts had ever been sent. Grace Metalious to Ollie Swan, November 24, 1962, Paul Reynolds Collection, Rare Book and Manuscript Room, Butler Library, Columbia University, New York; M. Colbert to Grace Metalious, Folder: *Les Plaisirs de l'Enfer*, Librairie Hachette, Paris.

67. Miller, "The Tragedy of Grace Metalious," 112.

68. Kathryn Messner to Grace Metalious, October 4, 1961, Paul Reynolds Collection, Rare Book and Manuscript Room, Butler Library, Columbia University, New York; Kathryn Messner to Grace Metalious, April 4, Paul Reynolds Collection; Messner to Metalious, October 4, ibid.

69. Quoted in Miller, "The Tragedy of Grace Metalious," 112.

70. "Dear Boss," undated letter, probably 1961, signatures illegible, Paul Reynolds Collection.

71. Metalious, "Me and Peyton Place," June 8, 1958, 24.

72. Bernard I. Snierson to Grace Metalious, October 26, 1960, Metalious Family Collection.

73. Metalious, "Why I Returned to My Husband," 6.

74. Grace Metalious to Oliver Swan, December 12, 1963, Paul Reynolds Collection, Rare Book and Manuscript Room, Butler Library, Columbia University, New York.

75. Friedrich, "Farewell to *Peyton Place*," 310.

76. Metalious, *Return to Peyton Place*, 238.

Epilogue: Memento Mori

1. Otto Friedrich, "Farewell to Peyton Place," *Esquire*, December 1971, 161.

2. Emily Nussbaum, "Difficult Women: How 'Sex and the City' Lost Its Good Name," *The New Yorker*, July 29, 2013, 66.

3. Quoted in Friedrich, "Farewell to Peyton Place," 160.

4. Margaret Widdemer, "Message and Middlebrow," *Saturday Review of Literature*, February 18, 1933.

5. Marsha Metalious, interview with the author, October 2001.

6. Bosley Crowther, "The Screen: Drama in 'Peyton Place,'" *New York Times*, December 13, 1957, 35.

7. Quoted in Emily Toth, *Inside Peyton Place: The Life of Grace Metalious* (1981; repr. Jackson: University Press of Mississippi, 2000), 195; quoted in a fan letter to Grace Metalious, October 28, 1960, Metalious Family Collection.

8. Crowther, "The Screen," 35.

9. Quoted in Leo Litwak, "Visit to a Town of the Mind: Peyton Place," *New York Times*, April 4, 1965.

10. Ibid.; Frank Judge, "A Cliff-Hanger That Makes a Better TV Mousetrap," *TV Magazine*, January 3, 1965, 24. While most series at the time produced twenty-six episodes per season, then repeated thirteen before the summer layoff, *Peyton Place* was on a "no-repeat, 52 week schedule for a total of 104 episodes a year." In June 1965 ABC decided to add another evening episode, increasing the series to an unprecedented three nights a week of viewing. See especially Al Salerno, "Is Peyton Place on Road to Expansion?" *New York World Telegram*, January 14, 1965; *Time*, August 20, 1965, 65; Richard Warren Lewis, "The Battle of Peyton Place," *TV Guide*, January 16–22, 1965, 6–9.

11. Quoted in Litwak, "Visit to a Town of the Mind," 54.

12. Known as the "queen of the soap opera writers," Irna Phillips was so impressed by the popularity of ABC's *Peyton Place* that she proposed to CBS that her daytime show *As the World Turns* be translated into a nighttime drama (Richard Doan, *New York Herald Tribune*, February 2, 1965). It was Phillips who completely dropped Selena Cross from the script. Bruce Morris, *Prime Time Network Serials: Episode Guides, Casts, and Credits for 37 Continuing Television Dramas, 1964–1993* (Jefferson, N.C.: McFarland & Co., 1994), 675.

13. It wasn't until the fifth season when, in the wake of the civil rights movement and the riots in Newark, New Jersey, producers introduced "a Negro family" to *Peyton Place*, hiring Canadian actor Percy Rodriguez as Dr. Harry Miles and Ruby Dee to play his wife. ABC news release, June 21, 1968, "Peyton Place" file, Paley Center, New York.

14. Quoted in Litwak, "Visit to a Town of the Mind," 64.

15. Ibid., 65.

16. Friedrich, "Farewell to Peyton Place," 162–63.

Index

Kinsey Reports (Kinsey, Alfred), 28, 65,
112–21, 126–28; *Sexual Behavior in the
Human Female*, 121, 126
Knopf, Alfred A., 95, 100, 201n27
Komarovsky, Mira, 115
Korda, Michael, 95, 102
Krafft-Ebing, Richard von, 64

Laconia, New Hampshire, 41–42, 54,
62–63, 109, 174
Laconia Evening Citizen, 56, 62, *152*
Laconia State School, 63
Ladies' Home Journal, 83, 116, 165
Lady Editor, The (Fuller), 93, 101
Lange, Hope, 180
League of American Writers, 84
Leave It to Beaver, 35
Left. *See* progressives
Leopard in My Lap (Denis), 76
Lepore, Jill, 25
lesbians, 120; lesbian novels, 36. *See also*
homosexuality; sex and sexuality
Les Plaisirs de l'Enfer ("The Pleasures of
Hell"), 33–34
Lester, Pauline, 83
Levin, Lawrence, 25
Lewis, Sinclair, 27, 111; *Main Street*, 33
Libbey, Laura Jean, 22, 78, 198n20
libraries, 21–22, 31–32, 61, 67, 79, 107
Life magazine, 56, 78, 89, 116, 165
Lippincott, J. B., 105
literacy, 9–10; increase in, 21
literary: definitions of, 12; and
regionalism, 87; standards, 85–86
literary agents, 85, 92, 94, 101–2
literary celebrity, 74–76, 88–90, 102, 112,
134, 146–51, 156–67, 170–71, 187
literary domestics, 198n19
literary taste, 25, 79, 96, 98–99, 108, 111,
178–79, 187
Literature, 21, 59, 67, 179;
commercialization of, 74, 79–86, 89,
96–97, 100–101, 111; and masculinity,
26, 80, 86
Little, Brown, 104–5

Liveright, Horace, 96
Loeb, William, 108
Lolita (Nabokov), 33, 104
Long, Elizabeth, 197n7
longing, 14, 24, 30, 33, 56, 68, 71, 89, 144,
160, 164–66, 180, 187. *See also* desire
Long Trail Boys, 83
Look magazine, 64, 116, 148, 152,
161–63, 162
love, 141, 145
Love Poems (Vanderbilt), 76
Lowell factory girls, *20*
Lowenthal, Leo, 88
Luce, Henry, 78

MacDonald, Betty, 77
Macmillan, 28, 83–84
Mademoiselle magazine, 84
Mad Men, 141
Magazine Institute, 84
magazines, 79–80, 82–84, 88–89; slicks,
79, 95
Maine, 154, 183; Camden, 123, 155,
180–81; illegitimacy rates, 205n6
Major, Floyd, 107
Makris, Tom, 173
male youth, 130, 138
Malone, Dorothy, 182
Manchester, New Hampshire, 60–61, 67,
183; Petit Canada, 61, 68
Mandingo, 9, 27, 100, 179
Manguel, Alberto, 32–33
mannish women, 120
Marcus, Greil: *A New Literary History of
America* (Marcus and Sollors), 12
Marjorie Dean series, 83
marketing, 96–98, 157; research, 98. *See
also* advertising; commercialization of
literature; publicity
married women, 128, 138–40, 143; sexual
behavior of, 126–27. *See also* sexual
affairs
Marrow, Parker, 17
Marsh, Mrs. John, 87
Marshall, David, 90

Printed in the USA
CPSIA information can be obtained
at www.ICGtesting.com
CBHW022323290424
7768CB00002B/200